797,885 Books
are available to read at

Forgotten Books

www.ForgottenBooks.com

Forgotten Books' App
Available for mobile, tablet & eReader

ISBN 978-1-330-71970-1
PIBN 10096644

This book is a reproduction of an important historical work. Forgotten Books uses state-of-the-art technology to digitally reconstruct the work, preserving the original format whilst repairing imperfections present in the aged copy. In rare cases, an imperfection in the original, such as a blemish or missing page, may be replicated in our edition. We do, however, repair the vast majority of imperfections successfully; any imperfections that remain are intentionally left to preserve the state of such historical works.

Forgotten Books is a registered trademark of FB &c Ltd.
Copyright © 2017 FB &c Ltd.
FB &c Ltd, Dalton House, 60 Windsor Avenue, London, SW19 2RR.
Company number 08720141. Registered in England and Wales.

For support please visit www.forgottenbooks.com

1 MONTH OF FREE READING

at

www.ForgottenBooks.com

By purchasing this book you are eligible for one month membership to ForgottenBooks.com, giving you unlimited access to our entire collection of over 700,000 titles via our web site and mobile apps.

To claim your free month visit:
www.forgottenbooks.com/free96644

* Offer is valid for 45 days from date of purchase. Terms and conditions apply.

English
Français
Deutsche
Italiano
Español
Português

www.forgottenbooks.com

Mythology Photography **Fiction**
Fishing Christianity **Art** Cooking
Essays Buddhism Freemasonry
Medicine **Biology** Music **Ancient Egypt** Evolution Carpentry Physics
Dance Geology **Mathematics** Fitness
Shakespeare **Folklore** Yoga Marketing
Confidence Immortality Biographies
Poetry **Psychology** Witchcraft
Electronics Chemistry History **Law**
Accounting **Philosophy** Anthropology
Alchemy Drama Quantum Mechanics
Atheism Sexual Health **Ancient History**
Entrepreneurship Languages Sport
Paleontology Needlework Islam
Metaphysics Investment Archaeology
Parenting Statistics Criminology
Motivational

ESSAYS AND STUDIES

PROSE SELECTIONS FOR COLLEGE READING

CHOSEN AND ARRANGED
BY
FREDERICK M. SMITH
ASSISTANT PROFESSOR OF ENGLISH, CORNELL UNIVERSITY

HOUGHTON MIFFLIN COMPANY
BOSTON NEW YORK CHICAGO SAN FRANCISCO
The Riverside Press Cambridge

COPYRIGHT, 1922, BY HOUGHTON MIFFLIN COMPANY

The selections reprinted in this book are used by permission of and special arrangement with the proprietors of their respective copyrights.

The Riverside Press
CAMBRIDGE · MASSACHUSETTS
PRINTED IN THE U.S.A.

PREFACE

IN a book of this kind a single name appears upon the title-page only by a sort of custom; for many persons have a hand in its making. I am indebted to my publishers for the use of much copyrighted material. Although due credit is given in the proper places I should like to acknowledge the kindness of Charles Scribner's Sons; Doubleday, Page & Company; D. Appleton & Company; the Yale University Press; and The Macmillan Company in permitting me to use material of which they control the copyrights.

To name those who have made suggestions with regard to the collection would be almost to print a directory of the English Department of Cornell University; but among those who have given particular assistance in the choice of selections I must mention Professor J. B. Reeves, of Westminster College, Missouri, and Mr. Seymour Long, Mr. Manning Smith, and Professor F. C. Prescott, of Cornell. Mr. J. H. Nelson has generously assisted me in reading the proof. To Professor Martin W. Sampson, of Cornell, I am indebted for advice and counsel on most matters connected with the book, and for permission to print his essay on Poetry.

F. M. S.

ITHACA, N.Y.
April 6, 1922

CONTENTS

BOOKS AND STUDY

OF STUDIES	*Francis Bacon*	1
OF KINGS' TREASURIES	*John Ruskin*	3
KNOWLEDGE VIEWED IN RELATION TO LEARNING	*John Henry Newman*	33
THE PRINCIPAL SUBJECTS OF EDUCATION	*Thomas Henry Huxley*	58
THE METHOD OF SCIENTIFIC INVESTIGATION	*Thomas Henry Huxley*	70
THE AMERICAN SCHOLAR	*Ralph Waldo Emerson*	80
A COLLEGE MAGAZINE	*Robert Louis Stevenson*	103
TRUTH OF INTERCOURSE	*Robert Louis Stevenson*	113
POETRY	*Martin Wright Sampson*	123

THE CONDUCT OF LIFE

WHERE I LIVED, AND WHAT I LIVED FOR	*Henry David Thoreau*	131
THE LAMP OF OBEDIENCE	*John Ruskin*	145
THE HERO AS DIVINITY	*Thomas Carlyle*	157
ÆS TRIPLEX	*Robert Louis Stevenson*	174
HOW TO OVERCOME THE OBSTACLES TO GOOD CITIZENSHIP	*James Bryce*	184
ABRAHAM LINCOLN	*Ralph Waldo Emerson*	193
A DEFINITION OF A GENTLEMAN	*John Henry Newman*	199

THE OUTDOORS

THE SKY	*John Ruskin*	202
ON GOING A JOURNEY	*William Hazlitt*	205
PHASES OF FARM LIFE	*John Burroughs*	218
THE INITIATION	*Joseph Conrad*	238
A NIGHT AMONG THE PINES	*Robert Louis Stevenson*	247
A RIVER REVERIE	*Lafcadio Hearn*	252

CONTENTS

CITIES AND MEN

OF TRAVEL	*Francis Bacon*	256
AN ENGLISH VILLAGE	*Tickner Edwardes*	259
MY FIRST DAY IN THE ORIENT	*Lafcadio Hearn*	263
TOURS	*Henry James*	269
A VERANDA IN THE ALCAZARIA	*F. Hopkinson Smith*	274
FIFTH AVENUE	*Frederick M. Smith*	279
POLK STREET	*Frank Norris*	285
KNOW THYSELF	*Samuel Johnson*	289
THE OLD AND THE NEW SCHOOLMASTER	*Charles Lamb*	294
OLD CHINA	*Charles Lamb*	304

A LITTLE GROUP OF INTERESTING PEOPLE

THE OLD GENTLEMAN	*Leigh Hunt*	311
THE OLD LADY	*Leigh Hunt*	316
ROSALIND	*Anna Jameson*	320
WOUTER VAN TWILLER	*Washington Irving*	325
THE MICAWBERS	*Charles Dickens*	329
AHAB	*Herman Melville*	334
MRS. TOUCHETT	*Henry James*	339
DOÑA RITA	*Joseph Conrad*	341
THE MISER	*Frank Norris*	343
MR. HASTINGS	*William Gilpin*	344
BOSWELL	*Thomas Carlyle*	346
TENNYSON	*Thomas Carlyle*	348
BOERHAAVE	*Samuel Johnson*	349

AN EXPLANATION

The man who presumes to add another to the myriad books intended to aid the college student in his writing and reading must, of course, preface his attempt with an explanation if not with an apology. This is an explanation: it is addressed particularly to those who are interested in the problem of "freshman English"; and it tells how we have tried to solve it in Cornell University. Reduced to its simplest terms the problem is, I take it, to teach young folk to think clearly, to write simple and correct English, and to like good books.

Like all others who have sought a solution we have made many experiments; and it would be fair to say that we have not had much success with those formal books on rhetoric or composition designed to lead the student gently but firmly from description through exposition to narrative and argument; books which, while laying down a multitude of rules for his guidance, seek to persuade him that writing is a delightful task. Many of these treatises are excellent, and can be used to good purpose by men who believe in them. But the very fact that there are so many shows that no one is altogether satisfactory, shows what variety of opinion there is on this difficult matter of teaching composition. And we all know that one man will have success with one method, and another with a system quite different. This suggests why, in a course handled by twenty or more instructors, we have thought it better to give a certain liberty to the teacher. For, on the whole, we have come to believe that the best way to teach composition is to lead the student to read a good deal and to write a good deal. In supervising the written work it is for the instructor to emphasize a few fundamental rules, and to make further suggestions to suit individual cases, referring repeatedly to some very simple manual like Strunk's *Elements of Style*.

It should be understood, then, that our freshman course combines literature and composition. And while we are quite aware of the many fine things in modern prose, we are so old-fashioned as to believe that such tried books as, say, the Bible and Shakespeare, give sounder training than the most up-to-date of weekly periodicals. So, in the course of the year, the student studies the Bible and Shakespeare, and *The Golden Treasury* and Browning and one or two of the greater novelists. And, at the very outset, he has in his hands a volume of selected essays which is intended as an induction to the study of English.

In assembling some essays for such use we have had two sorts in mind: first, essays which can be used in part or in whole as models; second, essays which will stimulate the student's interest in books, and give him ideas about life. It is the happy thing about good literature that it will nearly always serve both purposes.

Let me speak first of the prose as it is intended to help the writer. In his compositions he will, naturally, in the beginning, struggle with the eternal character sketch and the familiar description. Why, indeed, should he not, so long as he deals with subjects near to his own interests and experience? If, then, he is asked to portray a queer character, to write a description of his own town or village, to tell the story of a lively holiday, or to discuss some simple problem of his college life, it is worth while to send him to some bit of prose on a similar subject, by a trained writer: this will suggest words and method. When he is learning the more technical things about composition — to outline an essay, to construct an argument, to arrange paragraphs so that they will fit into a nice and forcible whole — he gets present help by a careful study of the work of men who are clear and logical.

With the intention of providing such models we have included many descriptive sketches, character pieces, and dramatic bits, besides longer and more important essays that lend themselves to analysis. For outdoor description he may go, among others, to Burroughs and Stevenson and Conrad; for city and village, to Norris and Henry James and Hearn; for construction, to Ruskin, Newman and Huxley.

This much for mere technique — for essays which serve as models and enrich the student's somewhat meager vocabulary. Quite apart from making him read for expression's sake, we must, if such a thing is possible, waken his interest in books, and induce him to read for the pure joy of reading: and we must direct his thoughts a little to the problems of his own life as a worker and a citizen. More than all we must hope to inspire him with the unshakable belief that life is a thoughtful man's job that must be faced cheerfully and courageously.

These important things have very much guided the selection. We want first to prove to youth the value of reading: Ruskin's "Of Kings' Treasuries" is a very clear appeal; it shows the real riches in books, and how one must earn his way to their treasures. Bacon enlarges the view of studies and suggests their practical value; while Newman and Emerson state the case for liberal study from two points of view — that of an English scholar and a cleric, and that of a man nearer to our common life, a thinker and an American. Huxley speaks as a scientist. Professor Sampson's essay was written to help the student to an understanding of the value of poetry in life — a thing that cannot be too much stressed in this day of machinery and clamant business.

If there are a good many outdoor essays, it is not merely that they shall serve as models of description, but because we believe there is real cultural value in the outdoors; and that perhaps Burroughs and Thoreau will open the reader's eyes to the charm of his own countryside and the poetry of simple living; or that Conrad will inspire him with a sense of the beauty and mystery of the wide sea, and the natural Universe.

But, when all is said, the chief business of books is to illustrate human nature. Most students are interested in people, whether those friendly persons who are met in history and novels and plays, or in real folk who go up and down in the world. They will do a good deal of writing about these different people; and to help them in observing, to give them a wider outlook, we have introduced a few of the more personal essays, and have hung a group of little portraits by master painters like Dickens and Melville and Leigh Hunt.

Last — and this most important of all — we have to speak of material which touches somewhat the conduct of life. Here we have grouped a few notable essays that, excellent as literature, stress some of the cardinal virtues. One reads Stevenson and is confirmed in courage and faith; one hears Thoreau's insistent call for simplicity. Emerson is sturdily individual and American. Ruskin says in no uncertain tones that obedience to law, either in art, or literature, or morals, is one of the foundation stones in any temple of righteousness. In "How to Overcome the Obstacles to Good Citizenship" James Bryce deals with some of the difficulties that confront the modern citizen.

If I have made clear what we have tried to do, the reason for the inclusion of every selection should be plain. The grouping, which is somewhat loose, is only intended to make a little more definite the plan I have outlined.

There is a feeling — just now very prevalent and noisy — that colleges should keep up with the times. And keeping up with the times means, to some apparently, that we must discard all the old and tried literature, study newspapers, write "movie" scenarios, and embrace the schemes of every gentleman who has a new fancy in education if so be he can call it by a fine name. This is, of course, very exciting; but may it not also be a little superficial and premature? Let me not be misunderstood. Keeping up with the times, testing new ideas for their truth or falsity, is the excellent and main duty of a young man in the world; but no young man can make tests without standards; or, to put it in the pleasant vernacular of our environment, no man can jump with any certainty of landing unless he has a firm take-off. It is the business of the college to show the students the old and the good that they may go on to welcome and to make things new and good. To follow a thing merely because it is new is to be like the valetudinarian who tries every patent medicine that is advertised. Standards — standards of taste, of right thinking, of ethics — these our young men and women must get somehow if they are to make *good* citizens; for good citizenship implies something more than mere enthusiasm. For many ardent reformers seem to overlook the fact that the way, and the *only* way, to make good citizens is first to make *good men.*

The world has not changed in fundamentals despite the upheaval it has suffered, and the sad face of it at present. If it is to be saved it will not be by the search for new and strange virtues, but by the practice of the old. Courage and honesty, unselfishness and faith, charity and common sense must still be the great stones of which we make our foundation.

"Taste," said Goethe to Eckermann, "is only to be educated by contemplation, not of the tolerably good, but of the truly excellent. I therefore show you only the best works, and when you are *grounded* in these you will have a standard for the rest, which you will know how to value without overrating them. And I show you the best in each class, that you may perceive that no class is to be despised, but that each gives delight when a man of genius attains the highest point."

It is because we believe this that we include in our first-year course the great English classics already mentioned. In this book of essays, however, there are presented some very modern writers (and some few of these are masters); for it is obvious that there are many reasons for acquainting students with some of the writing of their own time. But there is also a great weight of prose that has been tried by more than one generation and found good. The older men will not, on the whole, suffer by the comparison. "We are mighty fine fellows, nowadays," says Stevenson, "but we cannot write like Hazlitt." We cannot, indeed, nor like Bacon, nor like Newman, nor like Ruskin. And we make no mistake in giving to such men the greatest space. Only by the study of great writers are we ourselves made to strive for mastery.

ESSAYS AND STUDIES

OF STUDIES

FRANCIS BACON
1561-1626

"OF Studies," and "Of Travel" (page 256) are from that series of observations on life and character published in 1597, and known as "Bacon's Essays." Bacon's work repays study; he is a model of concision and point; his constant use of antithesis often gives a fine balance to his sentences, and much of his prose is made beautiful by an even more subtle rhythm.

STUDIES serve for delight, for ornament, and for ability. Their chief use for delight is in privateness and retiring; for ornament, is in discourse; and for ability, is in the judgement and disposition of business. For expert men can execute, and perhaps judge of particulars, one by one; but the general counsels, and the plots and marshalling of affairs, come best from those that are learned. To spend too much time in studies is sloth; to use them too much for ornament is affectation; to make judgement wholly by their rules is the humour of the scholar. They perfect nature, and are perfected by experience; for natural abilities are like natural plants, that need proyning by study; and studies themselves do give forth directions too much at large, except they be bounded in by experience. Crafty men contemn studies; simple men admire them; and wise men use them: for they teach not their own use; but that is a wisdom without them and above them, won by observation. Read not to contradict and confute; nor to believe and take for granted; nor to find talk and discourse; but to weigh and consider. Some books are to be tasted, others to be swallowed, and some few to be chewed and digested: that is, some books are to be read only in parts; others to be read, but not curiously; and some few to be read wholly, and with diligence and attention. Some books also may be read by deputy, and extracts made of them by others; but that would be only in the less important arguments, and the meaner sort of books; else distilled books are like common distilled waters, flashy things. Reading maketh a full man; conference a ready man; and writing an exact man. And therefore, if a man write little, he had need have a great memory; if he confer little, he had need have a present wit; and if he read little, he had need have much cunning, to seem to know that he doth not. Histories make men wise; poets witty; the mathematics subtile; natural philosophy deep; moral grave; logic and rhetoric able to contend. *Abeunt studia in mores.* Nay, there is no stond or impediment in the wit but may be wrought out by fit studies: like as diseases of the body may have appropriate exercises. Bowling is good for the stone and reins; shooting for the lungs and breast; gentle walking for the stomach; riding for the head; and the like. So if a man's wit be wandering, let him study the mathematics; for in demonstrations, if his wit be called away never so little, he must begin again. If his wit be not apt to distinguish or find differences, let him study the schoolmen; for they are *cymini sectores.* If he be not apt to beat over matters, and to call up one thing to prove and illustrate another, let him study the lawyers' cases. So every defect of the mind may have a special receipt.

OF KINGS' TREASURIES[1]

JOHN RUSKIN
1819–1900

THIS is a part of the first of two lectures which appeared under the title *Sesame and Lilies* in 1865. Profoundly interested in art and life, particularly in the life of the working-man, Ruskin wrote and lectured much on these subjects. *Modern Painters*, *The Seven Lamps of Architecture*, *The Stones of Venice*, *Time and Tide*, *Fors Clavigera*, and *Præterita* are among his important books.

"You shall each have a cake of sesame, — and ten pound."
LUCIAN: *The Fisherman*

1. My first duty this evening is to ask your pardon for the ambiguity of title under which the subject of lecture has been announced: for indeed I am not going to talk of kings, known as regnant, nor of treasuries, understood to contain wealth; but of quite another order of royalty, and another material of riches, than those usually acknowledged. I had even intended to ask your attention for a little while on trust, and (as sometimes one contrives, in taking a friend to see a favorite piece of scenery) to hide what I wanted most to show, with such imperfect cunning as I might, until we unexpectedly reached the best point of view by winding paths. But — and as also I have heard it said, by men practised in public address, that hearers are never so much fatigued as by the endeavor to follow a speaker who gives them no clue to his purpose — I will take the slight mask off at once, and tell you plainly that I want to speak to you about the treasures hidden in books; and about the way we

[1] For this essay the text of The Riverside Literature Series edition is used. The paragraph numbering is retained to aid the student in analysis.

find them, and the way we lose them. A grave subject, you will say; and a wide one! Yes; so wide that I shall make no effort to touch the compass of it. I will try only to bring before you a few simple thoughts about reading, which press themselves upon me every day more deeply, as I watch the course of the public mind with respect to our daily enlarging means of education; and the answeringly wider spreading on the levels, of the irrigation of literature.

2. It happens that I have practically some connection with schools for different classes of youth; and I receive many letters from parents respecting the education of their children. In the mass of these letters I am always struck by the precedence which the idea of a "position in life" takes above all other thoughts in the parents' — more especially in the mothers' — minds. "The education befitting such and such a *station in life*" — this is the phrase, this the object, always. They never seek, as far as I can make out, an education good in itself; even the conception of abstract rightness in training rarely seems reached by the writers. But, an education "which shall keep a good coat on my son's back; — which shall enable him to ring with confidence the visitors' bell at double-belled doors; which shall result ultimately in the establishment of a double-belled door to his own house; — in a word, which shall lead to advancement in life; — *this* we pray for on bent knees — and this is *all* we pray for." It never seems to occur to the parents that there may be an education which, in itself, *is* advancement in Life; — that any other than that may perhaps be advancement in Death; and that this essential education might be more easily got, or given, than they fancy, if they set about it in the right way; while it is for no price, and by no favor, to be got, if they set about it in the wrong.

3. Indeed, among the ideas most prevalent and effective in the mind of this busiest of countries, I suppose the first —

at least that which is confessed with the greatest frankness, and put forward as the fittest stimulus to youthful exertion — is this of "Advancement in life." May I ask you to consider with me, what this idea practically includes, and what it should include?

Practically, then, at present, "advancement in life" means, becoming conspicuous in life; obtaining a position which shall be acknowledged by others to be respectable or honorable. We do not understand by this advancement, in general, the mere making of money, but the being known to have made it; not the accomplishment of any great aim, but the being seen to have accomplished it. In a word, we mean the gratification of our thirst for applause. That thirst, if the last infirmity of noble minds, is also the first infirmity of weak ones; and on the whole, the strongest impulsive influence of average humanity: the greatest efforts of the race have always been traceable to the love of praise, as its greatest catastrophes to the love of pleasure.

4. I am not about to attack or defend this impulse. I want you only to feel how it lies at the root of effort; especially of all modern effort. It is the gratification of vanity which is, with us, the stimulus of toil and balm of repose; so closely does it touch the very springs of life that the wounding of our vanity is always spoken of (and truly) as in its measure *mortal;* we call it "mortification," using the same expression which we should apply to a gangrenous and incurable bodily hurt. And although few of us may be physicians enough to recognize the various effect of this passion upon health and energy, I believe most honest men know, and would at once acknowledge, its leading power with them as a motive. The seaman does not commonly desire to be made captain only because he knows he can manage the ship better than any other sailor on board. He wants to be made captain that he may be *called* captain.

The clergyman does not usually want to be made a bishop only because he believes that no other hand can, as firmly as his, direct the diocese through its difficulties. He wants to be made bishop primarily that he may be called "My Lord." And a prince does not usually desire to enlarge, or a subject to gain, a kingdom, because he believes that no one else can as well serve the State, upon its throne; but, briefly, because he wishes to be addressed as "Your Majesty," by as many lips as may be brought to such utterance.

5. This, then, being the main idea of "advancement in life," the force of it applies, for all of us, according to our station, particularly to that secondary result of such advancement which we call "getting into good society." We want to get into good society not that we may have it, but that we may be seen in it; and our notion of its goodness depends primarily on its conspicuousness.

Will you pardon me if I pause for a moment to put what I fear you may think an impertinent question? I never can go on with an address unless I feel, or know, that my audience are either with me or against me: I do not much care which, in beginning; but I must know where they are; and I would fain find out, at this instant, whether you think I am putting the motives of popular action too low. I am resolved, to-night, to state them low enough to be admitted as probable; for whenever, in my writings on Political Economy, I assume that a little honesty, or generosity — or what used to be called "virtue" — may be calculated upon as a human motive of action, people always answer me, saying, "You must not calculate on that: that is not in human nature: you must not assume anything to be common to men but acquisitiveness and jealousy; no other feeling ever has influence on them, except accidentally, and in matters out of the way of business." I begin, accordingly, to-night, low in the scale of motives; but I must know if you think me right in doing so. Therefore, let me ask those who admit the love of praise to be usually the strongest motive in men's minds in seeking advancement, and the honest desire of doing any kind of duty to be an entirely secondary one, to hold up their hands. (*About a dozen hands held up — the audience, partly, not being sure the lecturer is serious, and, partly, shy of expressing opinion.*) I am quite serious — I really do want to know what you think; however, I can judge by putting the reverse question. Will those who think that duty is generally the first, and love of praise the second, motive, hold up their hands? (*One hand reported to have been held up, behind the lecturer.*) Very good: I see you are with me, and that you think I have not begun too near the ground. Now, without teasing you by putting farther question, I venture to assume that you will admit duty as at least a secondary or tertiary motive. You think that the desire of doing something useful, or obtaining some real good, is indeed an existent collateral idea, though a secondary one, in most men's desire of advancement. You will grant that moderately honest men desire place and office, at least in some measure, for the sake of beneficent power; and would wish to associate rather with sensible and well-informed persons than with fools and ignorant persons, whether they are seen in the company of the sensible ones or not. And finally, without being troubled by repetition of any common truisms about the preciousness of friends, and the influence of companions, you will admit, doubtless, that according to the sincerity of our desire that our friends may be true, and our companions wise, — and in proportion to the earnestness and discretion with which we choose both, — will be the general chances of our happiness and usefulness.

6. But granting that we had both the will and the sense to choose our friends well, how few of us have the power! or,

at least, how limited, for most, is the sphere of choice! Nearly all our associations are determined by chance, or necessity; and restricted within a narrow circle. We cannot know whom we would; and those whom we know, we cannot have at our side when we most need them. All the higher circles of human intelligence are, to those beneath, only momentarily and partially open. We may, by good fortune, obtain a glimpse of a great poet, and hear the sound of his voice; or put a question to a man of science, and be answered good humoredly. We may intrude ten minutes' talk on a cabinet minister, answered probably with words worse than silence, being deceptive; or snatch, once or twice in our lives, the privilege of throwing a bouquet in the path of a princess, or arresting the kind glance of a queen. And yet these momentary chances we covet; and spend our years, and passions, and powers in pursuit of little more than these; while, meantime, there is a society, continually open to us, of people who will talk to us as long as we like, whatever our rank or occupation; — talk to us in the best words they can choose, and of the things nearest their hearts. And this society, because it is so numerous and so gentle, and can be kept waiting round us all day long, — kings and statesmen lingering patiently, not to grant audience, but to gain it! — in those plainly furnished and narrow anterooms, our bookcase shelves, — we make no account of that company, — perhaps never listen to a word they would say, all day long!

7. You may tell me, perhaps, or think within yourselves, that the apathy with which we regard this company of the noble, who are praying us to listen to them; and the passion with which we pursue the company, probably of the ignoble, who despise us, or who have nothing to teach us, are grounded in this, — that we can see the faces of the living men, and it is themselves, and not their sayings, with which we desire to become familiar. But it is not so. Suppose

you never were to see their faces: — suppose you could be put behind a screen in the statesman's cabinet, or the prince's chamber, would you not be glad to listen to their words. though you were forbidden to advance beyond the screen? And when the screen is only a little less, folded in two instead of four, and you can be hidden behind the cover of the two boards that bind a book, and listen all day long, not to the casual talk, but to the studied, determined, chosen addresses of the wisest of men; — this station of audience, and honorable privy council, you despise!

8. But perhaps you will say that it is because the living people talk of things that are passing, and are of immediate interest to you, that you desire to hear them. Nay; that cannot be so, for the living people will themselves tell you about passing matters, much better in their writings than in their careless talk. But I admit that this motive does influence you, so far as you prefer those rapid and ephemeral writings to slow and enduring writings — books, properly so called. For all books are divisible into two classes: the books of the hour, and the books of all time. Mark this distinction — it is not one of quality only. It is not merely the bad book that does not last, and the good one that does. It is a distinction of species. There are good books for the hour, and good ones for all time; bad books for the hour, and bad ones for all time. I must define the two kinds before I go farther.

9. The good book of the hour, then, — I do not speak of the bad ones, — is simply the useful or pleasant talk of some person whom you cannot otherwise converse with, printed for you. Very useful often, telling you what you need to know; very pleasant often, as a sensible friend's present talk would be. These bright accounts of travels; good-humored and witty discussions of question; lively or pathetic story-telling in the form of novel; firm fact-telling,

by the real agents concerned in the events of passing history;
— all these books of the hour, multiplying among us as education becomes more general, are a peculiar possession of the present age: we ought to be entirely thankful for them, and entirely ashamed of ourselves if we make no good use of them. But we make the worst possible use if we allow them to usurp the place of true books: for, strictly speaking, they are not books at all, but merely letters or newspapers in good print. Our friend's letter may be delightful, or necessary, to-day: whether worth keeping or not, is to be considered. The newspaper may be entirely proper at breakfast-time, but assuredly it is not reading for all day. So, though bound up in a volume, the long letter which gives you so pleasant an account of the inns, and roads, and weather last year at such a place, or which tells you that amusing story, or gives you the real circumstances of such and such events, however valuable for occasional reference, may not be, in the real sense of the word, a "book" at all, nor in the real sense, to be "read." A book is essentially not a talked thing, but a written thing; and written not with a view of mere communication, but of permanence. The book of talk is printed only because its author cannot speak to thousands of people at once; if he could, he would — the volume is mere *multiplication* of his voice. You cannot talk to your friend in India; if you could, you would; you write instead: that is mere *conveyance* of voice. But a book is written, not to multiply the voice merely, not to carry it merely, but to perpetuate it. The author has something to say which he perceives to be true and useful, or helpfully beautiful. So far as he knows, no one has yet said it; so far as he knows, no one else can say it. He is bound to say it, clearly and melodiously if he may; clearly, at all events. In the sum of his life he finds this to be the thing, or group of things, manifest to him; — this, the piece of true knowledge,

or sight, which his share of sunshine and earth has permitted him to seize. He would fain set it down forever; engrave it on rock, if he could; saying, "This is the best of me; for the rest, I ate, and drank, and slept, loved and hated, like another; my life was as the vapor, and is not; but this I saw and knew: this if anything of mine, is worth your memory." That is his "writing"; it is, in his small human way, and with whatever degree of true inspiration is in him, his inscription, or scripture. That is a "Book."

10. Perhaps you think no books were ever so written?

But, again, I ask you, do you at all believe in honesty, or at all in kindness? or do you think there is never any honesty or benevolence in wise people? None of us, I hope, are so unhappy as to think that. Well, whatever bit of a wise man's work is honestly and benevolently done, that bit is his book, or his piece of art. It is mixed always with evil fragments — ill-done, redundant, affected work. But if you read rightly, you will easily discover the true bits, and those *are* the book.

11. Now, books of this kind have been written in all ages by their greatest men, — by great readers, great statesmen, and great thinkers. These are all at your choice; and Life is short. You have heard as much before; — yet, have you measured and mapped out this short life and its possibilities? Do you know, if you read this, that you cannot read that — that what you lose to-day you cannot gain to-morrow? Will you go and gossip with your housemaid, or your stable-boy, when you may talk with queens and kings; or flatter yourselves that it is with any worthy consciousness of your own claims to respect, that you jostle with the hungry and common crowd for *entrée* here, and audience there, when all the while this eternal court is open to you, with its society, wide as the world, multitudinous as its days, the chosen, and the mighty, of every place and time? Into that

you may enter always; in that you may take fellowship and rank according to your wish; from that, once entered into it, you can never be an outcast but by your own fault; by your aristocracy of companionship there, your own inherent aristocracy will be assuredly tested, and the motives with which you strive to take high place in the society of the living, measured, as to all the truth and sincerity that are in them, by the place you desire to take in this company of the Dead.

12. "The place you desire," and the place *you fit yourself for*, I must also say; because, observe, this court of the past differs from all living aristocracy in this:— it is open to labor and to merit, but to nothing else. No wealth will bribe, no name overawe, no artifice deceive, the guardian of those Elysian gates. In the deep sense, no vile or vulgar person ever enters there. At the portières of that silent Faubourg St. Germain, there is but brief question: "Do you deserve to enter? Pass. Do you ask to be the companion of nobles? Make yourself noble, and you shall be. Do you long for the conversation of the wise? Learn to understand it, and you shall hear it. But on other terms?— no. If you will not rise to us, we cannot stoop to you. The living lord may assume courtesy, the living philosopher explain his thought to you with considerate pain; but here we neither feign nor interpret; you must rise to the level of our thoughts if you would be gladdened by them, and share our feelings if you would recognize our presence."

13. This, then, is what you have to do, and I admit that it is much. You must, in a word, love these people, if you are to be among them. No ambition is of any use. They scorn your ambition. You must love them, and show your love in these two following ways.

I. First, by a true desire to be taught by them, and to enter into their thoughts. To enter into theirs, observe;

not to find your own expressed by them. If the person who wrote the book is not wiser than you, you need not read it; if he be, he will think differently from you in many respects.

Very ready we are to say of a book, "How good this is — that's exactly what I think!" But the right feeling is, "How strange that is! I never thought of that before, and yet I see it is true; or if I do not now, I hope I shall, some day." But whether thus submissively or not, at least be sure that you go to the author to get at *his* meaning, not to find yours. Judge it afterwards if you think yourself qualified to do so; but ascertain it first. And be sure also, if the author is worth anything, that you will not get at his meaning all at once; — nay, that at his whole meaning you will not for a long time arrive in any wise. Not that he does not say what he means, and in strong words too; but he cannot say it all; and what is more strange, *will* not, but in a hidden way and in parable, in order that he may be sure you want it. I cannot quite see the reason of this, nor analyze that cruel reticence in the breasts of wise men which makes them always hide their deeper thought. They do not give it you by way of help, but of reward; and will make themselves sure that you deserve it before they allow you to reach it. But it is the same with the physical type of wisdom, gold. There seems, to you and me, no reason why the electric forces of the earth should not carry whatever there is of gold within it at once to the mountain tops, so that kings and people might know that all the gold they could get was there; and without any trouble of digging, or anxiety, or chance, or waste of time, cut it away, and coin as much as they needed. But Nature does not manage it so. She puts it in little fissures in the earth, nobody knows where; you may dig long and find none; you must dig painfully to find any.

14. And it **is** just the same with men's best wisdom.

When you come to a good book, you must ask yourself, "Am I inclined to work as an Australian miner would? Are my pickaxes and shovels in good order, and am I in good trim myself, my sleeves well up to the elbow, and my breath good, and my temper?" And, keeping the figure a little longer, even at cost of tiresomeness, for it is a thoroughly useful one, the metal you are in search of being the author's mind or meaning, his words are as the rock which you have to crush and smelt in order to get at it. And your pickaxes are your own care, wit, and learning; your smelting furnace is your own thoughtful soul. Do not hope to get at any good author's meaning without those tools and that fire; often you will need sharpest, finest chiselling, and patientest fusing, before you can gather one grain of the metal.

15. And, therefore, first of all, I tell you earnestly and authoritatively (I *know* I am right in this), you must get into the habit of looking intensely at words, and assuring yourself of their meaning, syllable by syllable — nay, letter by letter. For though it is only by reason of the opposition of letters in the function of signs, to sounds in the function of signs, that the study of books is called "literature," and that a man versed in it is called, by the consent of nations, a man of letters instead of a man of books, or of words, you may yet connect with that accidental nomenclature this real fact, — that you might read all the books in the British Museum (if you could live long enough), and remain an utterly "illiterate," uneducated person; but that if you read ten pages of a good book, letter by letter, — that is to say, with real accuracy, — you are forevermore in some measure an educated person. The entire difference between education and non-education (as regards the merely intellectual part of it) consists in this accuracy. A well-educated gentleman may not know many languages, — may not be able to speak any but his own, — may have read very few books.

But whatever language he knows, he knows precisely; whatever word he pronounces, he pronounces rightly; above all, he is learned in the *peerage* of words; knows the words of true descent and ancient blood, at a glance, from words of modern canaille; remembers all their ancestry, their intermarriages, distant relationships, and the extent to which they were admitted, and offices they held, among the national noblesse of words at any time, and in any country. But an uneducated person may know, by memory, many languages, and talk them all, and yet truly know not a word of any, — not a word even of his own. An ordinarily clever and sensible seaman will be able to make his way ashore at most ports; yet he has only to speak a sentence of any language to be known for an illiterate person; so also the accent, or turn of expression of a single sentence, will at once mark a scholar. And this is so strongly felt, so conclusively admitted, by educated persons, that a false accent or a mistaken syllable is enough, in the parliament of any civilized nation, to assign to a man a certain degree of inferior standing forever.

16. And this is right; but it is a pity that the accuracy insisted on is not greater, and required to a serious purpose. It is right that a false Latin quantity should excite a smile in the House of Commons; but it is wrong that a false English *meaning* should *not* excite a frown there. Let the accent of words be watched, and closely; let their meaning be watched more closely still, and fewer will do the work. A few words, well chosen and distinguished, will do work that a thousand cannot, when every one is acting, equivocally, in the function of another. Yes; and words, if they are not watched, will do deadly work sometimes. There are masked words droning and skulking about us in Europe just now — (there never were so many, owing to the spread of a shallow, blotching, blundering, infectious "information," or

rather deformation, everywhere, and to the teaching of catechisms and phrases at schools instead of human meanings) — there are masked words abroad, I say, which nobody understands, but which everybody uses, and most people will also fight for, live for, or even die for, fancying they mean this or that, or the other, of things dear to them: for such words wear chameleon cloaks — "ground-lion" cloaks, of the color of the ground of any man's fancy: on that ground they lie in wait, and rend him with a spring from it. There never were creatures of prey so mischievous, never diplomatists so cunning, never poisoners so deadly, as these masked words; they are the unjust stewards of all men's ideas: whatever fancy or favorite instinct a man most cherishes, he gives to his favorite masked word to take care of for him; the word at last comes to have an infinite power over him, — you cannot get at him but by its ministry.

17. And in languages so mongrel in breed as the English, there is a fatal power of equivocation put into men's hands, almost whether they will or no, in being able to use Greek or Latin words for an idea when they want it to be awful; and Saxon or otherwise common words when they want it to be vulgar. What a singular and salutary effect, for instance, would be produced on the minds of people who are in the habit of taking the Form of the "Word" they live by, for the Power of which that Word tells them, if we always either retained, or refused, the Greek form "biblos," or "biblion," as the right expression for "book" — instead of employing it only in the one instance in which we wish to give dignity to the idea, and translating it into English everywhere else. How wholesome it would be for many simple persons if, in such places (for instance) as Acts xix. 19, we retained the Greek expression, instead of translating it, and they had to read — "Many of them also which used curious arts, brought their bibles together, and burnt them before all

men; and they counted the price of them, and found it fifty thousand pieces of silver"! Or if, on the other hand, we translated where we retain it, and always spoke of "the Holy Book," instead of "Holy Bible," it might come into more heads than it does at present, that the Word of God, by which the heavens were, of old, and by which they are now kept in store, cannot be made a present of to anybody in morocco binding, nor sown on any wayside by help either of steam plough or steam press; but is nevertheless being offered to us daily, and by us with contumely refused; and sown in us daily, and by us, as instantly as may be, choked.

18. So, again, consider what effect has been produced on the English vulgar mind by the use of the sonorous Latin form "damno," in translating the Greek κατακρίνω, when people charitably wish to make it forcible; and the substitution of the temperate "condemn" for it, when they choose to keep it gentle; and what notable sermons have been preached by illiterate clergymen on — "He that believeth not shall be damned"; though they would shrink with horror from translating Heb. xi. 7, "The saving of his house, by which he damned the world," or John viii. 10-11, "Woman, hath no man damned thee? She saith, No man, Lord. Jesus answered her, Neither do I damn thee: go, and sin no more." And divisions in the mind of Europe, which have cost seas of blood, and in the defence of which the noblest souls of men have been cast away in frantic desolation, countless as forest leaves, — though, in the heart of them, founded on deeper causes, — have nevertheless been rendered practically possible, mainly, by the European adoption of the Greek word for a public meeting, "ecclesia," to give peculiar respectability to such meetings, when held for religious purposes; and other collateral equivocations, such as the vulgar English one of using the word "priest" as a contraction for "presbyter."

19. Now, in order to deal with words rightly, this is the habit you must form. Nearly every word in your language has been first a word of some other language — of Saxon, German, French, Latin, or Greek (not to speak of Eastern and primitive dialects). And many words have been all these; — that is to say, have been Greek first, Latin next, French or German next, and English last: undergoing a certain change of sense and use on the lips of each nation; but retaining a deep vital meaning, which all good scholars feel in employing them, even at this day. If you do not know the Greek alphabet, learn it; young or old — girl or boy — whoever you may be, if you think of reading seriously (which, of course, implies that you have some leisure at command), learn your Greek alphabet; then get good dictionaries of all these languages, and whenever you are in doubt about a word, hunt it down patiently. Read Max Müller's lectures thoroughly, to begin with; and, after that, never let a word escape you that looks suspicious. It is severe work; but you will find it, even at first, interesting, and at last, endlessly amusing. And the general gain to your character, in power and precision, will be quite incalculable.

Mind, this does not imply knowing, or trying to know, Greek, or Latin, or French. It takes a whole life to learn any language perfectly. But you can easily ascertain the meanings through which the English word has passed; and those which in a good writer's work it must still bear.

20. And now, merely for example's sake, I will, with your permission, read a few lines of a true book with you carefully; and see what will come out of them. I will take a book perfectly known to you all. No English words are more familiar to us, yet few perhaps have been read with less sincerity. I will take these few following lines of Lycidas.

"Last came, and last did go,
The Pilot of the Galilean lake.
Two massy keys he bore of metals twain
(The golden opes, the iron shuts amain).
He shook his mitred locks, and stern bespake: —
'How well could I have spared for thee, young swain,
Anow of such as, for their bellies' sake,
Creep, and intrude, and climb into the fold!
Of other care they little reckoning make
Than how to scramble at the shearers' feast,
And shove away the worthy bidden guest.
Blind mouths! that scarce themselves know how to hold
A sheep-hook, or have learned aught else the least
That to the faithful Herdman's art belongs!
What recks it them? What need they? They are sped
And when they list, their lean and flashy songs
Grate on their scrannel pipes of wretched straw;
The hungry sheep look up, and are not fed,
But swoln with wind and the rank mist they draw,
Rot inwardly, and foul contagion spread;
Besides what the grim Wolf with privy paw
Daily devours apace, and nothing said.'"

Let us think over this passage, and examine its words.

First, is it not singular to find Milton assigning to St. Peter, not only his full episcopal function, but the very types of it which Protestants usually refuse most passionately? His "mitred" locks! Milton was no bishop-lover; how comes St. Peter to be "mitred"? "Two massy keys he bore." Is this, then, the power of the keys claimed by the Bishops of Rome, and is it acknowledged here by Milton only in a poetical license, for the sake of its picturesqueness, that he may get the gleam of the golden keys to help his effect?

Do not think it. Great men do not play stage tricks with the doctrines of life and death: only little men do that. Milton means what he says; and means it with his might too — is going to put the whole strength of his spirit presently into the saying of it. For though not a lover of false bishops, he *was* a lover of true ones; and the Lake-pilot is here, in his thoughts, the type and head of true episcopal power. For Milton reads that text, "I will give unto thee the keys of the kingdom of Heaven," quite honestly. Puritan though he be, he would not blot it out of the book because there have been bad bishops; nay, in order to understand *him*, we must understand that verse first; it will not do to eye it askance, or whisper it under our breath, as if it were a weapon of an adverse sect. It is a solemn, universal assertion, deeply to be kept in mind by all sects. But perhaps we shall be better able to reason on it if we go on a little farther, and come back to it. For clearly this marked insistence on the power of the true episcopate is to make us feel more weightily what is to be charged against the false claimants of episcopate; or generally, against false claimants of power and rank in the body of the clergy: they who, "for their bellies' sake, creep, and intrude, and climb into the fold."

21. Never think Milton uses those three words to fill up his verse, as a loose writer would. He needs all the three; — specially those three, and no more than those — "creep," and "intrude," and "climb"; no other words would or could serve the turn, and no more could be added. For they exhaustively comprehend the three classes, correspondent to the three characters, of men who dishonestly seek ecclesiastical power. First, those who "creep" into the fold; who do not care for office, nor name, but for secret influence, and do all things occultly and cunningly, consenting to any servility of office or conduct, so only that they may intimately discern, and unawares direct, the minds of men. Then those who "intrude" (thrust, that is) themselves into the fold, who by natural insolence of heart, and stout eloquence of tongue, and fearlessly perseverant self-assertion, obtain hearing and authority with the common crowd. Lastly, those who "climb," who, by labor and learning, both stout and sound, but selfishly exerted in the cause of their own

ambition, gain high dignities and authorities, and become "lords over the heritage," though not "ensamples to the flock."

22. Now go on: —

> "Of other care they little reckoning make,
> Than how to scramble at the shearers' feast.
> *Blind mouths*" —

I pause again, for this is a strange expression: a broken metaphor, one might think, careless and unscholarly.

Not so; its very audacity and pithiness are intended to make us look close at the phrase and remember it. Those two monosyllables express the precisely accurate contraries of right character, in the two great offices of the Church — those of bishop and pastor.

A "Bishop" means "a person who sees."

A "Pastor" means "a person who feeds."

The most unbishoply character a man can have is therefore to be Blind.

The most unpastoral is, instead of feeding, to want to be fed, — to be a Mouth.

Take the two reverses together, and you have "blind mouths." We may advisably follow out this idea a little. Nearly all the evils in the Church have arisen from bishops desiring *power* more than *light*. They want authority, not outlook. Whereas their real office is not to rule; though it may be vigorously to exhort and rebuke; it is the king's office to rule; the bishop's office is to *oversee* the flock; to number it, sheep by sheep; to be ready always to give full account of it. Now, it is clear he cannot give account of the souls, if he has not so much as numbered the bodies of his flock. The first thing, therefore, that a bishop has to do is at least to put himself in a position in which, at any moment, he can obtain the history, from childhood, of every living soul in his diocese, and of its present state. Down in that back street, Bill and Nancy, knocking each other's teeth out! — Does the bishop know all about it? Has he his eye upon them? Has he *had* his eye upon them? Can he circumstantially explain to us how Bill got into the habit of beating Nancy about the head? If he cannot, he is no bishop, though he had a mitre as high as Salisbury steeple; he is no bishop, — he has sought to be at the helm instead of the mast-head; he has no sight of things. "Nay," you say, "it is not his duty to look after Bill in the back street." What! the fat sheep that have full fleeces — you think it is only those he should look after, while (go back to your Milton) "the hungry sheep look up, and are not fed, besides what the grim Wolf, with privy paw" (bishops knowing nothing about it), "daily devours apace, and nothing said"?

"But that's not our idea of a bishop." Perhaps not; but it was St. Paul's; and it was Milton's. They may be right, or we may be; but we must not think we are reading either one or the other by putting our meaning into their words.

23. I go on.

"But swoln with wind and the rank mist they draw."

This is to meet the vulgar answer that "if the poor are not looked after in their bodies, they are in their souls; they have spiritual food."

And Milton says, "They have no such thing as spiritual food; they are only swollen with wind." At first you may think that is a coarse type, and an obscure one. But again, it is a quite literally accurate one. Take up your Latin and Greek dictionaries, and find out the meaning of "Spirit." It is only a contraction of the Latin word "breath," and an indistinct translation of the Greek word for "wind." The same word is used in writing, "The wind bloweth where it listeth"; and in writing, "So is every one that is born of the Spirit"; born of the *breath*, that is; for it means the breath of

God, in soul and body. We have the true sense of it in our words "inspiration" and "expire." Now, there are two kinds of breath with which the flock may be filled; God's breath and man's. The breath of God is health, and life, and peace to them, as the air of heaven is to the flocks on the hills; but man's breath — the word which *he* calls spiritual — is disease and contagion to them, as the fog of the fen. They rot inwardly with it; they are puffed up by it, as a dead body by the vapors of its own decomposition. This is literally true of all false religious teaching; the first, and last, and fatalest sign of it is that "puffing up." Your converted children, who teach their parents; your converted convicts, who teach honest men; your converted dunces, who, having lived in cretinous stupefaction half their lives, suddenly awaking to the fact of there being a God, fancy themselves therefore his peculiar people and messengers; your sectarians of every species, small and great, Catholic or Protestant, of high church or low, in so far as they think themselves exclusively in the right and others wrong; and preëminently, in every sect, those who hold that men can be saved by thinking rightly instead of doing rightly, by word instead of act, and wish instead of work; — these are the true fog children — clouds, these, without water; bodies, these, of putrescent vapor and skin, without blood or flesh: blown bagpipes for the fiends to pipe with — corrupt, and corrupting — "Swoln with wind and the rank mist they draw."

24. Lastly, let us return to the lines respecting the power of the keys, for now we can understand them. Note the difference between Milton and Dante in their interpretation of this power; for once, the latter is weaker in thought; he supposes *both* the keys to be of the gate of heaven; one is of gold, the other of silver: they are given by St. Peter to the sentinel angel; and it is not easy to determine the meaning either of the substances of the three steps of the gate, or of

the two keys. But Milton makes one, of gold, the key of heaven; the other, of iron, the key of the prison in which the wicked teachers are to be bound who "have taken away the key of knowledge, yet entered not in themselves."

We have seen that the duties of bishop and pastor are to see, and feed; and of all who do so it is said, "He that watereth, shall be watered also himself." But the reverse is truth also. He that watereth not, shall be *withered* himself; and he that seeth not, shall himself be shut out of sight — shut into the perpetual prison-house. And that prison opens here, as well as hereafter; he who is to be bound in heaven must first be bound on earth. That command to the strong angels, of which the rock-apostle is the image, "Take him, and bind him hand and foot, and cast him out," issues, in its measure, against the teacher, for every help withheld, and for every truth refused, and for every falsehood enforced; so that he is more strictly fettered the more he fetters, and farther outcast, as he more and more misleads, till at last the bars of the iron cage close upon him, and as "the golden opes, the iron shuts amain."

25. We have got something out of the lines, I think, and much more is yet to be found in them; but we have done enough by way of example of the kind of word-by-word examination of your author which is rightly called "reading"; watching every accent and expression, and putting ourselves always in the author's place, annihilating our own personality, and seeking to enter into his, so as to be able assuredly to say, "Thus Milton thought," not "Thus *I* thought, in mis-reading Milton." And by this process you will gradually come to attach less weight to your own "Thus I thought" at other times. You will begin to perceive that what *you* thought was a matter of no serious importance; that your thoughts on any subject are not perhaps the clearest and wisest that could be arrived at thereupon: in fact,

that unless you are a very singular person, you cannot be
said to have any "thoughts" at all; that you have no materials for them, in any serious matters; — no right to "think,"
but only to try to learn more of the facts. Nay, most probably all your life (unless, as I said, you are a singular person)
you will have no legitimate right to an "opinion" on any
business, except that instantly under your hand. What
must of necessity be done, you can always find out, beyond
question, how to do. Have you a house to keep in order, a
commodity to sell, a field to plough, a ditch to cleanse?
There need be no two opinions about these proceedings; it is
at your peril if you have not much more than an "opinion"
on the way to manage such matters. And also, outside of
your own business, there are one or two subjects on which
you are bound to have but one opinion. That roguery and
lying are objectionable, and are instantly to be flogged out
of the way whenever discovered; that covetousness and love
of quarrelling are dangerous dispositions even in children,
and deadly dispositions in men and nations; that in the end,
the God of heaven and earth loves active, modest, and kind
people, and hates idle, proud, greedy, and cruel ones; — on
these general facts you are bound to have but one, and that
a very strong opinion. For the rest, respecting religions,
governments, sciences, arts, you will find that, on the whole,
you can know NOTHING, — judge nothing; that the best you
can do, even though you may be a well-educated person, is to
be silent, and strive to be wiser every day, and to understand
a little more of the thoughts of others, which so soon as you
try to do honestly, you will discover that the thoughts even
of the wisest are very little more than pertinent questions.
To put the difficulty into a clear shape, and exhibit to you
the grounds for *in*decision, that is all they can generally do
for you! — and well for them and for us, if indeed they are
able "to mix the music with our thoughts, and sadden us

with heavenly doubts." This writer, from whom I have been reading to you, is not among the first or wisest: he sees shrewdly as far as he sees, and therefore it is easy to find out his full meaning; but with the greater men, you cannot fathom their meaning; they do not even wholly measure it themselves, — it is so wide. Suppose I had asked you, for instance, to seek for Shakespeare's opinion, instead of Milton's, on this matter of Church authority? — or for Dante's? Have any of you, at this instant, the least idea what either thought about it? Have you ever balanced the scene with the bishops in Richard III. against the character of Cranmer? the description of St. Francis and St. Dominic against that of him who made Virgil wonder to gaze upon him, — "disteso, tanto vilmente, nell' eterno esilio";[1] or of him whom Dante stood beside, "come 'l frate che confessa lo perfido assassino"?[2] Shakespeare and Alighieri knew men better than most of us. I presume! They were both in the midst of the main struggle between the temporal and spiritual powers. They had an opinion, we may guess. But where is it? Bring it into court! Put Shakespeare's or Dante's creed into articles, and send *it* up for trial by the Ecclesiastical Courts!

26. You will not be able, I tell you again, for many and many a day, to come at the real purposes and teaching of these great men; but a very little honest study of them will enable you to perceive that what you took for your own "judgment" was mere chance prejudice, and drifted, helpless, entangled weed of castaway thought; nay, you will see

---

[1] Dante's *Inferno*, Canto xxiii. 125, 126.
  "O'er him who was extended on the cross
    So vilely in eternal banishment."]
[2] The same, Canto xix. 49, 50.
  "I stood even as the friar who is confessing
    The false assassin."
                    Longfellow's translation.]

that most men's minds are indeed little better than rough heath wilderness, neglected and stubborn, partly barren, partly overgrown with pestilent brakes, and venomous, wind-sown herbage of evil surmise; that the first thing you have to do for them, and yourself, is eagerly and scornfully to set fire to *this;* burn all the jungle into wholesome ash-heaps, and then plough and sow. All the true literary work before you, for life, must begin with obedience to that order, "Break up your fallow ground, and *sow not among thorns.*"

27. II. Having then faithfully listened to the great teachers, that you may enter into their Thoughts, you have yet this higher advance to make; — you have to enter into their Hearts. As you go to them first for clear sight, so you must stay with them, that you may share at last their just and mighty Passion. Passion, or "sensation." I am not afraid of the word; still less of the thing. You have heard many outcries against sensation lately; but, I can tell you, it is not less sensation we want, but more. The ennobling difference between one man and another — between one animal and another — is precisely in this, that one feels more than another. If we were sponges, perhaps sensation might not be easily got for us; if we were earth-worms, liable at every instant to be cut in two by the spade, perhaps too much sensation might not be good for us. But being human creatures, *it is* good for us; nay, we are only human in so far as we are sensitive, and our honor is precisely in proportion to our passion.

28. You know I said of that great and pure society of the Dead, that it would allow "no vain or vulgar person to enter there." What do you think I meant by a "vulgar" person? What do you yourselves mean by "vulgarity"? You will find it a fruitful subject of thought; but, briefly, the essence of all vulgarity lies in want of sensation. Simple and innocent vulgarity is merely an untrained and undeveloped

bluntness of body and mind; but in true inbred vulgarity, there is a deathful callousness, which, in extremity, becomes capable of every sort of bestial habit and crime, without fear, without pleasure, without horror, and without pity. It is in the blunt hand and the dead heart, in the diseased habit, in the hardened conscience, that men become vulgar; they are forever vulgar, precisely in proportion as they are incapable of sympathy — of quick understanding, — of all that, in deep insistence on the common but most accurate term, may be called the "tact," or "touch-faculty," of body and soul: that tact which the Mimosa has in trees, which the pure woman has above all creatures: fineness and fulness of sensation, beyond reason; the guide and sanctifier of reason itself. Reason can but determine what is true: — it is the God-given passion of humanity which alone can recognize what God has made good.

29. We come then to that great concourse of the Dead, not merely to know from them what is true, but chiefly to feel with them what is just. Now, to feel with them, we must be like them; and none of us can become that without pains. As the true knowledge is disciplined and tested knowledge, — not the first thought that comes, — so the true passion is disciplined and tested passion, — not the first passion that comes. The first that come are the vain, the false, the treacherous; if you yield to them, they will lead you wildly and far, in vain pursuit, in hollow enthusiasm, till you have no true purpose and no true passion left. Not that any feeling possible to humanity is in itself wrong, but only wrong when undisciplined. Its nobility is in its force and justice; it is wrong when it is weak, and felt for paltry cause. There is a mean wonder, as of a child who sees a juggler tossing golden balls, and this is base, if you will. But do you think that the wonder is ignoble, or the sensation less, with which every human soul is called to

watch the golden balls of heaven tossed through the night by the Hand that made them? There is a mean curiosity, as of a child opening a forbidden door, or a servant prying into her master's business; — and a noble curiosity, questioning, in the front of danger, the source of the great river beyond the sand, — the place of the great continent beyond the sea; — a nobler curiosity still, which questions of the source of the River of Life, and of the space of the Continent of Heaven — things which "the angels desire to look into." So the anxiety is ignoble, with which you linger over the course and catastrophe of an idle tale; but do you think the anxiety is less, or greater, with which you watch, or *ought* to watch, the dealings of fate and destiny with the life of an agonized nation? Alas! it is the narrowness, selfishness, minuteness, of your sensation that you have to deplore in England at this day; — sensation which spends itself in bouquets and speeches; in revellings and junketings; in sham fights and gay puppet shows, while you can look on and see noble nations murdered, man by man, without an effort or a tear.

30. I said "minuteness" and "selfishness" of sensation, but it would have been enough to have said "injustice" or 'unrighteousness" of sensation. For as in nothing is a gentleman better to be discerned from a vulgar person, so in nothing is a gentle nation (such nations have been) better to be discerned from a mob, than in this, — that their feelings are constant and just, results of due contemplation, and of equal thought. You can talk a mob into anything; its feelings may be — usually are — on the whole, generous and right; but it has no foundation for them, no hold of them; you may tease or tickle it into any, at your pleasure; it thinks by infection, for the most part, catching an opinion like a cold, and there is nothing so little that it will not roar itself wild about, when the fit is on; — nothing so great but it will

forget in an hour, when the fit is past. But a gentleman's, or a gentle nation's, passions are just, measured, and continuous. A great nation, for instance, does not spend its entire national wits for a couple of months in weighing evidence of a single ruffian's having done a single murder; and for a couple of years see its own children murder each other by their thousands or tens of thousands a day, considering only what the effect is likely to be on the price of cotton, and caring nowise to determine which side of battle is in the wrong. Neither does a great nation send its poor little boys to jail for stealing six walnuts; and allow its bankrupts to steal their hundreds of thousands with a bow, and its bankers rich with poor men's savings, to close their doors "under circumstances over which they have no control," with a "by your leave"; and large landed estates to be bought by men who have made their money by going with armed steamers up and down the China Seas, selling opium at the cannon's mouth, and altering, for the benefit of the foreign nation, the common highwayman's demand of "your money *or* your life," into that of "your money *and* your life." Neither does a great nation allow the lives of its innocent poor to be parched out of them by fog fever, and rotted out of them by dunghill plague, for the sake of sixpence a life extra per week to its landlords; and then debate, with drivelling tears, and diabolical sympathies, whether it ought not piously to save, and nursingly cherish, the lives of its murderers. Also, a great nation, having made up its mind that hanging is quite the wholesomest process for its homicides in general, can yet with mercy distinguish between the degrees of guilt in homicides; and does not yelp like a pack of frost-pinched wolf-cubs on the blood-track of an unhappy crazed boy, or gray-haired clodpate Othello, "perplexed i' the extreme," at the very moment that it is sending a Minister of the Crown to make polite speeches to a man who is bayoneting young girls in their fathers' sight, and killing noble youths in cool blood, faster than a country butcher kills lambs in spring. And, lastly, a great nation does not mock Heaven and its Powers, by pretending belief in a revelation which asserts the love of money to be the root of *all* evil, and declaring, at the same time, that it is actuated, and intends to be actuated, in all chief national deeds and measures, by no other love.

31. My friends, I do not know why any of us should talk about reading. We want some sharper discipline than that of reading; but, at all events, be assured, we cannot read. No reading is possible for a people with its mind in this state. No sentence of any great writer is intelligible to them. It is simply and sternly impossible for the English public, at this moment, to understand any thoughtful writing, — so incapable of thought has it become in its insanity of avarice. Happily, our disease is, as yet, little worse than this incapacity of thought; it is not corruption of the inner nature; we ring true still when anything strikes home to us; and though the idea that everything should "pay" has infected our every purpose so deeply, that even when we would play the good Samaritan, we never take out our twopence and give them to the host without saying, "When I come again, thou shalt give me fourpence," there is a capacity of noble passion left in our hearts' core. We show it in our work — in our war — even in those unjust domestic affections which make us furious at a small private wrong, while we are polite to a boundless public one: we are still industrious to the last hour of the day, though we add the gambler's fury to the laborer's patience; we are still brave to the death, though incapable of discerning true cause for battle; and are still true in affection to our own flesh, to the death, as the sea-monsters are, and the rock-eagles. And there is hope for a nation while this can be still said of it. As long as it holds its life in its hand, ready to give it for its honor (though a foolish honor),

for its love (though a selfish love), and for its business (though a base business), there is hope for it. But hope only; for this instinctive, reckless virtue cannot last. No nation can last, which has made a mob of itself, however generous at heart. It must discipline its passions, and direct them, or they will discipline *it*, one day, with scorpion-whips. Above all, a nation cannot last as a money-making mob: it cannot with impunity — it cannot with existence — go on despising literature, despising science, despising art, despising nature, despising compassion, and concentrating its soul on Pence. . . .

KNOWLEDGE VIEWED IN RELATION TO LEARNING

JOHN HENRY NEWMAN
1801–1890

THIS is the sixth of the nine *Discourses on University Teaching* that Cardinal Newman delivered in 1852, on the founding of a Catholic University in Dublin. In the early lectures he argued for the study of theology as proper to a university; but certain of the discourses were devoted to a plea for education as an end in itself, as a broadening influence and a builder of character. To this group the following essay belongs. Newman's rich and finely measured prose is characterized by logical method and deep sincerity.

IT were well if the English, like the Greek language, possessed some definite word to express, simply and generally, intellectual proficiency or perfection, such as "health," as used with reference to the animal frame, and "virtue," with reference to our moral nature. I am not able to find such a term; — talent, ability, genius, belong distinctly to the raw material, which is the subject-matter, not to that excellence which is the result of exercise and training. When we turn, indeed, to the particular kinds of intellectual perfection, words are forthcoming for our purpose, as, for instance, judgment, taste, and skill; yet even these belong, for the most part, to powers or habits bearing upon practice or upon art, and not to any perfect condition of the intellect, considered in itself. Wisdom, again, is certainly a more comprehensive word than any other, but it has a direct relation to conduct and to human life. Knowledge, indeed, and Science express purely intellectual ideas, but still not a state or quality of the intellect; for knowledge, in its ordinary sense, is but one of its circumstances, denoting a possession or a habit; and science has been appropriated to the subject-matter of the intellect, instead of belonging in English, as it ought to do, to the intellect itself. The consequence is that, on an occasion like this, many words are necessary, in order, first, to bring out and convey what surely is no difficult idea in itself, — that of the cultivation of the intellect as an end; next, in order to recommend what surely is no unreasonable object; and lastly, to describe and make the mind realize the particular perfection in which that object consists. Every one knows practically what are the constituents of health or of virtue; and every one recognizes health and virtue as ends to be pursued; it is otherwise with intellectual excellence, and this must be my excuse, if I seem to any one to be bestowing a good deal of labour on a preliminary matter.

In default of a recognized term, I have called the perfection or virtue of the intellect by the name of philosophy, philosophical knowledge, enlargement of mind, or illumination; terms which are not uncommonly given to it by writers of this day; but, whatever name we bestow on it, it is, I believe, as a matter of history, the business of a University to make this intellectual culture its direct scope, or to employ itself in the education of the intellect, — just as the work of a Hospital lies in healing the sick or wounded, of a Riding or Fencing School, or of a Gymnasium, in exercising the limbs, of an Almshouse, in aiding and solacing the old, of an Orphanage, in protecting innocence, of a Penitentiary, in restoring the guilty. I say, a University, taken in its bare idea, and before we view it as an instrument of the Church, has this object and this mission; it contemplates neither moral impression nor mechanical production; it professes to exercise the mind neither in art nor in duty; its function is intellectual culture; here it may leave its scholars, and it has done its work when it has done as much as this. It educates the intellect to reason well in all matters, to reach out towards truth, and to grasp it.

This, I said in my foregoing Discourse, was the object of a University, viewed in itself, and apart from the Catholic Church, or from the State, or from any other power which may use it; and I illustrated this in various ways. I said that the intellect must have an excellence of its own, for there was nothing which had not its specific good; that the word "educate" would not be used of intellectual culture, as it is used, had not the intellect had an end of its own; that, had it not such an end, there would be no meaning in calling certain intellectual exercises "liberal," in contrast with "useful," as is commonly done; that the very notion of a philosophical temper implied it, for it threw us back upon research and system as ends in themselves, distinct from effects and works of any kind; that a philosophical scheme of knowledge, or system of sciences, could not, from the nature of the case, issue in any one definite art or pursuit, as its end; and that, on the other hand, the discovery and contemplation of truth, to which research and systematizing led, were surely sufficient ends, though nothing beyond them were added, and that they had ever been accounted sufficient by mankind.

Here then I take up the subject; and, having determined that the cultivation of the intellect is an end distinct and sufficient in itself, and that, so far as words go it is an enlargement or illumination, I proceed to inquire what this mental breadth, or power, or light, or philosophy consists in. A Hospital heals a broken limb or cures a fever: what does an Institution effect, which professes the health, not of the body, not of the soul, but of the intellect? What is this good, which in former times, as well as our own, has been found worth the notice, the appropriation, of the Catholic Church?

I have then to investigate, in the Discourses which follow, those qualities and characteristics of the intellect in which its cultivation issues or rather consists; and, with a view of assisting myself in this undertaking, I shall recur to certain questions which have already been touched upon. These questions are three: viz. the relation of intellectual culture, first, to *mere* knowledge; secondly, to *professional* knowledge; and thirdly, to *religious* knowledge. In other words, are *acquirements* and *attainments* the scope of a University Education? or *expertness in particular arts and pursuits?* or *moral and religious proficiency?* or something besides these three? These questions I shall examine in succession, with the purpose I have mentioned; and I hope to be excused, if, in this anxious undertaking, I am led to repeat what, either in these Discourses or elsewhere, I have already put upon paper. And first, of *Mere Knowledge*, or Learning, and its connexion with intellectual illumination or Philosophy.

I suppose the *primâ-facie* view which the public at large would take of a University, considering it as a place of Education, is nothing more or less than a place for acquiring a great deal of knowledge on a great many subjects. Memory is one of the first developed of the mental faculties; a boy's business when he goes to school is to learn, that is, to store up things in his memory. For some years his intellect is little more than an instrument for taking in facts, or a receptacle for storing them; he welcomes them as fast as they come to him; he lives on what is without; he has his eyes ever about him; he has a lively susceptibility of impressions; he imbibes information of every kind; and little does he make his own in a true sense of the word, living rather upon his neighbours all around him. He has opinions, religious, political, and literary, and, for a boy, is very positive in them and sure about them; but he gets them from his schoolfellows, or his masters, or his parents, as the case may be. Such as he is in his other relations, such also is he in his school exercises; his mind is observant, sharp, ready, retentive: he is almost passive in the acquisition of knowledge. I say this in no disparagement of the idea of a clever boy. Geography, chronology, history, language, natural history, he heaps up the matter of these studies as treasures for a future day. It is the seven years of plenty with him: he gathers in by handfuls, like the Egyptians, without counting; and though, as time goes on, there is exercise for his argumentative powers in the Elements of Mathematics, and for his taste in the Poets and Orators, still, while at school, or at least, till quite the last years of his time, he acquires, and little more; and when he is leaving for the University, he is mainly the creature of foreign influences and circumstances, and made up of accidents, homogeneous or not, as the case may be. Moreover, the moral habits, which are a boy's praise, encourage and assist this result; that is, diligence, assiduity, regularity, despatch, persevering application; for these are the direct conditions of acquisition, and naturally lead to it. Acquirements, again, are emphatically producible, and at a moment; they are a something to show, both for master and scholar; an audience, even though ignorant themselves of the subjects of an examination, can comprehend when questions are answered and when they are not. Here again is a reason why mental culture is in the minds of men identified with the acquisition of knowledge.

The same notion possesses the public mind, when it passes on from the thought of a school to that of a University: and with the best of reasons so far as this, that there is no true culture without acquirements, and that philosophy presupposes knowledge. It requires a great deal of reading, or a wide range of information, to warrant us in putting forth our opinions on any serious subject; and without such learning the most original mind may be able indeed to dazzle, to amuse, to refute, to perplex, but not to come to any useful result or any trustworthy conclusion. There are indeed persons who profess a different view of the matter, and even act upon it. Every now and then you will find a person of vigorous or fertile mind, who relies upon his own resources, despises all former authors, and gives the world, with the utmost fearlessness, his views upon religion, or history, or any other popular subject. And his works may sell for a while; he may get a name in his day; but this will be all. His readers are sure to find in the long run that his doctrines are mere theories, and not the expression of facts, that they are chaff instead of bread, and then his popularity drops as suddenly as it rose.

Knowledge then is the indispensable condition of expansion of mind, and the instrument of attaining to it; this cannot be denied, it is ever to be insisted on; I begin with it as a first principle; however, the very truth of it carries men too far, and confirms to them the notion that it is the whole of the matter. A narrow mind is thought to be that which contains little knowledge; and an enlarged mind, that which holds a great deal; and what seems to put the matter beyond dispute is, the fact of the great number of studies which are pursued in a University, by its very profession. Lectures are given on every kind of subject; examinations are held; prizes awarded. There are moral, metaphysical, physical Professors; Professors of languages, of history, of mathematics, of experimental science. Lists of questions are published, wonderful for their range and depth, variety and difficulty; treatises are written, which carry upon their very face the evidence of extensive reading or multifarious information; what then is wanting for mental culture to a person of large reading and scientific attainments? what is grasp of mind but acquirement? where shall philosophical repose be found, but in the consciousness and enjoyment of large intellectual possessions?

And yet this notion is, I conceive, a mistake, and my present business is to show that it is one, and that the end of a Liberal Education is not mere knowledge, or knowledge considered in its *matter;* and I shall best attain my object, by actually setting down some cases, which will be generally granted to be instances of the process of enlightenment or enlargement of mind, and others which are not, and thus, by the comparison, you will be able to judge for yourselves, Gentlemen, whether Knowledge, that is, acquirement, is after all the real principle of the enlargement, or whether that principle is not rather something beyond it.

For instance,[1] let a person, whose experience has hitherto been confined to the more calm and unpretending scenery of these islands, whether here or in England, go for the first time into parts where physical nature puts on her wilder and more awful forms, whether at home or abroad, as into mountainous districts; or let one, who has ever lived in a quiet village, go for the first time to a great metropolis, — then I suppose he will have a sensation which perhaps he never had before. He has a feeling not in addition or increase of former feelings, but of something different in its nature. He will perhaps be borne forward, and find for a time that he has lost his bearings. He has made a certain progress, and he has a consciousness of mental enlargement; he does not stand where he did, he has a new centre, and a range of thoughts to which he was before a stranger.

[1] The pages which follow are taken almost *verbatim* from the author's 14th (Oxford) University Sermon, which, at the time of writing this Discourse, he did not expect ever to reprint.

Again, the view of the heavens which the telescope opens upon us, if allowed to fill and possess the mind, may almost whirl it round and make it dizzy. It brings in a flood of ideas, and is rightly called an intellectual enlargement, whatever is meant by the term.

And so again, the sight of beasts of prey and other foreign animals, their strangeness, the originality (if I may use the term) of their forms and gestures and habits and their variety and independence of each other, throw us out of ourselves into another creation, and as if under another Creator, if I may so express the temptation which may come on the mind. We seem to have new faculties, or a new exercise for our faculties, by this addition to our knowledge; like a prisoner, who, having been accustomed to wear manacles or fetters, suddenly finds his arms and legs free.

Hence Physical Science generally, in all its departments, as bringing before us the exuberant riches and resources, yet the orderly course, of the Universe, elevates and excites the student, and at first, I may say, almost takes away his breath, while in time it exercises a tranquillizing influence upon him.

Again, the study of history is said to enlarge and enlighten the mind, and why? because, as I conceive, it gives it a power of judging of passing events, and of all events, and a conscious superiority over them, which before it did not possess.

And in like manner, what is called seeing the world, entering into active life, going into society, travelling, gaining acquaintance with the various classes of the community, coming into contact with the principles and modes of thought of various parties, interests, and races, their views, aims, habits and manners, their religious creeds and forms of worship, — gaining experience how various yet how alike men are, how low-minded, how bad, how opposed, yet how confident in their opinions; all this exerts a perceptible influence upon the mind, which it is impossible to mistake, be it good or be it bad, and is popularly called its enlargement.

And then again, the first time the mind comes across the arguments and speculations of unbelievers, and feels what a novel light they cast upon what he has hitherto accounted sacred; and still more, if it gives in to them and embraces them, and throws off as so much prejudice what it has hitherto held, and, as if waking from a dream, begins to realize to its imagination that there is now no such thing as law and the transgression of law, that sin is a phantom, and punishment a bugbear, that it is free to sin, free to enjoy the world and the flesh; and still further, when it does enjoy them, and reflects that it may think and hold just what it will, that "the world is all before it where to choose," and what system to build up as its own private persuasion; when this torrent of wilful thoughts rushes over and inundates it, who will deny that the fruit of the tree of knowledge, or what the mind takes for knowledge, has made it one of the gods, with a sense of expansion and elevation, — an intoxication in reality, still, so far as the subjective state of the mind goes, an illumination? Hence the fanaticism of individuals or nations, who suddenly cast off their Maker. Their eyes are opened; and, like the judgment-stricken king in the Tragedy, they see two suns, and a magic universe, out of which they look back upon their former state of faith and innocence with a sort of contempt and indignation, as if they were then but fools, and the dupes of imposture.

On the other hand, Religion has its own enlargement, and an enlargement, not of tumult, but of peace. It is often remarked of uneducated persons, who have hitherto thought little of the unseen world, that, on their turning to God, looking into themselves, regulating their hearts, reforming their conduct, and meditating on death and judgment, heaven and hell, they seem to become, in point of intellect, different beings from what they were. Before, they took things as they came, and thought no more of one thing than another. But now every event has a meaning; they have their own estimate of whatever happens to them; they are mindful of times and seasons, and compare the present with the past; and the world, no longer dull, monotonous, unprofitable, and hopeless, is a various and complicated drama, with parts and an object, and an awful moral.

Now from these instances, to which many more might be added, it is plain, first, that the communication of knowledge certainly is either a condition or the means of that sense of enlargement or enlightenment, of which at this day we hear so much in certain quarters: this cannot be denied; but next, it is equally plain, that such communication is not the whole of the process. The enlargement consists, not merely in the passive reception into the mind of a number of ideas hitherto unknown to it, but in the mind's energetic and simultaneous action upon and towards and among those new ideas, which are rushing in upon it. It is the action of a formative power, reducing to order and meaning the matter of our acquirements; it is a making the objects of our knowledge subjectively our own, or, to use a familiar word, it is a digestion of what we receive, into the substance of our previous state of thought; and without this no enlargement is said to follow. There is no enlargement, unless there be a comparison of ideas one with another, as they come before the mind, and a systematizing of them. We feel our minds to be growing and expanding *then*, when we not only learn, but refer what we learn to what we know already. It is not the mere addition to our knowledge that is the illumination; but the locomotion, the movement onwards, of that mental centre, to which both what we know, and what we are learning, the accumulating mass of our acquirements, gravitates. And therefore a truly great intellect, and recognized to be such by the common opinion of mankind, such as the intellect of Aristotle, or of St. Thomas, or of Newton, or of Goethe, (I purposely take instances within and without the Catholic pale, when I would speak of the intellect as such,) is one which takes a connected view of old and new, past and present, far and near, and which has an insight into the influence of all these one on another; without which there is no whole, and no centre. It possesses the knowledge, not only of things, but also of their mutual and true relations; knowledge, not merely considered as acquirement, but as philosophy.

Accordingly, when this analytical, distributive, harmonizing process is away, the mind experiences no enlargement, and is not reckoned as enlightened or comprehensive, whatever it may add to its knowledge. For instance, a great memory, as I have already said, does not make a philosopher, any more than a dictionary can be called a grammar. There are men who embrace in their minds a vast multitude of ideas, but with little sensibility about their real relations towards each other. These may be antiquarians, annalists, naturalists; they may be learned in the law; they may be versed in statistics; they are most useful in their own place; I should shrink from speaking disrespectfully of them; still, there is nothing in such attainments to guarantee the absence of narrowness of mind. If they are nothing more than well-read men, or men of information, they have not what specially deserves the name of culture of mind, or fulfils the type of Liberal Education.

In like manner, we sometimes fall in with persons who have seen much of the world, and of the men who, in their day, have played a conspicuous part in it, but who generalize nothing, and have no observation, in the true sense of the word. They abound in information in detail, curious and entertaining, about men and things; and, having lived under the influence of no very clear or settled principles, religious or political, they speak of every one and every thing, only as so many phenomena, which are complete in themselves, and lead to nothing, not discussing them, or teaching any truth, or instructing the bearer, but simply talking. No one would say that these persons, well informed as they are, had attained to any great culture of intellect or to philosophy.

The case is the same still more strikingly where the persons in question are beyond dispute men of inferior powers and deficient education. Perhaps they have been much in foreign countries, and they receive, in a passive, otiose, unfruitful way, the various facts which are forced upon them there. Seafaring men, for example, range from one end of the earth to the other; but the multiplicity of external objects, which they have encountered, forms no symmetrical and consistent picture upon their imagination; they see the tapestry of human life, as it were on the wrong side, and it tells no story. They sleep, and they rise up, and they find themselves, now in Europe, now in Asia; they see visions of great cities and wild regions; they are in the marts of commerce, or amid the islands of the South; they gaze on Pompey's Pillar, or on the Andes; and nothing which meets them carries them forward or backward, to any idea beyond itself. Nothing has a drift or relation; nothing has a history or a promise. Every thing stands by itself, and comes and goes in its turn, like the shifting scenes of a show, which leave the spectator where he was. Perhaps you are near such a man on a particular occasion, and expect him to be shocked or perplexed at something which occurs; but one thing is much the same to him as another, or, if he is perplexed, it is as not knowing what to say, whether it is right to admire, or to ridicule, or to disapprove, while conscious that some expres-

KNOWLEDGE IN RELATION TO LEARNING 45

sion of opinion is expected from him; for in fact he has no standard of judgment at all, and no landmarks to guide him to a conclusion. Such is mere acquisition, and, I repeat, no one would dream of calling it philosophy.

Instances, such as these, confirm, by the contrast, the conclusion I have already drawn from those which preceded them. That only is true enlargement of mind which is the power of viewing many things at once as one whole, of referring them severally to their true place in the universal system, of understanding their respective values, and determining their mutual dependence. Thus is that form of Universal Knowledge, of which I have on a former occasion spoken, set up in the individual intellect, and constitutes its perfection. Possessed of this real illumination, the mind never views any part of the extended subject-matter of Knowledge without recollecting that it is but a part, or without the associations which spring from this recollection. It makes every thing in some sort lead to every thing else; it would communicate the image of the whole to every separate portion, till that whole becomes in imagination like a spirit, every where pervading and penetrating its component parts, and giving them one definite meaning. Just as our bodily organs, when mentioned, recall their function in the body, as the word "creation" suggests the Creator, and "subjects" a sovereign, so, in the mind of the Philosopher, as we are abstractedly conceiving of him, the elements of the physical and moral world, sciences, arts, pursuits, ranks, offices, events, opinions, individualities, are all viewed as one, with correlative functions, and as gradually by successive combinations converging, one and all, to the true centre.

To have even a portion of this illuminative reason and true philosophy is the highest state to which nature can aspire, in the way of intellect; it puts the mind above the influences of chance and necessity, above anxiety, suspense, unsettlement, and superstition, which is the lot of the many. Men, whose minds are possessed with some one object, take exaggerated views of its importance, are feverish in the pursuit of it, make it the measure of things which are utterly foreign to it, and are startled and despond if it happens to fail them. They are ever in alarm or in transport. Those, on the other hand, who have no object or principle whatever to hold by, lose their way, every step they take. They are thrown out, and do not know what to think or say, at every fresh juncture; they have no view of persons, or occurrences, or facts, which come suddenly upon them, and they hang upon the opinion of others, for want of internal resources. But the intellect, which has been disciplined to the perfection of its powers, which knows, and thinks while it knows, which has learned to leaven the dense mass of facts and events with the elastic force of reason, such an intellect cannot be partial, cannot be exclusive, cannot be impetuous, cannot be at a loss, cannot but be patient, collected, and majestically calm, because it discerns the end in every beginning, the origin in every end, the law in every interruption, the limit in each delay; because it ever knows where it stands, and how its path lies from one point to another. It is the τετράγωνος of the Peripatetic, and has the "nil admirari" of the Stoic, —

> "Felix qui potuit rerum cognoscere causas,
> Atque metus omnes, et inexorabile fatum
> Subjecit pedibus, strepitumque Acherontis avari."

There are men who, when in difficulties, originate at the moment vast ideas or dazzling projects; who, under the influence of excitement, are able to cast a light, almost as if from inspiration, on a subject or course of action which comes before them; who have a sudden presence of mind equal to any emergency, rising with the occasion, and an undaunted magnanimous bearing, and an energy and keenness which is but made intense by opposition. This is genius, this is heroism; it is the exhibition of a natural gift, which no culture can teach, at which no Institution can aim; here, on the contrary, we are concerned, not with mere nature, but with training and teaching. That perfection of the Intellect, which is the result of Education, and its *beau ideal*, to be imparted to individuals in their respective measures, is the clear, calm, accurate vision and comprehension of all things, as far as the finite mind can embrace them, each in its place, and with its own characteristics upon it. It is almost prophetic from its knowledge of history; it is almost heart-searching from its knowledge of human nature; it has almost supernatural charity from its freedom from littleness and prejudice; it has almost the repose of faith, because nothing can startle it; it has almost the beauty and harmony of heavenly contemplation, so intimate is it with the eternal order of things and the music of the spheres.

And now, if I may take for granted that the true and adequate end of intellectual training and of a University is not Learning or Acquirement, but rather, is Thought or Reason exercised upon Knowledge, or what may be called Philosophy, I shall be in a position to explain the various mistakes which at the present day beset the subject of University Education.

I say then, if we would improve the intellect, first of all, we must ascend; we cannot gain real knowledge on a level; we must generalize, we must reduce to method, we must have a grasp of principles, and group and shape our acquisitions by means of them. It matters not whether our field of operation be wide or limited; in every case, to command it, is to mount above it. Who has not felt the irritation of mind and impatience created by a deep, rich country, visited for the first time, with winding lanes, and high hedges, and green steeps, and tangled woods, and every thing smiling indeed, but in a maze? The same feeling comes upon us in a strange city, when we have no map of its streets. Hence you hear of practised travellers, when they first come into a place, mounting some high hill or church tower, by way of reconnoitring its neighbourhood. In like manner, you must be above your knowledge, not under it, or it will oppress you; and the more you have of it, the greater will be the load. The learning of a Salmasius or a Burman, unless you are its master, will be your tyrant. "Imperat aut servit"; if you can wield it with a strong arm, it is a great weapon; otherwise,

"Vis consili expers
Mole ruit suâ."

You will be overwhelmed, like Tarpeia, by the heavy wealth which you have exacted from tributary generations.

Instances abound; there are authors who are as pointless as they are inexhaustible in their literary resources. They measure knowledge by bulk, as it lies in the rude block, without symmetry, without design. How many commentators are there on the Classics, how many on Holy Scripture, from whom we rise up, wondering at the learning which has passed before us, and wondering why it passed! How many writers are there of Ecclesiastical History, such as Mosheim or Du Pin, who, breaking up their subject into details, destroy its life, and defraud us of the whole by their anxiety about the parts! The Sermons, again, of the English Divines in the seventeenth century, how often are they mere repertories of miscellaneous and officious learning! Of course Catholics also may read without thinking; and in their case, equally as with Protestants, it holds good, that such knowledge is unworthy of the name, knowledge which they have not thought through, and thought out. Such readers are only possessed by their knowledge, not possessed of it; nay, in matter of fact they are often even carried away by it, without any volition of their own. Recollect, the Memory can tyrannize, as well as the Imagination. Derangement, I believe, has been considered as a loss of control over the sequence of ideas. The mind, once set in motion, is henceforth deprived of the power of initiation, and becomes the victim of a train of associations, one thought suggesting another, in the way of cause and effect, as if by a mechanical process, or some physical necessity. No one, who has had experience of men of studious habits, but must recognize the existence of a parallel phenomenon in the case of those who have over-stimulated the Memory. In such persons Reason acts almost as feebly and as impotently as in the madman; once fairly started on any subject whatever, they have no power of self-control; they passively endure the succession of impulses which are evolved out of the original exciting cause; they are passed on from one idea to another and go steadily forward, plodding along one line of thought in spite of the amplest concessions of the hearer, or wandering from it in endless digression in spite of his remonstrances. Now, if, as is very certain, no one would envy the madman the glow and originality of his conceptions, why must we extol the cultivation of that intellect, which is the prey, not indeed of barren fancies but of barren facts, of random intrusions from without, though not of morbid imaginations from within? And in thus speaking, I am not denying that a strong and ready memory is in itself a real treasure; I am not disparaging a well-stored mind, though it be nothing besides, provided it be sober, any more than I would despise a bookseller's shop: — it is of great value to others, even when not so to the owner. Nor am I banishing, far from it, the possessors of deep and multifarious learning from my ideal University; they adorn it in the eyes of men; I do but say that they constitute no type of the results at which it aims; that it is no great gain to the intellect to have enlarged the memory at the expense of faculties which are indisputably higher.

Nor, indeed, am I supposing that there is any great danger, at least in this day, of over-education; the danger is on the other side. I will tell you, Gentlemen, what has been the practical error of the last twenty years, — not to load the memory of the student with a mass of undigested knowledge, but to force upon him so much that he has rejected all. It has been the error of distracting and enfeebling the mind by an unmeaning profusion of subjects; of implying that a smattering in a dozen branches of study is not shallowness, which it really is, but enlargement, which it is not; of considering an acquaintance with the learned names of things and persons, and the possession of clever duodecimos, and attendance on eloquent lecturers, and membership with scientific institutions, and the sight of the experiments of a platform and the specimens of a museum, that all this was not dissipation of mind, but progress. All things now are to be learned at once, not first one thing, then another, not one well, but many badly. Learning is to be without exertion, without attention, without toil; without grounding, without advance, without finishing. There is to be nothing individual in it; and this, forsooth, is the wonder of the age. What the steam engine does with matter, the printing press is to do with mind; it is to act mechanically, and the population is to be passively, almost unconsciously enlightened, by the mere multiplication and dissemination of volumes. Whether it be the school boy, or the school girl, or the youth at college, or the mechanic in the town, or the politician in the senate, all have been the victims in one way or other of this most preposterous and pernicious of delusions. Wise men have lifted up their voices in vain; and at length, lest their own institutions should be outshone and should disappear in the folly of the hour, they have been obliged, as far as they could with a good conscience, to humour a spirit which they could not withstand, and make temporizing concessions at which they could not but inwardly smile.

It must not be supposed that, because I so speak, therefore I have some sort of fear of the education of the people: on the contrary, the more education they have, the better, so that it is really education. Nor am I an enemy to the cheap publication of scientific and literary works, which is now in vogue: on the contrary, I consider it a great advantage, convenience, and gain; that is, to those to whom education has given a capacity for using them. Further, I consider such innocent recreations as science and literature are able to furnish will be a very fit occupation of the thoughts and the leisure of young persons, and may be made the means of keeping them from bad employments and bad companions. Moreover, as to that superficial acquaintance with chemistry, and geology, and astronomy, and political economy, and modern history, and biography, and other branches of knowledge, which periodical literature and occasioual lectures and scientific institutions diffuse through the community, I think it a graceful accomplishment, and a suitable, nay, in this day a necessary accomplishment, in the case of educated men. Nor, lastly, am I disparaging or discouraging the thorough acquisition of any one of these studies, or denying that, as far as it goes, such thorough acquisition is a real education of the mind. All I say is, call things by their right names, and do not confuse together ideas which are essentially different. A thorough knowledge of one science and a superficial acquaintance with many, are not the same thing; a smattering of a hundred things or a memory for detail, is not a philosophical or comprehensive view. Recreations are not education; accomplishments are not education. Do not say, the people must be educated, when, after all, you only mean, amused, refreshed, soothed, put into good spirits and good humour, or kept from vicious excesses. I do not say that such amusements, such occupations of mind, are not a great gain; but they are not education. You may as well call drawing and fencing education, as a general knowledge of botany or conchology. Stuffing birds or playing stringed instruments is an elegant pastime, and a resource to the idle, but it is not education; it does not form or cultivate the intellect. Education is a high word; it is the preparation for knowledge, and it is the imparting of knowledge in proportion to that preparation. We require intellectual eyes to know withal, as bodily eyes for sight. We need both objects and organs intellectual; we cannot gain them without setting about it; we cannot gain them in our sleep, or by hap-hazard. The best telescope does not dispense with eyes; the printing press or the lecture room will assist us greatly, but we must be true to ourselves, we must be parties in the work. A University is, according to the usual designation, an Alma Mater, knowing her children one by one, not a foundry, or a mint, or a treadmill.

I protest to yon, Gentlemen, that if I had to choose between a so-called University, which dispensed with residence and tutorial superintendence, and gave its degrees to any person who passed an examination in a wide range of subjects, and a University which had no professors or examinations at all, but merely brought a number of young men together for three or four years, and then sent them away as the University of Oxford is said to have done some sixty years since, if I were asked which of these two methods was the better discipline of the intellect, — mind, I do not say which is *morally* the better, for it is plain that compulsory study must be a good and idleness an intolerable mischief, — but if I must determine which of the two courses was the more successful in training, moulding, enlarging the mind, which sent out men the more fitted for their secular duties, which produced better public men, men of the world, men whose names would descend to posterity, I have no hesitation in giving the preference to that University which did nothing, over that which exacted of its members an acquaintance with every science under the sun. And, paradox as this may seem, still if results be the test of systems, the influence of the public schools and colleges of England, in the course of the last century, at least will bear out one side of the contrast as I have drawn it. What would come, on the other hand, of the ideal systems of education which have fascinated the imagination of this age, could they ever take effect, and whether they would not produce a generation frivolous, narrow-minded, and resourceless, intellectually considered, is a fair subject for debate; but so far is certain, that the Universities and scholastic establishments, to which I refer, and which did little more than bring together first boys and then youths in large numbers, these institutions, with miserable deformities on the side of morals, with a hollow profession of Christianity, and a heathen code of ethics, — I say, at least they can boast of a succession of heroes and statesmen, of literary men and philosophers, of men conspicuous for great natural virtues, for habits of business, for knowledge of life, for practical judgment, for cultivated tastes, for accomplishments, who have made England what it is, — able to subdue the earth, able to dominate over Catholics.

How is this to be explained? I suppose as follows: When a multitude of young men, keen, open-hearted, sympathetic, and observant, as young men are, come together and freely mix with each other, they are sure to learn one from another, even if there be no one to teach them; the conversation of all is a series of lectures to each, and they gain for themselves new ideas and views, fresh matter of thought, and distinct principles for judging and acting, day by day. An infant has to learn the meaning of the information which its senses convey to it, and this seems to be its employment. It fancies all that the eye presents to it to be close to it, till it actually learns the contrary, and thus by practice does it ascertain the relations and uses of those first elements of knowledge which are necessary for its animal existence. A parallel teaching is necessary for our social being, and it is secured by a large school or a college; and this effect may be fairly called in its own department an enlargement of mind. It is seeing the world on a small field with little trouble; for the pupils or students come from very different places, and with widely different notions, and there is much to generalize, much to adjust, much to eliminate, there are inter-relations to be defined, and conventional rules to be established, in the process, by which the whole assemblage is moulded together, and gains one tone and one character.

Let it be clearly understood, I repeat it, that I am not taking into account moral or religious considerations; I am but saying that that youthful community will constitute a whole, it will embody a specific idea, it will represent a doctrine, it will administer a code of conduct, and it will furnish principles of thought and action. It will give birth to a living teaching, which in course of time will take the shape of a self-perpetuating tradition, or a *genius loci*, as it is sometimes called; which haunts the home where it has been born, and which imbues and forms, more or less, and one by one, every individual who is successively brought under its shadow. Thus it is that, independent of direct instruction on the part of Superiors, there is a sort of self-education in the academic institutions of Protestant England; a characteristic tone of thought, a recognized standard of judgment is found in them, which, as developed in the individual who is submitted to it, becomes a twofold source of strength to him, both from the distinct stamp it impresses on his mind, and from the bond of union which it creates between him and others, — effects which are shared by the authorities of the place, for they themselves have been educated in it, and at all times are exposed to the influence of its ethical atmosphere. Here then is a real teaching, whatever be its standards and principles, true or false; and it at least tends towards cultivation of the intellect; it at least recognizes that knowledge is something more than a sort of passive reception of scraps and details; it is a something, and it does a something, which never will issue from the most strenuous efforts of a set of teachers, with no mutual sympathies and no inter-communion, of a set of examiners with no opinions which they dare profess, and with no common principles, who are teaching or questioning a set of youths who do not know them, and do not know each other, on a large number of subjects, different in kind, and connected by no wide philosophy, three times a week, or three times a year, or once in three years, in chill lecture-rooms or on a pompous anniversary.

Nay, self-education in any shape, in the most restricted sense, is preferable to a system of teaching which, professing so much, really does so little for the mind. Shut your College gates against the votary of knowledge, throw him back upon the searchings and the efforts of his own mind; he will gain by being spared an entrance into your Babel. Few, indeed, there are who can dispense with the stimulus and support of instructors, or will do any thing at all, if left to themselves. And fewer still (though such great minds are to be found), who will not, from such unassisted attempts, contract a self-reliance and a self-esteem, which are not only moral evils, but serious hindrances to the attainment of truth. And next to none, perhaps, or none, who will not be reminded from time to time of the disadvantage under which they lie, by their imperfect grounding, by the breaks, deficiencies, and irregularities of their knowledge, by the eccentricity of opinion and the confusion of principle which they exhibit. They will be too often ignorant of what every one knows and takes for granted, of that multitude of small truths which fall upon the mind like dust, impalpable and ever accumulating; they may be unable to converse, they may argue perversely, they may pride themselves on their worst paradoxes or their grossest truisms, they may be full of their own mode of viewing things, unwilling to be put out of their way, slow to enter into the minds of others; — but, with these and whatever other liabilities upon their heads, they are likely to have more thought, more mind, more philosophy, more true enlargement, than those earnest but ill-used persons, who are forced to load their minds with a score of subjects against an examination, who have too much on their hands to indulge themselves in thinking or investigation, who devour premiss and conclusion together with indiscriminate greediness, who hold whole sciences on faith, and commit demonstrations to memory, and who too often, as might be expected, when their period of education is passed, throw up all they have learned in disgust, having gained nothing really by their anxious labours, except perhaps the habit of application.

Yet such is the better specimen of the fruit of that ambitious system which has of late years been making way among us: for its result on ordinary minds, and on the common run of students, is less satisfactory still; they leave their place of education simply dissipated and relaxed by the multiplicity of subjects, which they have never really mastered, and so shallow as not even to know their shallowness. How much better, I say, is it for the active and thoughtful intellect, where such is to be found, to eschew the College and the University altogether, than to submit to a drudgery so ignoble, a mockery so contumelious! How much more profitable for the independent mind, after the mere rudiments of education, to range through a library at random, taking down books as they meet him, and pursuing the trains of thought which his mother wit suggests! How much healthier to wander into the fields, and there with the exiled Prince to find "tongues in the trees, books in the running brooks!" How much more genuine an education is that of the poor boy in the Poem [1] — a Poem, whether in conception or in execution, one of the most touching in our language — who, not in the wide world, but ranging day by day around his widowed mother's home, "a dexterous gleaner" in a narrow field, and with only such slender outfit

"as the village school and books a few
Supplied,"

contrived from the beach, and the quay, and the fisher's boat, and the inn's fireside, and the tradesman's shop, and the shepherd's walk, and the smuggler's hut, and the mossy moor, and the screaming gulls, and the restless waves, to fashion for himself a philosophy and a poetry of his own!

But in a large subject, I am exceeding my necessary limits. Gentlemen, I must conclude abruptly; and postpone any summing up of my argument, should that be necessary, to another day.

[1] Crabbe's "Tales of the Hall." This Poem, let me say, I read on its first publication, above thirty years ago, with extreme delight, and have never lost my love of it; and on taking it up lately, found I was even more touched by it than heretofore. A work which can please in youth and age, seems to fulfil (in logical language) the *accidental definition* of a Classic. [A further course of twenty years has past, and I bear the same witness in favour of this Poem.]

THE PRINCIPAL SUBJECTS OF EDUCATION[1]

THOMAS HENRY HUXLEY
1825–1895

THIS is an extract from the essay "Science and Art in Relation to Education," a subject upon which Huxley — one of the great scientists of the nineteenth century — had very decided opinions. He wanted to teach men "to think truly and to live rightly"; and he believed this could best be done by spreading a knowledge of the natural sciences and by inculcating a scientific method of study. In presenting his views he took the greatest pains to be clear; his best essays are models of form, and his style is simple and direct.

I KNOW quite well that launching myself into this discussion is a very dangerous operation; that it is a very large subject, and one which is difficult to deal with, however much I may trespass upon your patience in the time allotted to me. But the discussion is so fundamental, it is so completely impossible to make up one's mind on these matters until one has settled the question, that I will even venture to make the experiment. A great lawyer-statesman and philosopher of a former age — I mean Francis Bacon — said that truth came out of error much more rapidly than it came out of confusion. There is a wonderful truth in that saying. Next to being right in this world, the best of all things is to be clearly and definitely wrong, because you will come out somewhere. If you go buzzing about between right and wrong, vibrating and fluctuating, you come out nowhere; but if you are absolutely and thoroughly and persistently wrong, you must, some of these days, have the extreme

---

[1] Reprinted by courtesy of Messrs. D. Appleton and Company, the authorized publishers of Huxley's *Works*.

THE PRINCIPAL SUBJECTS OF EDUCATION 59

good fortune of knocking your head against a fact, and that sets you all straight again. So I will not trouble myself as to whether I may be right or wrong in what I am about to say, but at any rate I hope to be clear and definite; and then you will be able to judge for yourselves whether, in following out the train of thought I have to introduce, you knock your heads against facts or not.

I take it that the whole object of education is, in the first place, to train the faculties of the young in such a manner as to give their possessors the best chance of being happy and useful in their generation; and, in the second place, to furnish them with the most important portions of that immense capitalised experience of the human race which we call knowledge of various kinds. I am using the term knowledge in its widest possible sense; and the question is, what subjects to select by training and discipline, in which the object I have just defined may be best attained.

I must call your attention further to this fact, that all the subjects of our thoughts — all feelings and propositions (leaving aside our sensations as the mere materials and occasions of thinking and feeling), all our mental furniture — may be classified under one of two heads — as either within the province of the intellect, something that can be put into propositions and affirmed or denied; or as within the province of feeling, or that which, before the name was defiled, was called the æsthetic side of our nature, and which can neither be proved nor disproved, but only felt and known.

According to the classification which I have put before you, then, the subjects of all knowledge are divisible into the two groups, matters of science and matters of art; for all things with which the reasoning faculty alone is occupied, come under the province of science; and in the broadest sense, and not in the narrow and technical sense in which we are now accustomed to use the word art, all things feelable, all things which stir our emotions, come under the term of art, in the sense of the subject-matter of the æsthetic faculty. So that we are shut up to this — that the business of education is, in the first place, to provide the young with the means and the habit of observation; and, secondly, to supply the subject-matter of knowledge either in the shape of science or of art, or of both combined.

Now, it is a very remarkable fact — but it is true of most things in this world — that there is hardly anything one-sided, or of one nature; and it is not immediately obvious what of the things that interest us may be regarded as pure science, and what may be regarded as pure art. It may be that there are some peculiarly constituted persons who, before they have advanced far into the depths of geometry, find artistic beauty about it; but, taking the generality of mankind, I think it may be said that, when they begin to learn mathematics, their whole souls are absorbed in tracing the connection between the premises and the conclusion, and that to them geometry is pure science. So I think it may be said that mechanics and osteology are pure science. On the other hand, melody in music is pure art. You cannot reason about it; there is no proposition involved in it. So, again, in the pictorial art, an arabesque, or a "harmony in grey," touches none but the æsthetic faculty. But a great mathematician, and even many persons who are not great mathematicians, will tell you that they derive immense pleasure from geometrical reasonings. Everybody knows mathematicians speak of solutions and problems as "elegant," and they tell you that a certain mass of mystic symbols is "beautiful, quite lovely." Well, you do not see it. They do see it, because the intellectual process, the process of comprehending the reasons symbolised by these figures and these signs, confers upon them a sort of pleasure, such as an artist has in visual symmetry. Take a science of which

I may speak with more confidence, and which is the most attractive of those I am concerned with. It is what we call morphology, which consists in tracing out the unity in variety of the infinitely diversified structures of animals and plants. I cannot give you any example of a thorough æsthetic pleasure more intensely real than a pleasure of this kind — the pleasure which arises in one's mind when a whole mass of different structures run into one harmony as the expression of a central law. That is where the province of art overlays and embraces the province of intellect. And, if I may venture to express an opinion on such a subject, the great majority of forms of art are not in the sense what I just now defined them to be — pure art; but they derive much of their quality from simultaneous and even unconscious excitement of the intellect.

When I was a boy, I was very fond of music, and I am so now; and it so happened that I had the opportunity of hearing much good music. Among other things, I had abundant opportunities of hearing that great old master, Sebastian Bach. I remember perfectly well — though I knew nothing about music then, and, I may add, know nothing whatever about it now — the intense satisfaction and delight which I had in listening, by the hour together, to Bach's fugues. It is a pleasure which remains with me, I am glad to think; but, of late years, I have tried to find out the why and wherefore, and it has often occurred to me that the pleasure derived from musical compositions of this kind is essentially of the same nature as that which is derived from pursuits which are commonly regarded as purely intellectual. I mean, that the source of pleasure is exactly the same as in most of my problems in morphology — that you have the theme in one of the old master's works followed out in all its endless variations, always appearing and always reminding you of unity in variety. So in painting; what is called "truth to nature" is the intellectual element coming in, and truth to nature depends entirely upon the intellectual culture of the person to whom art is addressed. If you are in Australia, you may get credit for being a good artist — I mean among the natives — if you can draw a kangaroo after a fashion. But, among men of higher civilisation, the intellectual knowledge we possess brings its criticism into our appreciation of works of art, and we are obliged to satisfy it, as well as the mere sense of beauty in colour and in outline. And so, the higher the culture and information of those whom art addresses, the more exact and precise must be what we call its "truth to nature."

If we turn to literature, the same thing is true, and you find works of literature which may be said to be pure art. A little song of Shakespeare or of Goethe is pure art; it is exquisitely beautiful, although its intellectual content may be nothing. A series of pictures is made to pass before your mind by the meaning of words, and the effect is a melody of ideas. Nevertheless, the great mass of the literature we esteem is valued, not merely because of having artistic form, but because of its intellectual content; and the value is the higher the more precise, distinct, and true is that intellectual content. And, if you will let me for a moment speak of the very highest forms of literature, do we not regard them as highest simply because the more we know the truer they seem, and the more competent we are to appreciate beauty the more beautiful they are? No man ever understands Shakespeare until he is old, though the youngest may admire him, the reason being that he satisfies the artistic instinct of the youngest and harmonises with the ripest and richest experience of the oldest.

I have said this much to draw your attention to what, in my mind, lies at the root of all this matter, and at the understanding of one another by the men of science on the one hand, and the men of literature, and history, and art, on the other. It is not a question whether one order of study or another should predominate. It is a question of what topics of education you shall select which will combine all the needful elements in such due proportion as to give the greatest amount of food, support, and encouragement to those faculties which enable us to appreciate truth, and to profit by those sources of innocent happiness which are open to us, and, at the same time, to avoid that which is bad, and coarse, and ugly, and keep clear of the multitude of pitfalls and dangers which beset those who break through the natural or moral laws.

I address myself, in this spirit, to the consideration of the question of the value of purely literary education. Is it good and sufficient, or is it insufficient and bad? Well, here I venture to say that there are literary educations and literary educations. If I am to understand by that term the education that was current in the great majority of middle-class schools, and upper schools too, in this country when I was a boy, and which consisted absolutely and almost entirely in keeping boys for eight or ten years at learning the rules of Latin and Greek grammar, construing certain Latin and Greek authors, and possibly making verses which, had they been English verses, would have been condemned as abominable doggerel, — if that is what you mean by liberal education, then I say it is scandalously insufficient and almost worthless. My reason for saying so is not from the point of view of science at all, but from the point of view of literature. I say the thing professes to be literary education that is not a literary education at all. It was not literature at all that was taught, but science in a very bad form. It is quite obvious that grammar is science and not literature. The analysis of a text by the help of the rules of grammar is just as much a scientific operation as the analysis of a chemical compound by the help of the rules of chemical analysis. There is nothing that appeals to the æsthetic faculty in that operation; and I ask multitudes of men of my own age, who went through this process, whether they ever had a conception of art or literature until they obtained it for themselves after leaving school? Then you may say, "If that is so, if the education was scientific, why cannot you be satisfied with it?" I say, because although it is a scientific training, it is of the most inadequate and inappropriate kind. If there is any good at all in scientific education it is that men should be trained, as I said before, to know things for themselves at first hand, and that they should understand every step of the reason of that which they do.

I desire to speak with the utmost respect of that science — philology — of which grammar is a part and parcel; yet everybody knows that grammar, as it is usually learned at school, affords no scientific training. It is taught just as you would teach the rules of chess or draughts. On the other hand, if I am to understand by a literary education the study of the literatures of either ancient or modern nations — but especially those of antiquity, and especially that of ancient Greece; if this literature is studied, not merely from the point of view of philological science, and its practical application to the interpretation of texts, but as an exemplification of and commentary upon the principles of art; if you look upon the literature of a people as a chapter in the development of the human mind, if you work out this in a broad spirit, and with such collateral references to morals and politics, and physical geography, and the like as are needful to make you comprehend what the meaning of ancient literature and civilisation is, — then, assuredly, it affords a splendid and noble education. But I still think it is susceptible of improvement, and that no man will ever comprehend the **real** secret of the difference between the

THE PRINCIPAL SUBJECTS OF EDUCATION 65

ancient world and our present time, unless he has learned to see the difference which the late development of physical science has made between the thought of this day and the thought of that, and he will never see that difference, unless he has some practical insight into some branches of physical science; and you must remember that a literary education such as that which I have just referred to, is out of the reach of those whose school life is cut short at sixteen or seventeen.

But, you will say, all this is fault-finding; let us hear what you have in the way of positive suggestion. Then I am bound to tell you that, if I could make a clean sweep of everything — I am very glad I cannot because I might, and probably should, make mistakes, — but if I could make a clean sweep of everything and start afresh, I should, in the first place, secure that training of the young in reading and writing, and in the habit of attention and observation, both to that which is told them, and that which they see, which everybody agrees to. But in addition to that, I should make it absolutely necessary for everybody, for a longer or shorter period, to learn to draw. Now, you may say, there are some people who cannot draw, however much they may be taught. I deny that *in toto*, because I never yet met with anybody who could not learn to write. Writing is a form of drawing; therefore if you give the same attention and trouble to drawing as you do to writing, depend upon it, there is nobody who cannot be made to draw, more or less well. Do not misapprehend me. I do not say for one moment you would make an artistic draughtsman. Artists are not made; they grow. You may improve the natural faculty in that direction, but you cannot make it; but you can teach simple drawing, and you will find it an implement of learning of extreme value. I do not think its value can be exaggerated, because it gives you the means of training the young in attention and accuracy, which are the two things in which all mankind are more deficient than in any other mental quality whatever. The whole of my life has been spent in trying to give my proper attention to things and to be accurate, and I have not succeeded as well as I could wish; and other people, I am afraid, are not much more fortunate. You cannot begin this habit too early, and I consider there is nothing of so great a value as the habit of drawing, to secure those two desirable ends.

Then we come to the subject-matter, whether scientific or æsthetic, of education, and I should naturally have no question at all about teaching the elements of physical science of the kind I have sketched, in a practical manner; but among scientific topics, using the word scientific in the broadest sense, I would also include the elements of the theory of morals and of that of political and social life, which, strangely enough, it never seems to occur to anybody to teach a child. I would have the history of our own country, and of all the influences which have been brought to bear upon it, with incidental geography, not as a mere chronicle of reigns and battles, but as a chapter in the development of the race, and the history of civilisation.

Then with respect to æsthetic knowledge and discipline, we have happily in the English language one of the most magnificent storehouses of artistic beauty and of models of literary excellence which exists in the world at the present time. I have said before, and I repeat it here, that if a man cannot get literary culture of the highest kind out of his Bible, and Chaucer, and Shakespeare, and Milton, and Hobbes, and Bishop Berkeley, to mention only a few of our illustrious writers — I say, if he cannot get it out of those writers he cannot get it out of anything; and I would assuredly devote a very large portion of the time of every English child to the careful study of the models of English writing of such varied and wonderful kind as we possess, and, what is still more important and still more neglected, the habit of using that language with precision, with force, and with art. I fancy we are almost the only nation in the world who seem to think that composition comes by nature. The French attend to their own language, the Germans study theirs; but Englishmen do not seem to think it is worth their while. Nor would I fail to include, in the course of study I am sketching, translations of all the best works of antiquity, or of the modern world. It is a very desirable thing to read Homer in Greek; but if you don't happen to know Greek, the next best thing we can do is to read as good a translation of it as we have recently been furnished with in prose. You won't get all you would get from the original, but you may get a great deal; and to refuse to know this great deal because you cannot get all, seems to be as sensible as for a hungry man to refuse bread because he cannot get partridge. Finally, I would add instruction in either music or painting, or, if the child should be so unhappy, as sometimes happens, as to have no faculty for either of those, and no possibility of doing anything in any artistic sense with them, then I would see what could be done with literature alone; but I would provide, in the fullest sense, for the development of the æsthetic side of the mind. In my judgment, those are all the essentials of education for an English child. With that outfit, such as it might be made in the time given to education which is within the reach of nine-tenths of the population — with that outfit, an Englishman, within the limits of English life, is fitted to go anywhere, to occupy the highest positions, to fill the highest offices of the State, and to become distinguished in practical pursuits, in science, or in art. For, if he have the opportunity to learn all those things, and have his mind disciplined in the various directions the teaching of those topics would have necessitated, then, assuredly, he will be able to pick up, on his road through life, all the rest of the intellectual baggage he wants.

If the educational time at our disposition were sufficient, there are one or two things I would add to those I have just now called the essentials; and perhaps you will be surprised to hear, though I hope you will not, that I should add, not more science, but one, or, if possible, two languages. The knowledge of some other language than one's own is, in fact, of singular intellectual value. Many of the faults and mistakes of the ancient philosophers are traceable to the fact that they knew no language but their own, and were often led into confusing the symbol with the thought which it embodied. I think it is Locke who says that one-half of the mistakes of philosophers have arisen from questions about words; and one of the safest ways of delivering yourself from the bondage of words is, to know how ideas look in words to which you are not accustomed. That is one reason for the study of language; another reason is, that it opens new fields in art and in science. Another is the practical value of such knowledge; and yet another is this, that if your languages are properly chosen, from the time of learning the additional languages you will know your own language better than ever you did. So, I say, if the time given to education permits, add Latin and German. Latin, because it is the key to nearly one-half of English and to all the Romance languages; and German, because it is the key to almost all the remainder of English, and helps you to understand a race from whom most of us have sprung, and who have a character and a literature of a fateful force in the history of the world, such as probably has been allotted to those of no other people, except the Jews, the Greeks, and ourselves. Beyond these, the essential and the eminently desirable elements of all education, let each man take up his special line — the historian devote himself to his history, the man of science to his science, the man of letters to his culture of that kind, and the artist to his special pursuit.

Bacon has prefaced some of his works with no more than this: *Franciscus Bacon sic cogitavit;* let "sic cogitavi" be the epilogue to what I have ventured to address to you to-night.

THE METHOD OF SCIENTIFIC INVESTIGATION [1]

THOMAS HENRY HUXLEY

THIS is an extract from the lecture "The Causes of the Phenomena of Orgédanic Nature," printed in *Darwiniana*.

THE method of scientific investigation is nothing but the expression of the necessary mode of working of the human mind. It is simply the mode at which all phenomena are reasoned about, rendered precise and exact. There is no more difference, but there is just the same kind of difference, between the mental operations of a man of science and those of an ordinary person, as there is between the operations and methods of a baker or of a butcher weighing out his goods in common scales, and the operations of a chemist in performing a difficult and complex analysis by means of his balance and finely graduated weights. It is not that the action of the scales in the one case, and the balance in the other, differ in the principles of their construction or manner of working; but the beam of one is set on an infinitely finer axis than the other, and of course turns by the addition of a much smaller weight.

You will understand this better, perhaps, if I give you some familiar example. You have all heard it repeated, I dare say, that men of science work by means of induction and deduction, and that by the help of these operations, they, in a sort of sense, wring from Nature certain other things, which are called natural laws, and causes, and that out of these, by some cunning skill of their own, they build

[1] Reprinted by courtesy of Messrs. D. Appleton and Company, the authorized publishers of Huxley's *Works*.

up hypotheses and theories. And it is imagined by many, that the operations of the common mind can be by no means compared with these processes, and that they have to be acquired by a sort of special apprenticeship to the craft. To hear all these large words, you would think that the mind of a man of science must be constituted differently from that of his fellow men; but if you will not be frightened by terms, you will discover that you are quite wrong, and that all these terrible apparatus are being used by yourselves every day and every hour of your lives.

There is a well-known incident in one of Molière's plays, where the author makes the hero express unbounded delight on being told that he had been talking prose during the whole of his life. In the same way, I trust, that you will take comfort, and be delighted with yourselves, on the discovery that you have been acting on the principles of inductive and deductive philosophy during the same period. Probably there is not one here who has not in the course of the day had occasion to set in motion a complex train of reasoning, of the very same kind, though differing of course in degree, as that which a scientific man goes through in tracing the causes of natural phenomena.

A very trivial circumstance will serve to exemplify this. Suppose you go into a fruiterer's shop, wanting an apple, — you take up one, and, on biting it, you find it is sour; you look at it, and see that it is hard and green. You take up another one, and that too is hard, green, and sour. The shopman offers you a third; but, before biting it, you examine it, and find that it is hard and green, and you immediately say that you will not have it, as it must be sour, like those that you have already tried.

Nothing can be more simple than that, you think; but if you will take the trouble to analyse and trace out into its logical elements what has been done by the mind, you will be greatly surprised. In the first place you have performed the operation of induction. You found that, in two experiences, hardness and greenness in apples went together with sourness. It was so in the first case, and it was confirmed by the second. True, it is a very small basis, but still it is enough to make an induction from; you generalise the facts, and you expect to find sourness in apples where you get hardness and greenness. You found upon that a general law that all hard and green apples are sour; and that, so far as it goes, is a perfect induction. Well, having got your natural law in this way, when you are offered another apple which you find is hard and green, you say, "All hard and green apples are sour; this apple is hard and green, therefore this apple is sour." That train of reasoning is what logicians call a syllogism, and has all its various parts and terms, — its major premiss, its minor premiss and its conclusion. And, by the help of further reasoning, which, if drawn out, would have to be exhibited in two or three other syllogisms, you arrive at your final determination, "I will not have that apple." So that, you see, you have, in the first place, established a law by induction, and upon that you have founded a deduction, and reasoned out the special particular case. Well now, suppose, having got your conclusion of the law, that at some time afterwards, you are discussing the qualities of apples with a friend: you will say to him, "It is a very curious thing, — but I find that all hard and green apples are sour!" Your friend says to you, "But how do you know that?" You at once reply, "Oh, because I have tried them over and over again, and have always found them to be so." Well, if we were talking science instead of common sense, we should call that an experimental verification. And, if still opposed, you go further, and say, "I have heard from the people in Somersetshire and Devonshire, where a large number of apples are grown, that they have observed the same thing. It is also found to be the case in Normandy, and in North America. In short, I find it to be the universal experience of mankind wherever attention has been directed to the subject." Whereupon, your friend, unless he is a very unreasonable man, agrees with you, and is convinced that you are quite right in the conclusion you have drawn. He believes, although perhaps he does not know he believes it, that the more extensive verifications are, — that the more frequently experiments have been made, and results of the same kind arrived at, — that the more varied the conditions under which the same results are attained, the more certain is the ultimate conclusion, and he disputes the question no further. He sees that the experiment has been tried under all sorts of conditions, as to time, place, and people, with the same result; and he says with you, therefore, that the law you have laid down must be a good one, and he must believe it.

In science we do the same thing; — the philosopher exercises precisely the same faculties, though in a much more delicate manner. In scientific inquiry it becomes a matter of duty to expose a supposed law to every possible kind of verification, and to take care, moreover, that this is done intentionally, and not left to a mere accident, as in the case of the apples. And in science, as in common life, our confidence in a law is in exact proportion to the absence of variation in the result of our experimental verifications. For instance, if you let go your grasp of an article you may have in your hand, it will immediately fall to the ground. That is a very common verification of one of the best established laws of nature — that of gravitation. The method by which men of science establish the existence of that law is exactly the same as that by which we have established the trivial proposition about the sourness of hard and green apples. But we believe it in such an extensive, thorough, and unhesitating manner because the universal experience of mankind verifies it, and we can verify it ourselves at any time; and that is the strongest possible foundation on which any natural law can rest.

So much, then, by way of proof that the method of establishing laws in science is exactly the same as that pursued in common life. Let us now turn to another matter (though really it is but another phase of the same question), and that is, the method by which, from the relations of certain phenomena, we prove that some stand in the position of causes towards the others.

I want to put the case clearly before you, and I will therefore show you what I mean by another familiar example. I will suppose that one of you, on coming down in the morning to the parlor of your house, finds that a tea-pot and some spoons which had been left in the room on the previous evening are gone, — the window is open, and you observe the mark of a dirty hand on the window-frame, and perhaps, in addition to that, you notice the impress of a hob-nailed shoe on the gravel outside. All these phenomena have struck your attention instantly, and before two seconds have passed you say, "Oh, somebody has broken open the window, entered the room, and run off with the spoons and the tea-pot!" That speech is out of your mouth in a moment. And you will probably add, "I know there has; I am quite sure of it!" You mean to say exactly what you know; but in reality you are giving expression to what is, in all essential particulars, an hypothesis. You do not *know* it at all; it is nothing but an hypothesis rapidly framed in your own mind. And it is an hypothesis founded on a long train of inductions and deductions.

What are those inductions and deductions, and how have you got at this hypothesis? You have observed in the first place, that the window is open; but by a train of reasoning involving many inductions and deductions, you have probably arrived long before at the general law — and a very good one it is — that windows do not open of themselves; and you therefore conclude that something has opened the window. A second general law that you have arrived at in the same way is, that tea-pots and spoons do not go out of a window spontaneously, and you are satisfied that, as they are not now where you left them, they have been removed. In the third place, you look at the marks on the window-sill, and the shoe-marks outside, and you say that in all previous experience the former kind of mark has never been produced by anything else but the hand of a human being; and the same experience shows that no other animal but man at present wears shoes with hob-nails in them such as would produce the marks in the gravel. I do not know, even if we could discover any of those "missing links" that are talked about, that they would help us to any other conclusion! At any rate the law which states our present experience is strong enough for my present purpose. You next reach the conclusion that, as these kind of marks have not been left by any other animal than man, or are liable to be formed in any other way than a man's hand and shoe, the marks in question have been formed by a man in that way. You have, further, a general law, founded on observation and experience, and that, too, is, I am sorry to say, a very universal and unimpeachable one, — that some men are thieves; and you assume at once from all these premises — and that is what constitutes your hypothesis — that the man who made the marks outside and on the window-sill, opened the window, got into the room, and stole your tea-pot and spoons. You have now arrived at a *vera causa;* — you have assumed a cause which, it is plain, is competent to produce all the phenomena you have observed. You can explain all these phenomena only by the hypothesis of a thief. But that is a hypothetical conclusion, of the justice of which you have no absolute proof at all; it is only rendered highly probable by a series of inductive and deductive reasonings.

I suppose your first action, assuming that you are a man of ordinary common sense, and that you have established this hypothesis to your own satisfaction, will very likely be to go off for the police, and set them on the track of the burglar, with the view to the recovery of your property. But just as you are starting with this object, some person comes in, and on learning what you are about, says, "My good friend, you are going on a great deal too fast. How do you know that the man who really made the marks took the spoons? It might have been a monkey that took them, and the man may have merely looked in afterwards." You would probably reply, "Well, that is all very well, but you see it is contrary to all experience of the way tea-pots and spoons are abstracted; so that, at any rate, your hypothesis is less probable than mine." While you are talking the thing over in this way, another friend arrives, one of the good kind of people that I was talking of a little while ago. And he might say, "Oh, my dear sir, you are certainly going on a great deal too fast. You are most presumptuous. You admit that all these occurrences took place when you were fast asleep, at a time when you could not possibly have known anything about what was taking place. How do you know that the laws of Nature are not suspended during the night? It may be that there has been some kind of supernatural interference in this case." In point of fact, he declares that your hypothesis is one of which you cannot at all demonstrate the truth, and that you are by no means sure that the laws of Nature are the same when you are asleep as when you are awake.

Well, now, you cannot at the moment answer that kind of reasoning. You feel that your worthy friend has you some-

THE METHOD OF SCIENTIFIC INVESTIGATION 77

what at a disadvantage. You will feel perfectly convinced in your own mind, however, that you are quite right, and you say to him, "My good friend, I can only be guided by the natural probabilities of the case, and if you will be kind enough to stand aside and permit me to pass, I will go and fetch the police." Well, we will suppose that your journey is successful, and that by good luck you meet with a policeman; that eventually the burglar is found with your property on his person, and the marks correspond to his hand and to his boots. Probably any jury would consider those facts a very good experimental verification of your hypothesis, touching the cause of the abnormal phenomena observed in your parlor, and would act accordingly.

Now, in this supposititious case, I have taken phenomena of a very common kind, in order that you might see what are the different steps in an ordinary process of reasoning, if you will only take the trouble to analyse it carefully. All the operations I have described, you will see, are involved in the mind of any man of sense in leading him to a conclusion as to the course he should take in order to make good a robbery and punish the offender. I say that you are led, in that case, to your conclusion by exactly the same train of reasoning as that which a man of science pursues when he is endeavouring to discover the origin and laws of the most occult phenomena. The process is, and always must be, the same; and precisely the same mode of reasoning was employed by Newton and Laplace in their endeavours to discover and define the causes of the movements of the heavenly bodies, as you, with your own common sense, would employ to detect a burglar. The only difference is, that the nature of the inquiry being more abstruse, every step has to be most carefully watched, so that there may not be a single crack or flaw in your hypothesis. A flaw or crack in many of the hypotheses of daily life may be of little or no moment as affecting the general correctness of the conclusions at which we may arrive; but, in a scientific inquiry, a fallacy, great or small, is always of importance, and is sure to be in the long run constantly productive of mischievous if not fatal results.

Do not allow yourselves to be misled by the common notion that an hypothesis is untrustworthy simply because it is an hypothesis. It is often urged, in respect to some scientific conclusion, that, after all, it is only an hypothesis. But what more have we to guide us in nine-tenths of the most important affairs of daily life than hypotheses, and often very ill-based ones? So that in science, where the evidence of an hypothesis is subjected to the most rigid examination, we may rightly pursue the same course. You may have hypotheses, and hypotheses. A man may say, if he likes, that the moon is made of green cheese: that is an hypothesis. But another man, who has devoted a great deal of time and attention to the subject, and availed himself of the most powerful telescopes and the results of the observations of others, declares that in his opinion it is probably composed of materials very similar to those of which our own earth is made up: and that is also only an hypothesis. But I need not tell you that there is an enormous difference in the value of the two hypotheses. That one which is based on sound scientific knowledge is sure to have a corresponding value; and that which is a mere hasty random guess is likely to have but little value. Every great step in our progress in discovering causes has been made in exactly the same way as that which I have detailed to you. A person observing the occurrence of certain facts and phenomena asks, naturally enough, what process, what kind of operation known to occur in Nature applied to the particular case, will unravel and explain the mystery? Hence you have the scientific hypothesis; and its value will be proportionate to the care and completeness with which its basis had been tested and verified. It is in these matters as in the commonest affairs of practical life: the guess of the fool will be folly, while the guess of the wise man will contain wisdom. In all cases, you see that the value of the result depends on the patience and faithfulness with which the investigator applies to his hypothesis every possible kind of verification.

THE AMERICAN SCHOLAR[1]

RALPH WALDO EMERSON
1803-1882

THIS lecture was delivered before the Phi Beta Kappa Society, in Cambridge, Massachusetts, August 31, 1837. It has been called our intellectual declaration of independence. Emerson's simple, vigorous language, wide sympathy, lofty ideals and sane Americanism make this essay, and the one on Abraham Lincoln, of special and permanent value to Americans.

MR. PRESIDENT AND GENTLEMEN,

I GREET you on the recommencement of our literary year. Our anniversary is one of hope, and, perhaps, not enough of labor. We do not meet for games of strength or skill, for the recitation of histories, tragedies, and odes, like the ancient Greeks; for parliaments of love and poesy, like the Troubadours; nor for the advancement of science, like our contemporaries in the British and European capitals. Thus far, our holiday has been simply a friendly sign of the survival of the love of letters amongst a people too busy to give to letters any more. As such it is precious as the sign of an indestructible instinct. Perhaps the time is already come when it ought to be, and will be, something else; when the sluggard intellect of this continent will look from under its iron lids and fill the postponed expectation of the world with something better than the exertions of mechanical skill. Our day of dependence, our long apprenticeship to the learning of other lands, draws to a close. The millions that around us are rushing into life, cannot always be fed on the sere remains of foreign harvests. Events, actions arise, that must be sung, that will sing themselves. Who can doubt that poetry will revive and lead in a new age, as the star in the constellation Harp, which now flames in our zenith,

[1] Reprinted by arrangement with Houghton Mifflin Company.

astronomers announce, shall one day be the pole-star for a thousand years?

In this hope I accept the topic which not only usage but the nature of our association seem to prescribe to this day, — the AMERICAN SCHOLAR. Year by year we come up hither to read one more chapter of his biography. Let us inquire what light new days and events have thrown on his character and his hopes.

It is one of those fables which out of an unknown antiquity convey an unlooked-for wisdom, that the gods, in the beginning, divided Man into men, that he might be more helpful to himself; just as the hand was divided into fingers, the better to answer its end.

The old fable covers a doctrine ever new and sublime; that there is One Man, — present to all particular men only partially, or through one faculty; and that you must take the whole society to find the whole man. Man is not a farmer, or a professor, or an engineer, but he is all. Man is priest, and scholar, and statesman, and producer, and soldier. In the *divided* or social state these functions are parcelled out to individuals, each of whom aims to do his stint of the joint work, whilst each other performs his. The fable implies that the individual, to possess himself, must sometimes return from his own labor to embrace all the other laborers. But, unfortunately, this original unit, this fountain of power, has been so distributed to multitudes, has been so minutely subdivided and peddled out, that it is spilled into drops, and cannot be gathered. The state of society is one in which the members have suffered amputation from the trunk, and strut about so many walking monsters, — a good finger, a neck, a stomach, an elbow, but never a man.

Man is thus metamorphosed into a thing, into many things. The planter, who is Man sent out into the field to gather food, is seldom cheered by any idea of the true dignity of his ministry. He sees his bushel and his cart, and nothing beyond, and sinks into the farmer, instead of Man on the farm. The tradesman scarcely ever gives an ideal worth to his work, but is ridden by the routine of his craft, and the soul is subject to dollars. The priest becomes a form; the attorney a statute-book; the mechanic a machine; the sailor a rope of the ship.

In this distribution of functions the scholar is the delegated intellect. In the right state he is *Man Thinking*. In the degenerate state, when the victim of society, he tends to become a mere thinker, or still worse, the parrot of other men's thinking.

In this view of him, as Man Thinking, the theory of his office is contained. Him Nature solicits with all her placid, all her monitory pictures; him the past instructs; him the future invites. Is not indeed every man a student, and do not all things exist for the student's behoof? And, finally, is not the true scholar the only true master? But the old oracle said, "All things have two handles: beware of the wrong one." In life, too often, the scholar errs with mankind and forfeits his privilege. Let us see him in his school, and consider him in reference to the main influences he receives.

I. The first in time and the first in importance of the influences upon the mind is that of nature. Every day, the sun; and, after sunset, Night and her stars. Ever the winds blow; ever the grass grows. Every day, men and women, conversing, beholding and beholden. The scholar is he of all men whom this spectacle most engages. He must settle its value in his mind. What is nature to him? There is never a beginning, there is never an end, to the inexplicable continuity of this web of God, but always circular power returning into itself. Therein it resembles his own spirit, whose beginning, whose ending, he never can find, — so entire, so boundless. Far too as her splendors shine, system on system shooting like rays, upward, downward, without centre, without circumference, — in the mass and in the particle, Nature hastens to render account of herself to the mind. Classification begins. To the young mind every thing is individual, stands by itself. By and by, it finds how to join two things and see in them one nature; then three, then three thousand; and so, tyrannized over by its own unifying instinct, it goes on tying things together, diminishing anomalies, discovering roots running under ground whereby contrary and remote things cohere and flower out from one stem. It presently learns that since the dawn of history there has been a constant accumulation and classifying of facts. But what is classification but the perceiving that these objects are not chaotic, and are not foreign, but have a law which is also a law of the human mind? The astronomer discovers that geometry, a pure abstraction of the human mind, is the measure of planetary motion. The chemist finds proportions and intelligible method throughout matter; and science is nothing but the finding of analogy, identity, in the most remote parts. The ambitious soul sits down before each refractory fact; one after another reduces all strange constitutions, all new powers, to their class and their law, and goes on forever to animate the last fibre of organization, the outskirts of nature, by insight.

Thus to him, to this school-boy under the bending dome of day, is suggested that he and it proceed from one root; one is leaf and one is flower; relation, sympathy, stirring in every vein. And what is that root? Is not that the soul of his soul? A thought too bold; a dream too wild. Yet when this spiritual light shall have revealed the law of more earthly natures, — when he has learned to worship the soul, and to see that the natural philosophy that now is, is only the first gropings of its gigantic hand, he shall look forward to an ever expanding knowledge as to a becoming creator. He shall see that nature is the opposite of the soul, answering to it part for part. One is seal and one is print. Its beauty is the beauty of his own mind. Its laws are the laws of his own mind. Nature then becomes to him the measure of his attainments. So much of nature as he is ignorant of, so much of his own mind does he not yet possess. And, in fine, the ancient precept, "Know thyself," and the modern precept, "Study nature," become at last one maxim.

II. The next great influence into the spirit of the scholar is the mind of the Past, — in whatever form, whether of literature, of art, of institutions, that mind is inscribed. Books are the best type of the influence of the past, and perhaps we shall get at the truth, — learn the amount of this influence more conveniently, — by considering their value alone.

The theory of books is noble. The scholar of the first age received into him the world around; brooded thereon; gave it the new arrangement of his own mind, and uttered it again. It came into him life; it went out from him truth. It came to him short-lived actions; it went out from him immortal thoughts. It came to him business; it went from him poetry. It was dead fact; now, it is quick thought. It can stand, and it can go. It now endures, it now flies, it now inspires. Precisely in proportion to the depth of mind from which it issued, so high does it soar, so long does it sing.

Or, I might say, it depends on how far the process had gone, of transmuting life into truth. In proportion to the completeness of the distillation, so will the purity and imperishableness of the product be. But none is quite perfect. As no air-pump can by any means make a perfect vacuum, so neither can any artist entirely exclude the conventional, the local, the perishable from his book, or write a book of pure thought, that shall be as efficient, in all respects, to a remote posterity, as to contemporaries, or rather to the second age. Each age, it is found, must write its own books; or rather, each generation for the next succeeding. The books of an older period will not fit this.

Yet hence arises a grave mischief. The sacredness which attaches to the act of creation, the act of thought, is transferred to the record. The poet chanting was felt to be a divine man: henceforth the chant is divine also. The writer was a just and wise spirit: henceforward it is settled the book is perfect; as love of the hero corrupts into worship of his statue. Instantly the book becomes noxious: the guide is a tyrant. The sluggish and perverted mind of the multitude, slow to open to the incursions of Reason, having once so opened, having once received this book, stands upon it, and makes an outcry if it is disparaged. Colleges are built on it. Books are written on it by thinkers, not by Man Thinking; by men of talent, that is, who start wrong, who set out from accepted dogmas, not from their own sight of principles. Meek young men grow up in libraries, believing it their duty to accept the views which Cicero, which Locke, which Bacon, have given; forgetful that Cicero, Locke, and Bacon were only young men in libraries when they wrote these books.

Hence, instead of Man Thinking, we have the bookworm. Hence the book-learned class, who value books, as such; not as related to nature and the human constitution, but as making a sort of Third Estate with the world and the soul. Hence the restorers of readings, the emendators, the bibliomaniacs of all degrees.

Books are the best of things, well used; abused, among the worst. What is the right use? What is the one end which all means go to effect? They are for nothing but to inspire. I had better never see a book than to be warped by its attraction clean out of my own orbit, and made a satellite instead of a system. The one thing in the world, of value, is the active soul. This every man is entitled to; this every man contains within him, although in almost all men obstructed, and as yet unborn. The soul active sees absolute truth and utters truth, or creates. In this action it is genius; not the privilege of here and there a favorite, but the sound estate of every man. In its essence it is progressive. The book, the college, the school of art, the institution of any kind, stop with some past utterance of genius. This is good, say they, — let us hold by this. They pin me down. They look backward and not forward. But genius looks forward: the eyes of man are set in his forehead, not in his hindhead: man hopes: genius creates. Whatever talents may be, if the man create not, the pure efflux of the Deity is not his; — cinders and smoke there may be, but not yet flame. There are creative manners, there are creative actions, and creative words; manners, actions, words, that is, indicative of no custom or authority, but springing spontaneous from the mind's own sense of good and fair.

On the other part, instead of being its own seer, let it receive from another mind its truth, though it were in torrents of light, without periods of solitude, inquest, and self-recovery, and a fatal disservice is done. Genius is always sufficiently the enemy of genius by over-influence. The literature of every nation bears me witness. The English dramatic poets have Shakspearized now for two hundred years.

Undoubtedly there is a right way of reading, so it be sternly subordinated. Man Thinking must not be subdued by his instruments. Books are for the scholar's idle times. When he can read God directly, the hour is too precious to be wasted in other men's transcripts of their readings. But when the intervals of darkness come, as come they must, — when the sun is hid and the stars withdraw their shining, — we repair to the lamps which were kindled by their ray, to guide our steps to the East again, where the dawn is. We hear, that we may speak. The Arabian proverb says, "A fig tree, looking on a fig tree, becometh fruitful."

It is remarkable, the character of the pleasure we derive from the best books. They impress us with the conviction that one nature wrote and the same reads. We read the verses of one of the great English poets, of Chaucer, of Marvell, of Dryden, with the most modern joy, — with a pleasure, I mean, which is in great part caused by the abstraction of all *time* from their verses. There is some awe mixed with the joy of our surprise, when this poet, who lived in some past world, two or three hundred years ago, says that which lies close to my own soul, that which I also had well-nigh thought and said. But for the evidence thence afforded to the philosophical doctrine of the identity of all minds, we should suppose some preëstablished harmony, some foresight of souls that were to be, and some preparation of stores for their future wants, like the fact observed in insects, who lay up food before death for the young grub they shall never see.

I would not be hurried by any love of system, by any exaggeration of instincts, to underrate the Book. We all know, that as the human body can be nourished on any food, though it were boiled grass and the broth of shoes, so the human mind can be fed by any knowledge. And great and heroic men have existed who had almost no other information than by the printed page. I only would say that it needs a strong head to bear that diet. One must be an inventor to read well. As the proverb says, "He that would bring home the wealth of the Indies, must carry out the wealth of the Indies." There is then creative reading as well as creative writing. When the mind is braced by labor and invention, the page of whatever book we read becomes luminous with manifold allusion. Every sentence is doubly significant and the sense of our author is as broad as the world. We then see, what is always true, that as the seer's hour of vision is short and rare among heavy days and months, so is its record, perchance, the least part of his volume. The discerning will read, in his Plato or Shakspeare, only that least part, — only the authentic utterances of the oracle; — all the rest he rejects, were it never so many times Plato's and Shakspeare's.

Of course there is a portion of reading quite indispensable to a wise man. History and exact science he must learn by laborious reading. Colleges, in like manner, have their indispensable office, — to teach elements. But they can only highly serve us when they aim not to drill, but to create; when they gather from far every ray of various genius to their hospitable halls, and by the concentrated fires, set the hearts of their youth on flame. Thought and knowledge are natures in which apparatus and pretension avail nothing. Gowns and pecuniary foundations, though of towns of gold, can never countervail the least sentence or syllable of wit. Forget this, and our American colleges will recede in their public importance, whilst they grow richer every year.

III. There goes in the world a notion that the scholar should be a recluse, a valetudinarian, — as unfit for any handiwork or public labor as a penknife for an axe. The so-called "practical men" sneer at speculative men, as if, because they speculate or *see*, they could do nothing. I have heard it said that the clergy, — who are always, more universally than any other class, the scholars of their day, — are addressed as women; that the rough, spontaneous conversation of men they do not hear, but only a mincing and diluted speech. They are often virtually disfranchised; and indeed there are advocates for their celibacy. As far as this is true of the studious classes, it is not just and wise. Action is with the scholar subordinate, but it is essential. Without it he is not yet man. Without it thought can never ripen into truth. Whilst the world hangs before the eye as a cloud of beauty, we cannot even see its beauty. Inaction is cowardice, but there can be no scholar without the heroic mind. The preamble of thought, the transition through which it passes from the unconscious to the conscious, is action. Only so much do I know, as I have lived. Instantly we know whose words are loaded with life, and whose not.

The world, — this shadow of the soul, or *other me*, lies wide around. Its attractions are the keys which unlock my thoughts and make me acquainted with myself. I run eagerly into this resounding tumult. I grasp the hands of those next me, and take my place in the ring to suffer and to work, taught by an instinct that so shall the dumb abyss be vocal with speech. I pierce its order; I dissipate its fear; I dispose of it within the circuit of my expanding life. So much only of life as I know by experience, so much of the wilderness have I vanquished and planted, or so far have I extended my being, my dominion. I do not see how any man can afford, for the sake of his nerves and his nap, to spare any action in which he can partake. It is pearls and rubies to his discourse. Drudgery, calamity, exasperation, want, are instructors in eloquence and wisdom. The true scholar grudges every opportunity of action past by, as a loss of power.

It is the raw material out of which the intellect moulds her splendid products. A strange process too, this by which experience is converted into thought, as a mulberry leaf is converted into satin. The manufacture goes forward at all hours.

The actions and events of our childhood and youth are now matters of calmest observation. They lie like fair pictures in the air. Not so with our recent actions, — with the business which we now have in hand. On this we are quite unable to speculate. Our affections as yet circulate through it. We no more feel or know it than we feel the feet, or the hand, or the brain of our body. The new deed is yet a part of life, — remains for a time immersed in our unconscious life. In some contemplative hour it detaches itself from the life like a ripe fruit, to become a thought of the mind. Instantly it is raised, transfigured; the corruptible has put on incorruption. Henceforth it is an object of beauty, however base its origin and neighborhood. Observe too the impossibility of antedating this act. In its grub state, it cannot fly, it cannot shine, it is a dull grub. But suddenly, without observation, the selfsame thing unfurls beautiful wings, and is an angel of wisdom. So is there no fact, no event, in our private history, which shall not, sooner or later, lose its adhesive, inert form, and astonish us by soaring from our body into the empyrean. Cradle and infancy, school and playground, the fear of boys, and dogs, and ferules, the love of little maids and berries, and many another fact that once filled the whole sky, are gone already; friend and relative, profession and party, town and country, nation and world, must also soar and sing.

Of course, he who has put forth his total strength in fit actions has the richest return of wisdom. I will not shut myself out of this globe of action, and transplant an oak into a flower-pot, there to hunger and pine; nor trust the revenue of some single faculty, and exhaust one vein of thought, much like those Savoyards, who, getting their livelihood by carving shepherds, shepherdesses, and smoking Dutchmen, for all Europe, went out one day to the mountain to find stock, and discovered that they had whittled up the last of their pine-trees. Authors we have, in numbers, who have written out their vein, and who, moved by a commendable prudence, sail for Greece or Palestine, follow the trapper into the prairie, or ramble round Algiers, to replenish their merchantable stock.

If it were only for a vocabulary, the scholar would be covetous of action. Life is our dictionary. Years are well spent in country labors; in town; in the insight into trades and manufactures; in frank intercourse with many men and women; in science; in art; to the one end of mastering in all their facts a language by which to illustrate and embody our perceptions. I learn immediately from any speaker how much he has already lived, through the poverty or the splendor of his speech. Life lies behind us as the quarry from whence we get tiles and copestones for the masonry of today. This is the way to learn grammar. Colleges and books only copy the language which the field and the workyard made.

But the final value of action, like that of books, and better than books, is that it is a resource. That great principle of Undulation in nature, that shows itself in the inspiring and expiring of the breath; in desire and satiety; in the ebb and flow of the sea; in day and night; in heat and cold; and, as yet more deeply ingrained in every atom and every fluid, is known to us under the name of Polarity, — these "fits of easy transmission and reflection," as Newton called them, — are the law of nature because they are the law of spirit.

The mind now thinks, now acts, and each fit reproduces the other. When the artist has exhausted his materials, when the fancy no longer paints, when thoughts are no longer apprehended and books are a weariness, — he has always the resource *to live.* Character is higher than intellect. Thinking is the function. Living is the functionary. The stream retreats to its source. A great soul will be strong to live, as well as strong to think. Does he lack organ or medium to impart his truth? He can still fall back on this elemental force of living them. This is a total act. Thinking is a partial act. Let the grandeur of justice shine in his affairs. Let the beauty of affection cheer his lowly roof. Those "far from fame," who dwell and act with him, will feel the force of his constitution in the doings and passages of the day better than it can be measured by any public and designed display. Time shall teach him that the scholar loses no hour which the man lives. Herein he unfolds the sacred germ of his instinct, screened from influence. What is lost in seemliness is gained in strength. Not out of those on whom systems of education have exhausted their culture, comes the helpful giant to destroy the old or to build the new, but out of unhandselled savage nature; out of terrible Druids and Berserkers come at last Alfred and Shakspeare.

I hear therefore with joy whatever is beginning to be said of the dignity and necessity of labor to every citizen. There is virtue yet in the hoe and the spade, for learned as well as for unlearned hands. And labor is everywhere welcome; always we are invited to work; only be this limitation observed, that a man shall not for the sake of wider activity sacrifice any opinion to the popular judgments and modes of action.

I have now spoken of the education of the scholar by nature, by books, and by action. It remains to say somewhat of his duties.

They are such as become Man Thinking. They may all be comprised in self-trust. The office of the scholar is to cheer, to raise, and to guide men by showing them facts amidst appearances. He plies the slow, unhonored, and unpaid task of observation. Flamsteed and Herschel, in their glazed observatories, may catalogue the stars with the praise of all men, and the results being splendid and useful, honor is sure. But he, in his private observatory, cataloguing obscure and nebulous stars of the human mind, which as yet no man has thought of as such, — watching days and months sometimes for a few facts; correcting still his old records; — must relinquish display and immediate fame. In the long period of his preparation he must betray often an ignorance and shiftlessness in popular arts, incurring the disdain of the able who shoulder him aside. Long he must stammer in his speech; often forego the living for the dead. Worse yet, he must accept, — how often! poverty and solitude. For the ease and pleasure of treading the old road, accepting the fashions, the education, the religion of society, he takes the cross of making his own, and, of course, the self-accusation, the faint heart, the frequent uncertainty and loss of time, which are the nettles and tangling vines in the way of the self-relying and self-directed; and the state of virtual hostility in which he seems to stand to society, and especially to educated society. For all this loss and scorn, what offset? He is to find consolation in exercising the highest functions of human nature. He is one who raises himself from private considerations and breathes and lives on public and illustrious thoughts. He is the world's eye. He is the world's heart. He is to resist the vulgar prosperity that retrogrades ever to barbarism, by preserving and communicating heroic sentiments, noble biographies, melodious verse, and the conclusions of history. Whatsoever oracles the human heart, in all emergencies, in all solemn hours, has uttered as its commentary on the world of actions, — these he shall receive and impart. And whatsoever new verdict Reason from her inviolable seat pronounces on the passing men and events of to-day, — this he shall hear and promulgate.

These being his functions, it becomes him to feel all confidence in himself, and to defer never to the popular cry. He and he only knows the world. The world of any moment is the merest appearance. Some great decorum, some fetish of a government, some ephemeral trade, or war, or man, is cried up by half mankind and cried down by the other half, as if all depended on this particular up or down. The odds are that the whole question is not worth the poorest thought which the scholar has lost in listening to the controversy. Let him not quit his belief that a popgun is a popgun, though the ancient and honorable of the earth affirm it to be the crack of doom. In silence, in steadiness, in severe abstraction, let him hold by himself; add observation to observation, patient of neglect, patient of reproach, and bide his own time, — happy enough if he can satisfy himself alone that this day he has seen something truly. Success treads on every right step. For the instinct is sure, that prompts him to tell his brother what he thinks. He then learns that in going down into the secrets of his own mind he has descended into the secrets of all minds. He learns that he who has mastered any law in his private thoughts, is master to that extent of all men whose language he speaks, and of all into whose language his own can be translated. The poet, in utter solitude remembering his spontaneous thoughts and recording them, is found to have recorded that which men in crowded cities find true for them also. The orator distrusts at first the fitness of his frank confessions, his want of knowledge of the persons he addresses, until he finds that he is the complement of his hearers; — that they drink his words because he fulfils for them their own nature; the deeper he dives into his privatest, secretest presentiment, to his wonder he finds this is the most acceptable, most public, and universally true. The people delight in it; the better part of every man feels, This is my music; this is myself.

In self-trust all the virtues are comprehended. Free should the scholar be, — free and brave. Free even to the definition of freedom, "without any hindrance that does not arise out of his own constitution." Brave; for fear is a thing which a scholar by his very function puts behind him. Fear always springs from ignorance. It is a shame to him if his tranquillity, amid dangerous times, arise from the presumption that like children and women his is a protected class; or if he seek a temporary peace by the diversion of his thoughts from politics or vexed questions, hiding his head like an ostrich in the flowering bushes, peeping into microscopes, and turning rhymes, as a boy whistles to keep his courage up. So is the danger a danger still; so is the fear worse. Manlike let him turn and face it. Let him look into its eye and search its nature, inspect its origin, — see the whelping of this lion, — which lies no great way back; he will then find in himself a perfect comprehension of its nature and extent; he will have made his hands meet on the other side, and can henceforth defy it and pass on superior. The world is his who can see through its pretension. What deafness, what stone-blind custom, what overgrown error you behold is there only by sufferance, — by your sufferance. See it to be a lie, and you have already dealt it its mortal blow.

Yes, we are the cowed, — we the trustless. It is a mischievous notion that we are come late into nature; that the world was finished a long time ago. As the world was plastic and fluid in the hands of God, so it is ever to so much of his attributes as we bring to it. To ignorance and sin, it is flint. They adapt themselves to it as they may; but in proportion as a man has any thing in him divine, the firmament flows before him and takes his signet and form. Not he is great who can alter matter, but he who can alter my state of mind. They are the kings of the world who give the color of their present thought to all nature and all art, and persuade men by the cheerful serenity of their carrying the matter, that this thing which they do is the apple which the ages have desired to pluck, now at last ripe, and inviting nations to the harvest. The great man makes the great thing. Wherever Macdonald sits, there is the head of the table. Linnæus makes botany the most alluring of studies, and wins it from the farmer and the herb-woman; Davy, chemistry; and Cuvier, fossils. The day is always his who works in it with serenity and great aims. The unstable estimates of men crowd to him whose mind is filled with a truth, as the heaped waves of the Atlantic follow the moon.

For this self-trust, the reason is deeper than can be fathomed, — darker than can be enlightened. I might not carry with me the feeling of my audience in stating my own belief, but I have already shown the ground of my hope, in adverting to the doctrine that man is one. I believe man has been wronged; he has wronged himself. He has almost lost the light that can lead him back to his prerogatives. Men are become of no account. Men in history, men in the world of to-day, are bugs, are spawn, and are called "the mass" and "the herd." In a century, in a millennium, one or two men; that is to say, one or two approximations to the right state of every man. All the rest behold in the hero or the poet their own green and crude being, — ripened; yes, and are content to be less, so *that* may attain to its full stature. What a testimony, full of grandeur, full of pity, is borne to the demands of his own nature, by the poor clansman, the poor partisan, who rejoices in the glory of his chief. The poor and the low find some amends to their immense moral capacity, for their acquiescence in a political and social inferiority. They are content to be brushed like flies from the path of a great person, so that justice shall be done by him to that common nature which it is the dearest desire of all to see enlarged and glorified. They sun themselves in the great man's light, and feel it to be their own element. They cast the dignity of man from their downtrod selves upon the shoulders of a hero, and will perish to add one drop of blood to make that great heart beat, those giant sinews combat and conquer. He lives for us, and we live in him.

Men such as they are, very naturally seek money or power; and power because it is as good as money, — the "spoils," so called, "of office." And why not? for they aspire to the highest, and this, in their sleep-walking, they dream is highest. Wake them and they shall quit the false good and leap to the true, and leave governments to clerks and desks. This revolution is to be wrought by the gradual domestication of the idea of Culture. The main enterprise of the world for splendor, for extent, is the upbuilding of a man. Here are the materials strewn along the ground. The private life of one man shall be a more illustrious monarchy, more formidable to its enemy, more sweet and serene in its influence to its friend, than any kingdom in history. For a man, rightly viewed, comprehendeth the particular natures of all men. Each philosopher, each bard, each actor has only done for me, as by a delegate, what one day I can do for myself. The books which once we valued more than the apple of the eye, we have quite exhausted. What is that but saying that we have come up with the point of view which the universal mind took through the eyes of one scribe; we have been that man, and have passed on. First, one, then another, we drain all cisterns, and waxing greater by all these supplies, we crave a better and more abundant food. The man has never lived that can feed us ever. The human mind cannot be enshrined in a person who shall set a barrier on any one side to this unbounded, unboundable empire. It is one central fire, which, flaming now out of the lips of Etna, lightens the capes of Sicily, and now out of the throat of Vesuvius, illuminates the towers and vineyards of Naples. It is one light which beams out of a thousand stars. It is one soul which animates all men.

But I have dwelt perhaps tediously upon this abstraction of the Scholar. I ought not to delay longer to add what I have to say of nearer reference to the time and to this country.

Historically, there is thought to be a difference in the ideas which predominate over successive epochs, and there are data for marking the genius of the Classic, of the Romantic, and now of the Reflective or Philosophical age. With the views I have intimated of the oneness or the identity of the mind through all individuals, I do not much dwell on these differences. In fact, I believe each individual passes through all three. The boy is a Greek; the youth, romantic; the adult, reflective. I deny not however that a revolution in the leading idea may be distinctly enough traced.

Our age is bewailed as the age of Introversion. Must that needs be evil? We, it seems, are critical; we are embarrassed with second thoughts; we cannot enjoy any thing for hankering to know whereof the pleasure consists; we are lined with eyes; we see with our feet; the time is infected with Hamlet's unhappiness, —

"Sicklied o'er with the pale cast of thought."

It is so bad then? Sight is the last thing to be pitied. Would we be blind? Do we fear lest we should outsee nature and God, and drink truth dry? I look upon the discontent of the literary class as a mere announcement of the fact that they find themselves not in the state of mind of their fathers, and regret the coming state as untried; as a boy dreads the water before he has learned that he can swim. If there is any period one would desire to be born in, is it not the age of Revolution; when the old and the new stand side by side and admit of being compared; when the energies of all men are searched by fear and by hope; when the historic glories of the old can be compensated by the rich possibilities of the new era? This time, like all times, is a very good one, if we but know what to do with it.

I read with some joy of the auspicious signs of the coming days, as they glimmer already through poetry and art, through philosophy and science, through church and state.

One of these signs is the fact that the same movement which affected the elevation of what was called the lowest class in the state, assumed in literature a very marked and as benign an aspect. Instead of the sublime and beautiful, the near, the low, the common, was explored and poetized. That which had been negligently trodden under foot by those who were harnessing and provisioning themselves for long journeys into far countries, is suddenly found to be richer than all foreign parts. The literature of the poor, the feelings of the child, the philosophy of the street, the meaning of household life, are the topics of the time. It is a great stride. It is a sign, — is it not? of new vigor when the extremities are made active, when currents of warm life run into the hands and the feet. I ask not for the great, the remote, the romantic; what is doing in Italy or Arabia; what is Greek art, or Provençal minstrelsy; I embrace the common, I explore and sit at the feet of the familiar, the low. Give me insight into to-day, and you may have the antique and future worlds. What would we really know the meaning of? The meal in the firkin; the milk in the pan; the ballad in the street; the news of the boat; the glance of the eye; the form and the gait of the body; — show me the ultimate reason of these matters; show me the sublime presence of the highest spiritual cause lurking, as always it does lurk, in these suburbs and extremities of nature; let me see every trifle bristling with the polarity that ranges it instantly on an eternal law; and the shop, the plough, and the ledger referred to the like cause by which light undulates and poets sing; — and the world lies no longer a dull miscellany and lumber-room, but has form and order; there is **no trifle,** there is no puzzle, but one design unites and animates the farthest pinnacle and the lowest trench.

This idea has inspired the genius of Goldsmith, Burns, Cowper, and, in a newer time, of Goethe, Wordsworth, and Carlyle. This idea they have differently followed and with various success. In contrast with their writing, the style of Pope, of Johnson, of Gibbon, looks cold and pedantic. This writing is blood-warm. Man is surprised to find that things near are not less beautiful and wondrous than things remote. The near explains the far. The drop is a small ocean. A man is related to all nature. This perception of the worth of the vulgar is fruitful in discoveries. Goethe, in this very thing the most modern of the moderns, has shown us, as none ever did, the genius of the ancients.

There is one man of genius who has done much for this philosophy of life, whose literary value has never yet been rightly estimated; — I mean Emanuel Swedenborg. The most imaginative of men, yet writing with the precision of a mathematician, he endeavored to engraft a purely philosophical Ethics on the popular Christianity of his time. Such an attempt of course must have difficulty which no genius could surmount. But he saw and showed the connection between nature and the affections of the soul. He pierced the emblematic or spiritual character of the visible, audible, tangible world. Especially did his shade-loving muse hover over and interpret the lower parts of nature; he showed the mysterious bond that allies moral evil to the foul material forms, and has given in epical parables a theory of insanity, of beasts, of unclean and fearful things.

Another sign of our times, also marked by an analogous political movement, is the new importance given to the single person. Every thing that tends to insulate the individual, — to surround him with barriers of natural respect, so that each man shall feel the world is his, and man shall treat with man as a sovereign state with a sovereign state, — tends to true union as well as greatness. "I learned," said the melancholy Pestalozzi, "that no man in God's wide earth is either willing or able to help any other man." Help must come from the bosom alone. The scholar is that man who must take up into himself all the ability of the time, all the contributions of the past, all the hopes of the future. He must be an university of knowledges. If there be one lesson more than another which should pierce his ear, it is, The world is nothing, the man is all; in yourself is the law of all nature, and you know not yet how a globule of sap ascends; in yourself slumbers the whole of Reason; it is for you to know all; it is for you to dare all. Mr. President and Gentlemen, this confidence in the unsearched might of man belongs, by all motives, by all prophecy, by all preparation, to the American Scholar. We have listened too long to the courtly muses of Europe. The spirit of the American freeman is already suspected to be timid, imitative, tame. Public and private avarice make the air we breathe thick and fat. The scholar is decent, indolent, complaisant. See already the tragic consequence. The mind of this country, taught to aim at low objects, eats upon itself. There is no work for any but the decorous and the complaisant. Young men of the fairest promise, who begin life upon our shores, inflated by the mountain winds, shined upon by all the stars of God, find the earth below not in unison with these, but are hindered from action by the disgust which the principles on which business is managed inspire, and turn drudges, or die of disgust, some of them suicides. What is the remedy? They did not yet see, and thousands of young men as hopeful now crowding to the barriers for the career do not yet see, that if the single man plant himself indomitably on his instincts, and there abide, the huge world will come round to him. Patience, — patience; with the shades of all the good and great for company; and for solace the perspective of your own infinite life; and for work the study and the communication of principles, the making those instincts prevalent, the conversion of the world. Is it not the chief disgrace in the world, not to be an unit; — not to be reckoned one character; — not to yield that peculiar fruit which each man was created to bear, but to be reckoned in the gross, in the hundred, or the thousand, of the party, the section, to which we belong; and our opinion predicted geographically, as the north, or the south? Not so, brothers and friends,— please God, ours shall not be so. We will walk on our own feet; we will work with our own hands; we will speak our own minds. The study of letters shall be no longer a name for pity, for doubt, and for sensual indulgence. The dread of man and the love of man shall be a wall of defence and a wreath of joy around all. A nation of men will for the first time exist, because each believes himself inspired by the Divine Soul which also inspires all men.

A COLLEGE MAGAZINE [1]
ROBERT LOUIS STEVENSON
1850-1894

STEVENSON has taken his place as one of the English stylists. His suggestions in this essay, published in 1887, and in "Truth of Intercourse," 1879, are of particular value to writers because he speaks as one having authority. Stevenson was successful in nearly every form of writing — in verse, the novel, the short story, the essay, the travel sketch: *A Child's Garden of Verses, Treasure Island,* "A Lodging for the Night," "Æs Triplex," and *Travels with a Donkey,* are masterpieces of their kind.

I

ALL through my boyhood and youth, I was known and pointed out for the pattern of an idler; and yet I was always busy on my own private end, which was to learn to write. I kept always two books in my pocket, one to read, one to write in. As I walked, my mind was busy fitting what I saw with appropriate words; when I sat by the roadside, I would either read, or a pencil and a penny version-book would be in my hand, to note down the features of the scene or commemorate some halting stanzas. Thus I lived with words. And what I thus wrote was for no ulterior use, it was written consciously for practice. It was not so much that I wished to be an author (though I wished that too) as that I had vowed that I would learn to write. That was a proficiency that tempted me; and I practised to acquire it, as men learn to whittle, in a wager with myself. Description was the principal field of my exercise; for to any one with senses there is always something worth describing, and town and country are but one continuous subject. But I worked in other ways also; often accompanied my walks with dramatic

[1] From *Memories and Portraits*, by permission of the publishers, Charles Scribner's Sons.

dialogues, in which I played many parts; and often exercised myself in writing down conversations from memory.

This was all excellent, no doubt; so were the diaries I sometimes tried to keep, but always and very speedily discarded, finding them a school of posturing and melancholy self-deception. And yet this was not the most efficient part of my training. Good though it was, it only taught me (so far as I have learned them at all) the lower and less intellectual elements of the art, the choice of the essential note and the right word: things that to a happier constitution had perhaps come by nature. And regarded as training, it had one grave defect; for it set me no standard of achievement. So that there was perhaps more profit, as there was certainly more effort, in my secret labors at home. Whenever I read a book or a passage that particularly pleased me, in which a thing was said or an effect rendered with propriety, in which there was either some conspicuous force or some happy distinction in the style, I must sit down at once and set myself to ape that quality. I was unsuccessful, and I knew it; and tried again, and was again unsuccessful and always unsuccessful; but at least in these vain bouts, I got some practice in rhythm, in harmony, in construction, and in the co-ordination of parts. I have thus played the sedulous ape to Hazlitt, to Lamb, to Wordsworth, to Sir Thomas Browne, to Defoe, to Hawthorne, to Montaigne, to Baudelaire, and to Obermann. I remember one of these monkey tricks, which was called *The Vanity of Morals;* it was to have had a second part, *The Vanity of Knowledge;* and as I had neither morality nor scholarship, the names were apt; but the second part was never attempted, and the first part was written (which is my reason for recalling it, ghostlike, from its ashes) no less than three times: first in the manner of Hazlitt, second in the manner of Ruskin, who had cast on me a passing spell, and third, in a laborious pasticcio of Sir

Thomas Browne. So with my other works: *Cain*, an epic, was (save the mark!) an imitation of *Sordello; Robin Hood*, a tale in verse, took an eclectic middle course among the fields of Keats, Chaucer, and Morris; in *Monmouth*, a tragedy, I reclined on the bosom of Mr. Swinburne; in my innumerable gouty-footed lyrics, I followed many masters; in the first draft of *The King's Pardon*, a tragedy, I was on the trail of no lesser man than John Webster; in the second draft of the same piece, with staggering versatility, I had shifted my allegiance to Congreve, and of course conceived my fable in a less serious vein — for it was not Congreve's verse, it was his exquisite prose, that I admired and sought to copy. Even at the age of thirteen I had tried to do justice to the inhabitants of the famous city of Peebles in the style of the *Book of Snobs*. So I might go on forever, through all my abortive novels, and down to my later plays, of which I think more tenderly, for they were not only conceived at first under the bracing influence of old Dumas, but have met with resurrections: one, strangely bettered by another hand, came on the stage itself and was played by bodily actors; the other, originally known as *Semiramis: A Tragedy*, I have observed on book-stalls under the *alias* of *Prince Otto*. But enough has been said to show by what arts of impersonation, and in what purely ventriloquial efforts I first saw my words on paper.

That, like it or not, is the way to learn to write; whether I have profited or not, that is the way. It was so Keats learned, and there was never a finer temperament for literature than Keats's; it was so, if we could trace it out, that all men have learned; and that is why a revival of letters is always accompanied or heralded by a cast back to earlier and fresher models. Perhaps I hear some one cry out: But this is not the way to be original! It is not; nor is there any way but to be born so. Nor yet, if you are born original, is there anything in this training that shall clip the wings of your originality. There can be none more original than Montaigne, neither could any be more unlike Cicero; yet no craftsman can fail to see how much the one must have tried in his time to imitate the other. Burns is the very type of a prime force in letters; he was of all men the most imitative. Shakespeare himself, the imperial, proceeds directly from a school. It is only from a school that we can expect to have good writers; it is almost invariably from a school that great writers, these lawless exceptions, issue. Nor is there anything here that should astonish the considerate. Before he can tell what cadences he truly prefers, the student should have tried all that are possible; before he can choose and preserve a fitting key of words, he should long have practised the literary scales; and it is only after years of such gymnastic that he can sit down at last, legions of words swarming to his call, dozens of turns of phrase simultaneously bidding for his choice, and he himself knowing what he wants to do and (within the narrow limit of a man's ability) able to do it.

And it is the great point of these imitations that there still shines beyond the student's reach his inimitable model. Let him try as he please, he is still sure of failure; and it is a very old and a very true saying that failure is the only high road to success. I must have had some disposition to learn; for I clear-sightedly condemned my own performances. I liked doing them indeed; but when they were done, I could see they were rubbish. In consequence, I very rarely showed them even to my friends; and such friends as I chose to be my confidants I must have chosen well, for they had the friendliness to be quite plain with me. "Padding," said one. Another wrote: "I cannot understand why you do lyrics so badly." No more could I! Thrice I put myself in the way of a more authoritative rebuff, by sending a paper to a magazine. These were returned; and I was not surprised nor even pained. If they had not been looked at, as (like all amateurs) I suspected was the case, there was no good in repeating the experiment; if they had been looked at — well, then I had not yet learned to write, and I must keep on learning and living. Lastly, I had a piece of good fortune, which is the occasion of this paper, and by which I was able to see my literature in print, and to measure experimentally how far I stood from the favor of the public.

II

THE Speculative Society is a body of some antiquity, and has counted among its members Scott, Brougham, Jeffrey, Horner, Benjamin Constant, Robert Emmet, and many a legal and local celebrity besides. By an accident, variously explained, it has its rooms in the very buildings of the University of Edinburgh: a hall, Turkey-carpeted, hung with pictures, looking, when lighted up at night with fire and candle, like some goodly dining-room; a passage-like library, walled with books in their wire cages; and a corridor with a fireplace, benches, a table, many prints of famous members, and a mural tablet to the virtues of a former secretary. Here a member can warm himself and loaf and read; here, in defiance of Senatus-consults, he can smoke. The Senatus looks askance at these privileges; looks even with a somewhat vinegar aspect on the whole society; which argues a lack of proportion in the learned mind, for the world, we may be sure, will prize far higher this haunt of dead lions than all the living dogs of the professorate.

I sat one December morning in the library of the Speculative; a very humble-minded youth, though it was a virtue I never had much credit for; yet proud of my privileges as a member of the Spec.; proud of the pipe I was smoking in the teeth of the Senatus; and in particular, proud of being in the next room to three very distinguished students, who were then conversing beside the corridor fire. One of these has now his name on the back of several volumes, and his voice, I learn, is influential in the law courts. Of the death of the second, you have just been reading what I had to say. And the third also has escaped out of that battle of life in which he fought so hard, it may be so unwisely. They were all three, as I have said, notable students; but this was the most conspicuous. Wealthy, handsome, ambitious, adventurous, diplomatic, a reader of Balzac, and of all men that I have known, the most like to one of Balzac's characters, he led a life, and was attended by an ill fortune, that could be properly set forth only in the *Comédie Humaine*. He had then his eye on Parliament; and soon after the time of which I write, he made a showy speech at a political dinner, was cried up to heaven next day in the *Courant*, and the day after was dashed lower than earth with a charge of plagiarism in the *Scotsman*. Report would have it (I dare say, very wrongly) that he was betrayed by one in whom he particularly trusted, and that the author of the charge had learned its truth from his own lips. Thus, at least, he was up one day on a pinnacle, admired and envied by all; and the next, though still but a boy, he was publicly disgraced. The blow would have broken a less finely tempered spirit; and even him I suppose it rendered reckless; for he took flight to London, and there, in a fast club, disposed of the bulk of his considerable patrimony in the space of one winter. For years thereafter he lived I know not how; always well dressed, always in good hotels and good society, always with empty pockets. The charm of his manner may have stood him in good stead; but though my own manners are very agreeable, I have never found in them a source of livelihood; and to explain the miracle of his continued existence, I must fall back upon the theory of the philosopher, that in his case, as in all of the same kind, "there was a suffering relative in the background." From this genteel eclipse he reappeared upon the scene, and presently sought me out in the character of a generous editor. It is in this part that I best remember him; tall, slender, with a not ungraceful stoop; looking quite like a refined gentleman, and quite like an urbane adventurer; smiling with an engaging ambiguity; cocking at you one peaked eyebrow with a great appearance of finesse; speaking low and sweet and thick, with a touch of burr; telling strange tales with singular deliberation and, to a patient listener, excellent effect. After all these ups and downs, he seemed still, like the rich student that he was of yore, to breathe of money; seemed still perfectly sure of himself and certain of his end. Yet he was then upon the brink of his last overthrow. He had set himself to found the strangest thing in our society: one of those periodical sheets from which men suppose themselves to learn opinions; in which young gentlemen from the universities are encouraged, at so much a line, to garble facts, insult foreign nations, and calumniate private individuals; and which are now the source of glory, so that if a man's name be often enough printed there, he becomes a kind of demigod; and people will pardon him when he talks back and forth, as they do for Mr. Gladstone; and crowd him to suffocation on railway platforms, as they did the other day to General Boulanger; and buy his literary works, as I hope you have just done for me. Our fathers, when they were upon some great enterprise, would sacrifice a life; building, it may be, a favorite slave into the foundations of their palace. It was with his own life that my companion disarmed the envy of the gods. He fought his paper single-handed; trusting no one, for he was something of a cynic; up early and down late, for he was nothing of a sluggard; daily ear-wigging influential men, for he was a master of ingratiation. In that slender and silken fellow there must have been a rare vein of courage, that he should thus have died at his employment; and doubtless ambition spoke loudly in his ear, and doubtless love also, for it seems there was a marriage in his view had he succeeded. But he died, and his paper died after him; and of all this grace, and tact, and courage, it must seem to our blind eyes as if there had come literally nothing.

These three students sat, as I was saying, in the corridor, under the mural tablet that records the virtues of Macbean, the former secretary. We would often smile at that ineloquent memorial, and thought it a poor thing to come into the world at all and leave no more behind one than Macbean. And yet of these three, two are gone and have left less; and this book, perhaps, when it is old and foxy, and some one picks it up in a corner of a book-shop, and glances through it, smiling at the old, graceless turns of speech, and perhaps for the love of *Alma Mater* (which may be still extant and flourishing) buys it, not without haggling, for some pence — this book may alone preserve a memory of James Walter Ferrier and Robert Glasgow Brown.

Their thoughts ran very differently on that December morning; they were all on fire with ambition; and when they had called me in to them, and made me a sharer in their design, I too became drunken with pride and hope. We were to found a University magazine. A pair of little, active brothers — Livingstone by name, great skippers on the foot, great rubbers of the hands, who kept a book-shop over against the University building — had been debauched to play the part of publishers. We four were to be conjunct editors and, what was the main point of the concern, to print our own works; while, by every rule of arithmetic — that flatterer of credulity — the adventure must succeed and bring great profit. Well, well: it was a bright vision. I went home that morning walking upon air. To have been chosen by these three distinguished students was to me the most unspeakable advance; it was my first draught of consideration; it reconciled me to myself and to my fellowmen; and as I steered round the railings at the Tron, I could not withhold my lips from smiling publicly. Yet, in the bottom of my heart, I knew that magazine would be a grim fiasco; I knew it would not be worth reading; I knew, even if it were, that nobody would read it; and I kept wondering how I should be able, upon my compact income of twelve pounds per annum, payable monthly, to meet my share in the expense. It was a comfortable thought to me that I had a father.

The magazine appeared, in a yellow cover which was the best part of it, for at least it was unassuming; it ran four months in undisturbed obscurity, and died without a gasp. The first number was edited by all four of us with prodigious bustle; the second fell principally into the hands of Ferrier and me; the third I edited alone; and it has long been a solemn question who it was that edited the fourth. It would perhaps be still more difficult to say who read it. Poor yellow sheet, that looked so hopefully in the Livingstones' window! Poor, harmless paper, that might have gone to print a *Shakespeare* on, and was instead so clumsily defaced with nonsense! And, shall I say, Poor Editors? I cannot pity myself, to whom it was all pure gain. It was no news to me, but only the wholesome confirmation of my judgment, when the magazine struggled into half-birth, and instantly sickened and subsided into night. I had sent a copy to the lady with whom my heart was at that time somewhat engaged, and who did all that in her lay to break it; and she, with some tact, passed over the gift and my cherished contributions in silence. I will not say that I was pleased at this; but I will tell her now, if by any chance she takes up the work of her former servant, that I thought the better of her taste. I cleared the decks after this lost engagement; had the necessary interview with my father, which passed off not amiss; paid over my share of the expense to the two little, active brothers, who rubbed their hands as much, but methought skipped rather less than formerly, having perhaps, these two also, embarked upon the enterprise with some graceful illusions; and then, reviewing the whole episode, I told myself that the time was not yet ripe, nor the man ready; and to work I went again with my penny version-books, having fallen back in one day from the printed author to the manuscript student.

TRUTH OF INTERCOURSE [1]

ROBERT LOUIS STEVENSON

This was first published as a magazine essay in 1879. It is now included in the volume *Virginibus Puerisque*.

Among sayings that have a currency in spite of being wholly false upon the face of them for the sake of a half-truth upon another subject which is accidentally combined with the error, one of the grossest and broadest conveys the monstrous proposition that it is easy to tell the truth and hard to tell a lie. I wish heartily it were. But the truth is one; it has first to be discovered, then justly and exactly uttered. Even with instruments specially contrived for such a purpose — with a foot rule, a level, or a theodolite — it is not easy to be exact; it is easier, alas! to be inexact. From those who mark the divisions on a scale to those who measure the boundaries of empires or the distance of the heavenly stars, it is by careful method and minute, unwearying attention that men rise even to material exactness or to sure knowledge even of external and constant things. But it is easier to draw the outline of a mountain than the changing appearance of a face; and truth in human relations is of this more intangible and dubious order: hard to seize, harder to communicate. Veracity to facts in a loose, colloquial sense — not to say that I have been in Malabar when as a matter of fact I was never out of England, not to say that I have read Cervantes in the original when as a matter of fact I know not one syllable of Spanish — this, indeed, is easy and to the same degree unimportant in itself. Lies of this sort, according to circumstances, may or may not be important; in a

---

[1] From *Virginibus Puerisque*, by permission of the publishers, Charles Scribner's Sons.

certain sense even they may or may not be false. The habitual liar may be a very honest fellow, and live truly with his wife and friends; while another man who never told a formal falsehood in his life may yet be himself one lie — heart and face, from top to bottom. This is the kind of lie which poisons intimacy. And, *vice versa,* veracity to sentiment, truth in a relation, truth to your own heart and your friends, never to feign or falsify emotion — that is the truth which makes love possible and mankind happy.

L'art de bien dire is but a drawing-room accomplishment unless it be pressed into the service of the truth. The difficulty of literature is not to write, but to write what you mean; not to affect your reader, but to affect him precisely as you wish. This is commonly understood in the case of books or set orations; even in making your will, or writing an explicit letter, some difficulty is admitted by the world. But one thing you can never make Philistine natures understand; one thing, which yet lies on the surface, remains as unseizable to their wits as a high flight of metaphysics — namely, that the business of life is mainly carried on by means of this difficult art of literature, and according to a man's proficiency in that art shall be the freedom and the fulness of his intercourse with other men. Anybody, it is supposed, can say what he means; and, in spite of their notorious experience to the contrary, people so continue to suppose. Now, I simply open the last book I have been reading — Mr. Leland's captivating *English Gipsies.* "It is said," I find on p. 7, "that those who can converse with Irish peasants in their own native tongue form far higher opinions of their appreciation of the beautiful, and of *the elements of humor and pathos in their hearts,* than do those who know their thoughts only through the medium of English. I know from my own observations that this is quite the case with the Indians of North America, and it is unquestionably so with the gipsy." In short, where a man has not a full possession of the language, the most important, because the most amiable, qualities of his nature have to lie buried and fallow; for the pleasure of comradeship, and the intellectual part of love, rest upon these very "elements of humor and pathos." Here is a man opulent in both, and for lack of a medium he can put none of it out to interest in the market of affection! But what is thus made plain to our apprehensions in the case of a foreign language is partially true even with the tongue we learned in childhood. Indeed, we all speak different dialects; one shall be copious and exact, another loose and meagre; but the speech of the ideal talker shall correspond and fit upon the truth of fact — not clumsily, obscuring lineaments, like a mantle, but clearly adhering, like an athlete's skin. And what is the result? That the one can open himself more clearly to his friends, and can enjoy more of what makes life truly valuable — intimacy with those he loves. An orator makes a false step; he employs some trivial, some absurd, some vulgar phrase; in the turn of a sentence he insults, by a side wind, those whom he is laboring to charm; in speaking to one sentiment he unconsciously ruffles another in parenthesis; and you are not surprised, for you know his task to be delicate and filled with perils. "O frivolous mind of man, light ignorance!" As if yourself, when you seek to explain some misunderstanding or excuse some apparent fault, speaking swiftly and addressing a mind still recently incensed, were not harnessing for a more perilous adventure; as if yourself required less tact and eloquence; as if an angry friend or a suspicious lover were not more easy to offend than a meeting of indifferent politicians! Nay, and the orator treads in a beaten round; the matters he discusses have been discussed a thousand times before; language is ready-shaped to his purpose; he speaks out of a cut and dry vocabulary. But you —

may it not be that your defence reposes on some subtlety of feeling, not so much as touched upon in Shakespeare, to express which, like a pioneer, you must venture forth into zones of thought still unsurveyed, and become yourself a literary innovator? For even in love there are unlovely humors; ambiguous acts, unpardonable words, may yet have sprung from a kind sentiment. If the injured one could read your heart, you may be sure that he would understand and pardon; but, alas! the heart cannot be shown — it has to be demonstrated in words. Do you think it is a hard thing to write poetry? Why, that is to write poetry, and of a high, if not the highest, order.

I should even more admire "the lifelong and heroic literary labors" of my fellowmen, patiently clearing up in words their loves and their contentions, and speaking their autobiography daily to their wives, were it not for a circumstance which lessens their difficulty and my admiration by equal parts. For life, though largely, is not entirely carried on by literature. We are subject to physical passions and contortions; the voice breaks and changes, and speaks by unconscious and winning inflections; we have legible countenances, like an open book; things that cannot be said look eloquently through the eyes; and the soul, not locked into the body as a dungeon, dwells ever on the threshold with appealing signals. Groans and tears, looks and gestures, a flush or a paleness, are often the most clear reporters of the heart, and speak more directly to the hearts of others. The message flies by these interpreters in the least space of time, and the misunderstanding is averted in the moment of its birth. To explain in words takes time and a just and patient hearing; and in the critical epochs of a close relation, patience and justice are not qualities on which we can rely. But the look or the gesture explains things in a breath; they tell their message without ambiguity; unlike speech, they cannot stumble, by the way, on a reproach or an illusion that should steel your friend against the truth; and then they have a higher authority, for they are the direct expression of the heart, not yet transmitted through the unfaithful and sophisticating brain. Not long ago I wrote a letter to a friend which came near involving us in quarrel; but we met, and in personal talk I repeated the worst of what I had written, and added worse to that; and with the commentary of the body it seemed not unfriendly either to hear or say. Indeed, letters are in vain for the purposes of intimacy; an absence is a dead break in the relation; yet two who know each other fully and are bent on perpetuity in love, may so preserve the attitude of their affections that they may meet on the same terms as they had parted.

Pitiful is the case of the blind, who cannot read the face; pitiful that of the deaf, who cannot follow the changes of the voice. And there are others also to be pitied; for there are some of an inert, uneloquent nature, who have been denied all the symbols of communication, who have neither a lively play of facial expression, nor speaking gestures, nor a responsive voice, nor yet the gift of frank, explanatory speech: people truly made of clay, people tied for life into a bag which no one can undo. They are poorer than the gipsy, for their heart can speak no language under heaven. Such people we must learn slowly by the tenor of their acts, or through yea and nay communications; or we take them on trust on the strength of a general air, and now and again, when we see the spirit breaking through in a flash, correct or change our estimate. But these will be uphill intimacies, without charm or freedom, to the end; and freedom is the chief ingredient in confidence. Some minds, romantically dull, despise physical endowments. That is a doctrine for a misanthrope; to those who like their fellow-creatures it must always be meaningless; and, for my part, I can see few things more desirable, after the possession of such radical qualities as honor and humor and pathos, than to have a lively and not a stolid countenance; to have looks to correspond with every feeling; to be elegant and delightful in person, so that we shall please even in the intervals of active pleasing, and may never discredit speech with uncouth manners or become unconsciously our own burlesques. But of all unfortunates there is one creature (for I will not call him man) conspicuous in misfortune. This is he who has forfeited his birthright of expression, who has cultivated artful intonations, who has taught his face tricks, like a pet monkey, and on every side perverted or cut off his means of communication with his fellowmen. The body is a house of many windows: there we all sit, showing ourselves and crying on the passers-by to come and love us. But this fellow has filled his windows with opaque glass, elegantly colored. His house may be admired for its design, the crowd may pause before the stained windows, but meanwhile the poor proprietor must lie languishing within uncomforted, unchangeably alone.

Truth of intercourse is something more difficult than to refrain from open lies. It is possible to avoid falsehood and yet not tell the truth. It is not enough to answer formal questions. To reach the truth by yea and nay communications implies a questioner with a share of inspiration, such as is often found in mutual love. *Yea* and *nay* mean nothing; the meaning must have been related in the question. Many words are often necessary to convey a very simple statement; for in this sort of exercise we never hit the gold; the most that we can hope is by many arrows, more or less far off on different sides, to indicate, in the course of time, for what target we are aiming, and after an hour's talk, back and forward, to convey the purport of a single principle or a single thought. And yet while the curt, pithy speaker misses the point entirely, a wordy, prolegomenous babbler will often add three new offences in the process of excusing one. It is really a most delicate affair. The world was made before the English language, and seemingly upon a different design. Suppose we held our converse not in words, but in music; those who have a bad ear would find themselves cut off from all near commerce, and no better than foreigners in this big world. But we do not consider how many have "a bad ear" for words, nor how often the most eloquent find nothing to reply. I hate questioners and questions; there are so few that can be spoken to without a lie. "*Do you forgive me?*" Madam and sweetheart, so far as I have gone in life, I have never yet been able to discover what forgiveness means. "*Is it still the same between us?*" Why, how can it be? It is eternally different; and yet you are still the friend of my heart. "*Do you understand me?*" God knows; I should think it highly improbable.

The cruellest lies are often told in silence. A man may have sat in a room for hours and not opened his teeth, and yet come out of that room a disloyal friend or a vile calumniator. And how many loves have perished because, from pride, or spite, or diffidence, or that unmanly shame which withholds a man from daring to betray emotion, a lover, at the critical point of the relation, has but hung his head and held his tongue? And, again, a lie may be told by a truth, or a truth conveyed through a lie. Truth to facts is not always truth to sentiment; and part of the truth, as often happens in answer to a question, may be the foulest calumny. A fact may be an exception; but the feeling is the law, and it is that which you must neither garble nor belie. The whole tenor of a conversation is a part of the meaning of each separate statement; the beginning and the end define and travesty the intermediate conversation. You never speak to

God; you address a fellowman, full of his own tempers; and to tell truth, rightly understood, is not to state the true facts, but to convey a true impression; truth in spirit, not truth to letter, is the true veracity. To reconcile averted friends a Jesuitical discretion is often needful, not so much to gain a kind hearing as to communicate sober truth. Women have an ill name in this connection; yet they live in as true relations; the lie of a good woman is the true index of her heart.

"It takes," says Thoreau, in the noblest and most useful passage I remember to have read in any modern author,[1] "two to speak truth — one to speak and another to hear." He must be very little experienced, or have no great zeal for truth, who does not recognize the fact. A grain of anger or a grain of suspicion produces strange acoustical effects, and makes the ear greedy to remark offence. Hence we find those who have once quarrelled carry themselves distantly, and are ever ready to break the truce. To speak truth there must be moral equality or else no respect; and hence between parent and child intercourse is apt to degenerate into a verbal fencing bout, and misapprehensions to become ingrained. And there is another side to this, for the parent begins with an imperfect notion of the child's character, formed in early years or during the equinoctial gales of youth; to this he adheres, noting only the facts which suit with his preconception; and wherever a person fancies himself unjustly judged, he at once and finally gives up the effort to speak truth. With our chosen friends, on the other hand, and still more between lovers (for mutual understanding is love's essence), the truth is easily indicated by the one and aptly comprehended by the other. A hint taken, a look understood, conveys the gist of long and delicate explana-

---

[1] *A Week on the Concord and Merrimack Rivers*, Wednesday, p. 283.

tions; and where the life is known even *yea* and *nay* become luminous. In the closest of all relations — that of a love well founded and equally shared — speech is half discarded, like a roundabout, infantile process or a ceremony of formal etiquette; and the two communicate directly by their presences, and with few looks and fewer words contrive to share their good and evil and uphold each other's hearts in joy. For love rests upon a physical basis; it is a familiarity of nature's making and apart from voluntary choice. Understanding has in some sort outrun knowledge, for the affcetion perhaps began with the acquaintance; and as it was not made like other relations, so it is not, like them, to be perturbed or clouded. Each knows more than can be uttered; each lives by faith, and believes by a natural compulsion; and between man and wife the language of the body is largely developed and grown strangely eloquent. The thought that prompted and was conveyed in a caress would only lose to be set down in words — ay, although Shakespeare himself should be the scribe.

Yet it is in these dear intimacies, beyond all others, that we must strive and do battle for the truth. Let but a doubt arise, and alas! all the previous intimacy and confidence is but another charge against the person doubted. "*What a monstrous dishonesty is this if I have been deceived so long and so completely!*" Let but that thought gain entrance, and you plead before a deaf tribunal. Appeal to the past; why, that is your crime! Make all clear, convince the reason; alas! speciousness is but a proof against you. "*If you can abuse me now, the more likely that you have abused me from the first.*"

For a strong affection such moments are worth supporting, and they will end well; for your advocate is in your lover's heart, and speaks her own language; it is not you but she herself who can defend and clear you of the charge. But in slighter intimacies, and for a less stringent union? Indeed, is it worth while? We are all *incompris*, only more or less concerned for the mischance; all trying wrongly to do right; all fawning at each other's feet like dumb, neglected lapdogs. Sometimes we catch an eye — this is our opportunity in the ages — and we wag our tail with a poor smile. "*Is that all?*" All? If you only knew! But how can they know? They do not love us; the more fools we to squander life on the indifferent.

But the morality of the thing, you will be glad to hear, is excellent; for it is only by trying to understand others that we can get our own hearts understood; and in matters of human feeling the clement judge is the most successful pleader.

POETRY [1]

MARTIN WRIGHT SAMPSON

Professor of English Literature, Cornell University

I REMEMBER that as a small boy I used to wonder what there would be left to discover when the waste places on my maps were dotted with names, when from pole to pole we should be familiar with this round world of ours. The thought that we had not yet explored everything appealed to my sense of adventure, when lifting my head out of the enchanting pages of Jules Verne, I could see myself, larger and sterner than life, crossing vast deserts, penetrating mysterious jungles, scaling impending cliffs, and winning the fair daughter of an incredible king. I was boyishly glad that there were unexplored tracts in Africa and Australia and about the frozen limits of the poles — they were old Earth's pledges to her little son that glory and loveliness had not passed away. The vacant stretches were not vacant, for in them romance lay hid.

The childish notion of romance quietly fades, and in its place there comes the true romance. I did not need to grow all the way to manhood to learn that if the wastes of the world gave fewer and fewer opportunities for discovery, yet there was before me the known world, more mysterious in what it had done than any wild expanse of land that had no history. The thought of the past made magical the present. Europe — word of potent charm that sent visions racing through my brain — was ready to be revealed to me. What if it had been known through old centuries? to me it would be new. What if mankind were older still? to me it was unspeakably new.

[1] Condensed from a lecture at Cornell University. Printed by courtesy of the author.

After all, it was the child's notion still, but real now and lasting. For what was, and what is, romance to me but the possibility of discovering new things? A dreaming boy might look for them in the fantastic, in the remote, but a man shall find them in the things long since found out, and in his own heart. Romance does not pass, for man is a poet. Steeped in reverie, or thrilling with power, he yearns for the things that are waiting to be discovered by him. I care not if this dream be of a Jacob's ladder from heaven, or of a railroad from Cairo to the Cape, the dream is the romance of life, and we cling to it by an instinct surer than reason. Certain men who could look within and without themselves and write, have written a myriad of visions whose name is poetry, and in behalf of this I speak.

What is poetry? The question appears quickly with no quick and cogent answer accompanying it. In the way of the spirit we can reach a common meaning; in the way of the letter, probably not. For poetry has as yet eluded definition. Those marks that commonly seem to distinguish it fail as touchstones when we make the final test. Poetry lies not solely in the use of metre — is not the English translation of Job a poem? not in continuous felicity of style — is not Wordsworth a poet? not in a great theme nor in a deep conception — is not some of the most beautiful poetry as irresponsible as a flower? Such qualities are, to be sure, oftenest present in poetry, but they do not separately ensure the name of poetry to the writings in which they appear. Poems succeed by virtue of something other than the outward and visible sign, and each of us preserves in his heart his criterion, the inward and spiritual grace. That which indefinably touches us is poetry to us, though to others it be doggerel or rant. That which others proclaim great or beautiful is not poetry to us if it does not wind its way into our souls. In the main, because we are like one another, we agree; and when we agree that the thing which has spoken to us is poetry, then truly it is poetry — for who else shall judge? The poet writes for the world to read, and when the world is deeply touched and again and again reaffirms its judgment, it has given in its practical way an answer to our question. The answer is not a definition: we may define it if we can.

Now that which is at the bottom of all our attempted definitions of poetry is a sense of something personal and precious. And because of its very intimacy, this personal and precious something is both variable and constant. It may change, as mood shifts into mood; but it persists, as our identity persists. As this poetical nature of ours varies, we feel the futility of defining it; while it remains, we know that to question its power is vain. It is an elusive and lasting part of us, which we can neither master nor escape from, to which we are not slave and from which we desire no release.

This deep-seated element is one of which we have no cause to be ashamed. We do not talk of it in the market-place, but we are inwardly proud of it and must preserve it at all hazards. For although it is lasting, it is not everlasting, and sometimes may linger hidden and hardly subject to our call. If this tender and almost sacred element is not kept safe, something of the sweetness goes out of our waking hours, and our dreams are only the disordered fantasies of sleep.

I am speaking seriously when I say it is at our high peril that we allow to become dormant this poetic sensibility. Our natures are none so rich that we can afford to let go even a little of their wealth. I say this seriously, and yet, I hope, temperately; for I am by no means ready to urge that the poetical in us is our very best part. It yields, if it can so be separated, to the religious, to the heroic, to the contrite in us; and spells beauty more than it does serene steadfastness of purpose. But saying that says the worst thing that can be said against it. If it may seem at times to be nothing more than beauty, it is always, assuredly, nothing less. Life would be poor without it.

Poetry, then, to which this profound element in us responds, might seem to need no support or defense. But we all know that poetry is not, on the whole, very widely read; that when highly thought of, it is often respected rather than made to enter fully into daily life; and that it is often completely misunderstood.

One misunderstanding, which may stand for them all, is that poetry is essentially opposed to common sense, an affair of dreamers, a weak and rather maudlin thing. Now poetry is, to be sure, an affair of dreamers; but all dreamers are not maudlin; and dreams are chiefly of two classes, the silly and the true, and poetry at bottom deals with the true. Instead of being the opposite of common sense, poetry is therefore the superlative of common sense. The misconception of poetry as a rather effeminate thing may have arisen in several ways: for instance, many poems deal with things that at a given time may be uninteresting to mature men and women, and impatience leads to sweeping judgment. Thus all poetry suffers in their minds from the casual inadequacy of specific examples.

Indifference is probably a more serious obstacle than misconception, indifference of those who really apprehend poetry and who have at one time been genuinely fond of it. The habit of reading poetry has not been kept up; and one cannot long remain susceptible to any art if the appreciation of it is not habitual. The failure to keep on reading is partly due to an ignorance of the scope of poetry. We read certain kinds of verse in school and suppose them to be entirely representative of poetry, when indeed they are not. And we read certain kinds of poetry somewhat ignorantly in youth, and trusting our youthful judgment never recur to them again. "Paradise Lost" has often been sacrificed to immaturity.

The best way of remaining open to the appeal of poetry is to study it seriously. One who has mastered the fundamental laws of a process is unlikely to lose whatever enjoyment the result can give him. Out of continuous, thoughtful reading comes understanding. Out of understanding comes a renovation of heart and soul.

Perhaps we are assuming too easily that the thesis is established: that poetry has a peculiarly great value to us. Let us consider some of the things that poetry may do for a reader. Poetry makes external nature more delightful to us. The violet, the rose, the song-birds, clouds and streams and mountains, mean more to us because poets have spoken of them. I do not mean that the poets may have seen more in nature than other men see. Some men see more than the poets. It is not merely what the poet sees, but what he says, that makes his comment on nature inspiring. To the daffodil Shakespeare and Wordsworth add a charm: their words are as much a part of the flower as if they were petals. I cannot look at daffodils without seeing more than their yellow. They tell me Shakespeare's words anew:

"Daffodils,
That come before the swallow dares, and take
The winds of March with beauty."

They sing again to me Wordsworth's imperishable song,

"And then my heart with pleasure fills,
And dances with the daffodils."

A brook under the trees makes me hear Coleridge as well as the brook's noise.

"A noise like of a hidden brook,
In the leafy month of June,
That to the sleeping woods all night
Singeth a quiet tune."

Nature is richer to me because a poet has said the right word for all time. Poetry is full of these fleeting secrets fastened into steadfast words. Shakespeare and Shelley, Keats and Browning, have added to the music of the lark, the nightingale, the thrush, true words that the unknowing birds carelessly sing to all who love poetry.

But what poetry does for external nature, that, in far greater degree, it does for human nature. It reveals the human spirit, that means more than flowers or mountains, even when these arise before us through words of consummate tenderness or majesty. And human nature must mean more to us still, when we have heard poetry's word about it. I do not know in how many ways, in how many accents, this word may be spoken, but I do know that the message is so large that even the message of nature seems small beside it. In his own way the poet tells us of life; and I, his reader, come away liking life better, feeling that its joys and sorrows have been made lucid to me.

If a poet make individual men stand before us, his characters enter into the close circle of our acquaintance. Our horizon widens as we hear their stories, receive their confidences, love, struggle, and suffer with them. We step from out the cramping present into some spacious hall where Hamlet or Launcelot awaits our coming and for a brief space is ours in spite of all the world. The moving figures do not take the place of life, but they reveal endless possibilities of life. It is hard to imagine a mood in which there shall be no personage from the high realm of poetry ready to speak to me if I am willing to listen. Thus I escape my hereditary and social limitations and add to my experience, experience I never shall have; and it may be with a stouter heart I can face the conflicts that must be mine, if I have held my breath when heroes flung their challenge, and have stared all eyes when they struggled with doubts or passions or dragons and came out with the glory of victory on their brows.

And even more than such figures of heroic and kindly men, drawn by the poet's fancy, I value the revelation of that unassailable reality, the soul of the poet himself, who tells with penetrating candor his yearnings, temptations, failures, and triumphs; who speaks because he cannot keep silent; who speaks beautifully because his thought finds no expression in the repulsive and ugly; who speaks nobly because his nature is noble; who speaks in poetry because by the grace of God a poet he was born.

Such revelations hearten and strengthen a man. They make him know his own heart better, they give him a better own heart to know. He who has shared with sympathy the recounted experience of another man is thereby the more fitted to share in the actual lives of his fellows, and knowing mankind better is thereby more human.

I know that it needs not poetry thus to delight and deepen and broaden a man. Life itself may give a man abiding knowledge of life. To life, poetry is essentially secondary: no verses can take the place of living. But in a deeper sense poetry is a part of life: a poem is a personal fact to writer and reader, every whit as much as pleasure and pain. A fancied adventure is not a real adventure, but a poem's effect is intensely real. One would ten thousand times rather do something heroic than read or write of heroism, but is it utterly vain to read of heroism? Will a man's thoughts grow noble the more surely if you take away from him the noble pages of literature? Of a certainty such reading is real experience.

The practical advantage of letting poetry enter into one's life is easily possible to show. Over and over again one is thrown on his own resources and meets emergencies in which his character is crucially tested. He must make decisions, he must act; and all that there is to prompt and back him is what he is at the moment of need. What he is determines what he shall be. At his best he can do things only to the limit of what that best may be. Now if there has entered into his life, as a valid part of it, the vision, the insight, that poetry may give, there will be a lift in his nature that will add something to what used to be his best: and because of his assimilation of the spirit of poetry; because the happy words, the shining phrases, the glowing passion, of poetry have many a time cleared up a dull hour and become part of his habit; because day by day his brain will have been fitted with better thoughts and feelings than he could have created for himself — the man will have behind him an inspired and strengthened character to guide his choosing mind, his eager hand. To live with beauty is not only to give oneself a joy, it is to have the power of beauty at one's call. A man's life would be in a deep and manly way purified and sweetened if each day he could gain a little of the inspiration that poets fuse into their verse and have it share his visions for that day. The wise poet was right who advised us, daily to see a beautiful picture, daily to read a beautiful poem. He was right, he was practical.

Continually to be a sharer in the wholesome gifts of art, of the most accessible and broadest of the arts, literature, to partake freely of the bounty of our sage and generous brethren, the poets of our race, this is to cherish well the immortal part of us, this is to preserve the soul from the stupefying commonplace, this is to use wisely the talents the Master has lent us.

WHERE I LIVED, AND WHAT I LIVED FOR

HENRY DAVID THOREAU
1817-1862

THOREAU'S friend Channing called him the "poet-naturalist," and there is no better characterization of this sturdy individualist and outdoor man. In 1845 he built himself a hut on the shores of Walden Pond, near Concord, Massachusetts, and lived there alone for nearly two years. *Walden* gives an account of this experience; the extract here is part of the second chapter of that book. Other notable books by Thoreau are *A Week on the Concord and Merrimack Rivers*, *Excursions*, *The Maine Woods*, *A Yankee in Canada*, and his *Journals*. The authorized editions are published by Houghton Mifflin Company.

WHEN first I took up my abode in the woods, that is, began to spend my nights as well as days there, which, by accident, was on Independence Day, or the Fourth of July, 1845, my house was not finished for winter, but was merely a defence against the rain, without plastering or chimney, the walls being of rough, weather-stained boards, with wide chinks, which made it cool at night. The upright white hewn studs and freshly planed door and window casings gave it a clean and airy look, especially in the morning, when its timbers were saturated with dew, so that I fancied that by noon some sweet gum would exude from them. To my imagination it retained throughout the day more or less of this auroral character, reminding me of a certain house on a mountain which I had visited a year before. This was an airy and unplastered cabin, fit to entertain a travelling god, and where a goddess might trail her garments. The winds which passed over my dwelling were such as sweep over the ridges of mountains, bearing the broken strains, or celestial parts only, of terrestrial music. The morning wind forever blows, the poem of creation is uninterrupted; but few are the ears that hear it. Olympus is but the outside of the earth everywhere.

The only house I had been the owner of before, if I except a boat, was a tent, which I used occasionally when making excursions in the summer, and this is still rolled up in my garret; but the boat, after passing from hand to hand, has gone down the stream of time. With this more substantial shelter about me, I had made some progress toward settling in the world. This frame, so slightly clad, was a sort of crystallization around me, and reacted on the builder. It was suggestive somewhat as a picture in outlines. I did not need to go outdoors to take the air, for the atmosphere within had lost none of its freshness. It was not so much within-doors as behind a door where I sat, even in the rainiest weather. The Harivansa says, "An abode without birds is like a meat without seasoning." Such was not my abode, for I found myself suddenly neighbor to the birds; not by having imprisoned one, but having caged myself near them. I was not only nearer to some of those which commonly frequent the garden and the orchard, but to those wilder and more thrilling songsters of the forest which never, or rarely, serenade a villager, — the wood thrush, the veery, the scarlet tanager, the field sparrow, the whip-poor-will, and many others.

I was seated by the shore of a small pond, about a mile and a half south of the village of Concord and somewhat higher than it, in the midst of an extensive wood between that town and Lincoln, and about two miles south of that our only field known to fame, Concord Battle Ground; but I was so low in the woods that the opposite shore, half a mile off, like the rest, covered with wood, was my most distant horizon. For the first week, whenever I looked out on the pond it impressed me like a tarn high up on the side of a mountain, its bottom far above the surface of other lakes, and, as the sun arose, I saw it throwing off its nightly clothing of mist, and here and there, by degrees, its soft ripples or its smooth reflecting surface was revealed, while the mists, like ghosts, were stealthily withdrawing in every direction into the woods, as at the breaking up of some nocturnal conventicle. The very dew seemed to hang upon the trees later into the day than usual, as on the sides of mountains.

This small lake was of most value as a neighbor in the intervals of a gentle rain-storm in August, when, both air and water being perfectly still, but the sky overcast, mid-afternoon had all the serenity of evening, and the wood thrush sang around, and was heard from shore to shore. A lake like this is never smoother than at such a time; and the clear portion of the air above it being shallow and darkened by clouds, the water, full of light and reflections, becomes a lower heaven itself so much the more important. From a hill-top near by, where the wood had been recently cut off, there was a pleasing vista southward across the pond, through a wide indentation in the hills which form the shore there, where their opposite sides sloping toward each other suggested a stream flowing out in that direction through a wooded valley, but stream there was none. That way I looked between and over the near green hills to some distant and higher ones in the horizon, tinged with blue. Indeed, by standing on tiptoe I could catch a glimpse of some of the peaks of the still bluer and more distant mountain ranges in the northwest, those true-blue coins from heaven's own mint, and also of some portion of the village. But in other directions, even from this point, I could not see over or beyond the woods which surrounded me. It is well to have some water in your neighborhood, to give buoyancy to and float the earth. One value even of the smallest well is, that when you look into it you see that earth is not continent but insular. This is as important as that it keeps butter cool.

When I looked across the pond from this peak toward the Sudbury meadows, which in time of flood I distinguished elevated perhaps by a mirage in their seething valley, like a coin in a basin, all the earth beyond the pond appeared like a thin crust insulated and floated even by this small sheet of intervening water, and I was reminded that this on which I dwelt was but *dry land.*

Though the view from my door was still more contracted, I did not feel crowded or confined in the least. There was pasture enough for my imagination. The low shrub oak plateau to which the opposite shore arose stretched away toward the prairies of the West and the steppes of Tartary, affording ample room for all the roving families of men. "There are none happy in the world but beings who enjoy freely a vast horizon," — said Damodara, when his herds required new and larger pastures.

Both place and time were changed, and I dwelt nearer to those parts of the universe and to those eras in history which had most attracted me. Where I lived was as far off as many a region viewed nightly by astronomers. We are wont to imagine rare and delectable places in some remote and more celestial corner of the system, behind the constellation of Cassiopeia's Chair, far from noise and disturbance. I discovered that my house actually had its site in such a withdrawn, but forever new and unprofaned, part of the universe. If it were worth the while to settle in those parts near to the Pleiades or the Hyades, to Aldebaran or Altair, then I was really there, or at an equal remoteness from the life which I had left behind, dwindled and twinkling with as fine a ray to my nearest neighbor, and to be seen only in moonless nights by him. Such was that part of creation where I had squatted

" There was a shepherd that did live,
And held his thoughts as high
As were the mounts whereon his flocks
Did hourly feed him by."

What should we think of the shepherd's life if his flocks always wandered to higher pastures than his thoughts?

Every morning was a cheerful invitation to make my life of equal simplicity, and I may say innocence, with Nature herself. I have been as sincere a worshipper of Aurora as the Greeks. I got up early and bathed in the pond; that was a religious exercise, and one of the best things which I did. They say that characters were engraven on the bathing tub of King Tching-thang to this effect: "Renew thyself completely each day; do it again, and again, and forever again." I can understand that. Morning brings back the heroic ages. I was as much affected by the faint hum of a mosquito making its invisible and unimaginable tour through my apartment at earliest dawn, when I was sitting with door and windows open, as I could be by any trumpet that ever sang of fame. It was Homer's requiem; itself an Iliad and Odyssey in the air, singing its own wrath and wanderings. There was something cosmical about it; a standing advertisement, till forbidden, of the everlasting vigor and fertility of the world. The morning, which is the most memorable season of the day, is the awakening hour. Then there is least somnolence in us; and for an hour, at least, some part of us awakes which slumbers all the rest of the day and night. Little is to be expected of that day, if it can be called a day, to which we are not awakened by our Genius, but by the mechanical nudgings of some servitor, are not awakened by our own newly acquired force and aspirations from within, accompanied by the undulations of celestial music, instead of factory bells, and a fragrance filling the air — to a higher life than we fell asleep from; and thus the darkness bear its fruit, and prove itself to be good, no less than the light. That man who does not believe that each day contains an earlier, more sacred, and auroral hour than he has yet profaned, has despaired of life, and is pursuing a descending and darkening way. After a partial cessation of his sensuous life, the soul of man, or its organs rather, are reinvigorated each day, and his Genius tries again what noble life it can make. All memorable events, I should say, transpire in morning time and in a morning atmosphere. The Vedas say, "All intelligences awake with the morning." Poetry and art, and the fairest and most memorable of the actions of men, date from such an hour. All poets and heroes, like Memnon, are the children of Aurora, and emit their music at sunrise. To him whose elastic and vigorous thought keeps pace with the sun, the day is a perpetual morning. It matters not what the clocks say or the attitudes and labors of men. Morning is when I am awake and there is a dawn in me. Moral reform is the effort to throw off sleep. Why is it that men give so poor an account of their day if they have not been slumbering? They are not such poor calculators. If they had not been overcome with drowsiness, they would have performed something. The millions are awake enough for physical labor; but only one in a million is awake enough for effective intellectual exertion, only one in a hundred millions to a poetic or divine life. To be awake is to be alive. I have never yet met a man who was quite awake. How could I have looked him in the face?

We must learn to reawaken and keep ourselves awake, not by mechanical aids, but by an infinite expectation of the dawn, which does not forsake us in our soundest sleep. I know of no more encouraging fact than the unquestionable ability of man to elevate his life by a conscious endeavor. It is something to be able to paint a particular picture, or to carve a statue, and so to make a few objects beautiful; but it is far more glorious to carve and paint the very atmosphere and medium through which we look, which morally we can do. To affect the quality of the day, that is the highest of arts. Every man is tasked to make his life, even in its details, worthy of the contemplation of his most elevated and critical hour. If we refused, or rather used up, such paltry information as we get, the oracles would distinctly inform us how this might be done.

I went to the woods because I wished to live deliberately, to front only the essential facts of life, and see if I could not learn what it had to teach, and not, when I came to die, discover that I had not lived. I did not wish to live what was not life, living is so dear; nor did I wish to practise resignation, unless it was quite necessary. I wanted to live deep and suck out all the marrow of life, to live so sturdily and Spartan-like as to put to rout all that was not life, to cut a broad swath and shave close, to drive life into a corner, and reduce it to its lowest terms, and, if it proved to be mean, why then to get the whole and genuine meanness of it, and publish its meanness to the world; or if it were sublime, to know it by experience, and be able to give a true account of it in my next excursion. For most men, it appears to me, are in a strange uncertainty about it, whether it is of the devil or of God, and have *somewhat hastily* concluded that it is the chief end of man here to "glorify God and enjoy him forever."

Still we live meanly, like ants; though the fable tells us that we were long ago changed into men; like pygmies we fight with cranes; it is error upon error, and clout upon clout, and our best virtue has for its occasion a superfluous and evitable wretchedness. Our life is frittered away by detail. An honest man has hardly need to count more than his ten fingers, or in extreme cases he may add his ten toes, and lump the rest. Simplicity, simplicity, simplicity! I say, let your affairs be as two or three, and not a hundred or a thousand; instead of a million count half a dozen, and keep your accounts on your thumb-nail. In the midst of this chopping sea of civilized life, such are the clouds and storms and quicksands and thousand-and-one items to be allowed for, that a man has to live, if he would not founder and go to the bottom and not make his port at all, by dead reckoning, and he must be a great calculator indeed who succeeds. Simplify, simplify. Instead of three meals a day, if it be necessary eat but one; instead of a hundred dishes, five; and reduce other things in proportion. Our life is like a German Confederacy, made up of petty states, with its boundary forever fluctuating, so that even a German cannot tell you how it is bounded at any moment. The nation itself, with all its so-called internal improvements, which, by the way are all external and superficial, is just such an unwieldy and overgrown establishment, cluttered with furniture and tripped up by its own traps, ruined by luxury and heedless expense, by want of calculation and a worthy aim, as the million households in the land; and the only cure for it, as for them, is in a rigid economy, a stern and more than Spartan simplicity of life and elevation of purpose. It lives too fast. Men think that it is essential that the *Nation* have commerce, and export ice, and talk through a telegraph, and ride thirty miles an hour, without a doubt, whether *they* do or not; but whether we should live like baboons or like men, is a little uncertain. If we do not get out sleepers, and forge rails, and devote days and nights to the work, but go to tinkering upon our *lives* to improve *them*, who will build railroads? And if railroads are not built, how shall we get to heaven in season? But if we stay at home and mind our business, who will want railroads? We do not ride on the railroad; it rides upon us. Did you ever think what those sleepers are that underlie the railroad? Each one is a man, an Irishman, or a Yankee man. The rails are laid on them, and they are covered with sand, and the cars run smoothly over them. They are sound sleepers, I assure you. And every few years a new lot is laid down and run over; so that, if some have the pleasure of riding on a rail, others have the misfortune to be ridden upon. And when they run over a man that is walking in his sleep, a supernumerary sleeper in the wrong position, and wake him up, they suddenly stop the cars, and make a hue and cry about it, as if this were an exception. I am glad to know that it takes a gang of men for every five miles to keep the sleepers down and level in their beds as it is, for this is a sign that they may sometime get up again.

Why should we live with such hurry and waste of life? We are determined to be starved before we are hungry. Men say that a stitch in time saves nine, and so they take a thousand stitches to-day to save nine to-morrow. As for *work*, we have n't any of any consequence. We have the Saint Vitus' dance, and cannot possibly keep our heads still. If I should only give a few pulls at the parish bell-rope, as for a fire, that is, without setting the bell, there is hardly a man on his farm in the outskirts of Concord, notwithstanding that press of engagements which was his excuse so many times this morning, nor a boy, nor a woman, I might almost say, but would forsake all and follow that sound, not mainly to save property from the flames, but, if we will confess the truth, much more to see it burn, since burn it must, and we, be it known, did not set it on fire, — or to see it put out, and have a hand in it, if that is done as handsomely; yes, even if it were the parish church itself. Hardly a man takes a half hour's nap after dinner, but when he wakes he holds up his head and asks, "What's the news?" as if the rest of mankind had stood his sentinels. Some give directions to be waked every half-hour, doubtless for no other purpose; and then, to pay for it, they tell what they have dreamed. After a night's sleep the news is as indispensable as the breakfast "Pray tell me anything new that has happened to a man anywhere on this globe," — and he reads it over his coffee and rolls, that a man has had his eyes gouged out this morning on the Wachito River; never dreaming the while that he lives in the dark unfathomed mammoth cave of this world, and has but the rudiment of an eye himself.

For my part, I could easily do without the post-office. I think that there are very few important communications made through it. To speak critically, I never received more than one or two letters in my life — I wrote this some years ago — that were worth the postage. The penny-post is, commonly, an institution through which you seriously offer a man that penny for his thoughts which is so often safely offered in jest. And I am sure that I never read any memorable news in a newspaper. If we read of one man robbed, or murdered, or killed by accident, or one house burned, or one vessel wrecked, or one steamboat blown up, or one cow run over on the Western Railroad, or one mad dog killed, or one lot of grasshoppers in the winter, — we never need read of another. One is enough. If you are acquainted with the principle, what do you care for a myriad instances and applications? To a philosopher all *news*, as it is called, is gossip, and they who edit and read it are old women over their tea. Yet not a few are greedy after this gossip. There was such a rush, as I hear, the other day at one of the offices to learn the foreign news by the last arrival, that several large squares of plate glass belonging to the establishment were broken by the pressure, — news which I seriously think a ready wit might write a twelvemonth, or twelve years, beforehand with sufficient accuracy. As for Spain, for instance, if you know how to throw in Don Carlos and the Infanta, and Don Pedro and Seville and Granada, from time to time in the right proportions, — they may have changed the names a little since I saw the papers, — and serve up a bull-fight when other entertainments fail, it will be true to the letter, and give us as good an idea of the exact state or ruin of things in Spain as the most succinct and lucid reports under this head in the newspapers: and as for England, almost the last significant scrap of news from that quarter was the revolution of 1649; and if you have learned the history of her crops for an average year, you never need attend to that thing again, unless your speculations are of a merely pecuniary character. If one may judge who rarely looks into the newspapers, nothing new does ever happen in foreign parts, a French revolution not excepted.

What news! how much more important to know what that is which was never old! "Kieou-he-yu (great dignitary of the state of Wei) sent a man to Khoung-tseu to know his news. Khoung-tseu caused the messenger to be seated near him, and questioned him in these terms: What is your master doing? The messenger answered with respect: My master desires to diminish the number of his faults, but he cannot come to the end of them. The messenger being gone, the philosopher remarked: What a worthy messenger! What a worthy messenger!" The preacher, instead of vexing the ears of drowsy farmers on their day of rest at the end of the week, — for Sunday is the fit conclusion of an ill-spent week, and not the fresh and brave beginning of a new one, — with this one other draggle-tail of a sermon, should shout with thundering voice, "Pause! Avast! Why so seeming fast, but deadly slow?"

Shams and delusions are esteemed for soundest truths, while reality is fabulous. If men would steadily observe realities only, and not allow themselves to be deluded, life, to compare it with such things as we know, would be like a fairy tale and the Arabian Nights' Entertainments. If we respected only what is inevitable and has a right to be, music and poetry would resound along the streets. When we are unhurried and wise, we perceive that only great and worthy things have any permanent and absolute existence, that petty fears and petty pleasures are but the shadow of the reality. This is always exhilarating and sublime. By closing the eyes and slumbering, and consenting to be deceived by shows, men establish and confirm their daily life of routine and habit everywhere, which still is built on purely illusory foundations. Children, who play life, discern its true law and relations more clearly than men, who fail to live it worthily, but who think that they are wiser by experience, that is, by failure. I have read in a Hindoo book, that "there was a king's son, who, being expelled in infancy from his native city, was brought up by a forester, and, growing up to maturity in that state, imagined himself to belong to the barbarous race with which he lived. One of his father's ministers having discovered him, revealed to him what he was, and the misconception of his character was removed, and he knew himself to be a prince. So soul," continues the Hindoo philosopher, "from the circumstances in which it is placed, mistakes its own character, until the truth is revealed to it by some holy teacher, and then it knows itself to be *Brahme*." I perceive that we inhabitants of New England live this mean life that we do because our vision does not penetrate the surface of things. We think that that *is* which *appears* to be. If a man should walk through this town and see only the reality, where, think you, would the "Mill-dam" go to? If he should give us an account of the realities he beheld there, we should not recognize the place in his description. Look at a meeting-house, or a court-house, or a jail, or a shop, or a dwelling-house, and say what that thing really is before a true gaze, and they would all go to pieces in your account of them. Men esteem truth remote, in the outskirts of the system, behind the farthest star, before Adam and after the last man. In eternity there is indeed something true and sublime. But all these times and places and occasions are now and here.

God himself culminates in the present moment, and will never be more divine in the lapse of all the ages. And we are enabled to apprehend at all what is sublime and noble only by the perpetual instilling and drenching of the reality that surrounds us. The universe constantly and obediently answers to our conceptions; whether we travel fast or slow, the track is laid for us. Let us spend our lives in conceiving then. The poet or the artist never yet had so fair and noble a design but some of his posterity at least could accomplish it.

Let us spend one day as deliberately as Nature, and not be thrown off the track by every nutshell and mosquito's wing that falls on the rails. Let us rise early and fast, or break fast, gently and without perturbation; let company come and let company go, let the bells ring and the children cry, — determined to make a day of it. Why should we knock under and go with the stream? Let us not be upset and overwhelmed in that terrible rapid and whirlpool called a dinner, situated in the meridian shallows. Weather this danger and you are safe, for the rest of the way is down hill. With unrelaxed nerves, with morning vigor, sail by it, looking another way, tied to the mast like Ulysses. If the engine whistles, let it whistle till it is hoarse for its pains. If the bell rings, why should we run? We will consider what kind of music they are like. Let us settle ourselves, and work and wedge our feet downward through the mud and slush of opinion, and prejudice, and tradition, and delusion, and appearance, that alluvion which covers the globe, through Paris and London, through New York and Boston and Concord, through Church and State, through poetry and philosophy and religion, till we come to a hard bottom and rocks in place, which we can call *reality* and say, This is, and no mistake; and then begin, having a *point d'appui*, below freshet and frost and fire, a place where you might found a wall or a state, or set a lamp-post safely, or perhaps a gauge, not a Nilometer, but a Realometer, that future ages might know how deep a freshet of shams and appearances had gathered from time to time. If you stand right fronting and face to face to a fact, you will see the sun glimmer on both its surfaces, as if it were a cimeter, and feel its sweet edge dividing you through the heart and marrow, and so you will happily conclude your mortal career. Be it life or death, we crave only reality. If we are really dying, let us hear the rattle in our throats and feel cold in the extremities; if we are alive, let us go about our business.

" Time is but the stream I go a-fishing in. I drink at it; but while I drink I see the sandy bottom and detect how shallow it is. Its thin current slides away, but eternity remains. I would drink deeper; fish in the sky, whose bottom is pebbly with stars. I cannot count one. I know not the first letter of the alphabet. I have always been regretting that I was not as wise as the day I was born. The intellect is a cleaver; it discerns and rifts its way into the secret of things. I do not wish to be any more busy with my hands than is necessary. My head is hands and feet. I feel all my best faculties concentrated in it. My instinct tells me that my head is an organ for burrowing, as some creatures use their snout and fore paws, and with it I would mine and burrow my way through these hills. I think that the richest vein is somewhere hereabouts; so by the divining-rod and thin rising vapors I judge; and here I will begin to mine.

THE LAMP OF OBEDIENCE
JOHN RUSKIN
1819–1900

The Seven Lamps of Architecture was published in 1849. The extract here given is a part of the last one of these essays. Ruskin's love of beauty and of right thinking, his stress on the moral attitude of men as the fundamental and important thing in all work, make what he has to say about art bear strongly on the conduct of life.

I. It has been my endeavor to show in the preceding pages how every form of noble architecture is in some sort the embodiment of the Polity, Life, History, and Religious Faith of nations. Once or twice in doing this, I have named a principle to which I would now assign a definite place among those which direct that embodiment; the last place, not only as that to which its own humility would incline, but rather as belonging to it in the aspect of the crowning grace of all the rest: that principle, I mean, to which Polity owes its stability, Life its happiness, Faith its acceptance, Creation its continuance, — Obedience.

Nor is it the least among the sources of more serious satisfaction which I have found in the pursuit of a subject that at first appeared to bear but slightly on the grave interests of mankind, that the conditions of material perfection which it leads me in conclusion to consider, furnish a strange proof how false is the conception, how frantic the pursuit, of that treacherous phantom which men call Liberty: most treacherous, indeed, of all phantoms; for the feeblest ray of reason might surely show us, that not only its attainment, but its being, was impossible. There is no such thing in the universe. There can never be. The stars have it not; the earth has it not; the sea has it not; and we men have the mockery and semblance of it only for our heaviest punishment.

In one of the noblest poems for its imagery and its music belonging to the recent school of our literature, the writer has sought in the aspect of inanimate nature the expression of that Liberty which, having once loved, he had seen among men in its true dyes of darkness. But with what strange fallacy of interpretation! since in one noble line of his invocation he has contradicted the assumptions of the rest, and acknowledged the presence of a subjection, surely not less severe because eternal? How could he otherwise? since if there be any one principle more widely than another confessed by every utterance, or more sternly than another imprinted on every atom, of the visible creation, that principle is not Liberty, but Law.

II. The enthusiast would reply that by Liberty he meant the Law of Liberty. Then why use the single and misunderstood word? If by liberty you mean chastisement of the passions, discipline of the intellect, subjection of the will; if you mean the fear of inflicting, the shame of committing, a wrong; if you mean respect for all who are in authority, and consideration for all who are in dependence; veneration for the good, mercy to the evil, sympathy with the weak; if you mean watchfulness over all thoughts, temperance in all pleasures, and perseverance in all toils; if you mean, in a word, that Service which is defined in the liturgy of the English church to be perfect Freedom, why do you name this by the same word by which the luxurious mean license, and the reckless mean change; by which the rogue means rapine, and the fool, equality, by which the proud mean anarchy, and the malignant mean violence? Call it by any name rather than this, but its best and truest is, Obedience. Obedience is, indeed, founded on a kind of freedom, else it would become mere subjugation, but that freedom is only granted that obedience may be more perfect; and thus, while a measure of license is necessary to exhibit the individual energies of things, the fairness and pleasantness and perfection of them all consist in their Restraint. Compare a river that has burst its banks with one that is bound by them, and the clouds that are scattered over the face of the whole heaven with those that are marshalled into ranks and orders by its winds. So that though restraint, utter and unrelaxing, can never be comely, this is not because it is in itself an evil, but only because, when too great, it overpowers the nature of the thing restrained, and so counteracts the other laws of which that nature is itself composed. And the balance wherein consists the fairness of creation is between the laws of life and being in the things governed and the laws of general sway to which they are subjected; and the suspension or infringement of either kind of law, or, literally, disorder, is equivalent to, and synonymous with, disease; while the increase of both honor and beauty is habitually on the side of restraint (or the action of superior law) rather than of character (or the action of inherent law). The noblest word in the catalogue of social virtue is "Loyalty," and the sweetest which men have learned in the pastures of the wilderness is "Fold."

III. Nor is this all; but we may observe, that exactly in proportion to the majesty of things in the scale of being, is the completeness of their obedience to the laws that are set over them. Gravitation is less quietly, less instantly obeyed by a grain of dust than it is by the sun and moon; and the ocean falls and flows under influences which the lake and river do not recognize. So also in estimating the dignity of any action or occupation of men, there is perhaps no better test than the question "are its laws strait?" For their severity will probably be commensurate with the greatness of the numbers whose labor it concentrates or whose interest it concerns.

This severity must be singular, therefore, in the case of that art, above all others, whose productions are the most vast and the most common; which requires for its practice the co-operation of bodies of men, and for its perfection the perseverance of successive generations. And taking into account also what we have before so often observed of Architecture, her continual influence over the emotions of daily life, and her realism, as opposed to the two sister arts which are in comparison but the picturing of stories and of dreams, we might beforehand expect that we should find her healthy state and action dependent on far more severe laws than theirs: that the license which they extend to the workings of individual mind would be withdrawn by her; and that, in assertion of the relations which she holds with all that is universally important to man, she would set forth, by her own majestic subjection, some likeness of that on which man's social happiness and power depend. We might, therefore, without the light of experience, conclude, that Architecture never could flourish except when it was subjected to a national law as strict and as minutely authoritative as the laws which regulate religion, policy, and social relations; nay, even more authoritative than these, because both capable of more enforcement, as over more passive matter; and needing more enforcement, as the purest type not of one law nor of another, but of the common authority of all. But in this matter experience speaks more loudly than reason. If there be any one condition which, in watching the progress of architecture, we see distinct and general; if, amidst the counter evidence of success attending opposite accidents of character and circumstance, any one conclusion may be constantly and indisputably drawn, it is this; that the architecture of a nation is great only when it is as universal and as established as its language; and when provincial differences of style are nothing more than so many dialects. Other necessities are matters of doubt: nations have been alike successful in their architecture in times of poverty and of wealth; in times of war and of peace; in times of barbarism and of refinement; under governments the most liberal or the most arbitrary; but this one condition has been constant, this one requirement clear in all places and at all times, that the work shall be that of a *school*, that no individual caprice shall dispense with, or materially vary, accepted types and customary decorations; and that from the cottage to the palace, and from the chapel to the basilica, and from the garden fence to the fortress wall, every member and feature of the architecture of the nation shall be as commouly current, as frankly accepted, as its language or its coin.

IV. A day never passes without our hearing our English architects called upon to be original, and to invent a new style: about as sensible and necessary an exhortation as to ask of a man who has never had rags enough on his back to keep out cold, to invent a new mode of cutting a coat. Give him a whole coat first, and let him concern himself about the fashion of it afterwards. We want no new style of architecture. Who wants a new style of painting or sculpture? But we want *some* style. It is of marvellously little importance, if we have a code of laws and they be good laws, whether they be new or old, foreign or native, Roman or Saxon, or Norman or English laws. But it is of considerable importance that we should have a code of laws of one kind or another, and that code accepted and enforced from one side of the island to another, and not one law made ground of judgment at York and another in Exeter. And in like manner it does not matter one marble splinter whether we have an old or new architecture, but it matters everything whether we have an architecture truly so called or not; that is, whether an architecture whose laws might be taught at our schools from Cornwall to Northumberland, as we teach English spelling and English grammar, or an architecture which is to be invented fresh every time we build a workhouse or a parish school. There seems to me to be a wonderful misunderstanding among the majority of architects at the present day as to the very nature and meaning of Originality, and of all wherein it consists. Originality in expression does not depend on invention of new words; nor originality in poetry on invention of new measures; nor, in painting, on invention of new colors, or new modes of using them. The chords of music, the harmonies of color, the general principles of the arrangement of sculptural masses, have been determined long ago, and, in all probability, cannot be added to any more than they can be altered. Granting that they may be, such additions or alterations are much more the work of time and of multitudes than of individual inventors. We may have one Van Eyck, who will be known as the introducer of a new style once in ten centuries, but he himself will trace his invention to some accidental bye-play or pursuit; and the use of that invention will depend altogether on the popular necessities or instincts of the period. Originality depends on nothing of the kind. A man who has the gift, will take up any style that is going, the style of his day, and will work in that, and be great in that, and make everything that he does in it look as fresh as if every thought of it had just come down from heaven. I do not say that he will not take liberties with his materials, or with his rules: I do not say that strange changes will not sometimes be wrought by his efforts, or his fancies, in both. But those changes will be instinctive, natural, facile, though sometimes marvellous; they will never be sought after as things necessary to his dignity or to his independence; and those liberties will be like the liberties that a great speaker takes with the language, not a defiance of its rules for the sake of singularity; but inevitable, uncalculated, and brilliant consequences of an effort to express what the language, without such infraction, could not. There may be times when, as I have above described, the life of an art is manifested in its changes, and in its refusal of ancient limitations: so there are in the life of an insect; and there is great interest in the state of both the art and the insect at those periods when, by their natural progress and constitutional power, such changes are about to be wrought. But as that would be both an uncomfortable and foolish caterpillar which, instead of being contented with a caterpillar's life and feeding on caterpillar's food, was always striving to turn itself into a chrysalis; and as that would be an unhappy chrysalis which should lie awake at night and roll restlessly in its cocoon, in efforts to turn itself prematurely into a moth; so will that art be unhappy and unprosperous which, instead of supporting itself on the food, and contenting itself with the customs which have been enough for the support and guidance of other arts before it and like it, is struggling and fretting under the natural limitations of its existence, and striving to become something other than it is. And though it is the nobility of the highest creatures to look forward to, and partly to understand the changes which are appointed for them, preparing for them beforehand; and if, as is usual with *appointed* changes, they be into a higher state, even desiring them, and rejoicing in the hope of them, yet it is the strength of every creature, be it changeful or not, to rest for the time being, contented with the conditions of its existence, and striving only to bring about the changes which it desires, by fulfilling to the uttermost the duties for which its present state is appointed and continued.

V. Neither originality, therefore, nor change, good though

both may be, and this is commonly a most merciful and enthusiastic supposition with respect to either, are ever to be sought in themselves, or can ever be healthily obtained by any struggle or rebellion against common laws. We want neither the one or the other. The forms of architecture already known are good enough for us, and for far better than any of us: and it will be time enough to think of changing them for better when we can use them as they are. But there are some things which we not only want, but cannot do without; and which all the struggling and raving in the world, nay more, which all the real talent and resolution in England, will never enable us to do without: and these are Obedience, Unity, Fellowship, and Order. And all our schools of design, and committees of tastes; all our academies and lectures, and journalisms, and essays; all the sacrifices which we are beginning to make, all the truth which there is in our English nature, all the power of our English will, and the life of our English intellect, will in this matter be as useless as efforts and emotions in a dream, unless we are contented to submit architecture and all art, like other things, to English law.

VI. I say architecture and all art; for I believe architecture must be the beginning of arts, and that the others must follow her in their time and order; and I think the prosperity of our schools of painting and sculpture, in which no one will deny the life, though many the health, depends upon that of our architecture. I think that all will languish until that takes the lead, and (this I do not *think*, but I proclaim, as confidently as I would assert the necessity, for the safety of society, of an understood and strongly administered legal government) our architecture *will* languish, and that in the very dust, until the first principle of common sense be manfully obeyed, and an universal system of form and workmanship be everywhere adopted and enforced. It may be said that this is impossible. It may be so — I fear it is so: I have nothing to do with the possibility or impossibility of it; I simply know and assert the necessity of it. If it be impossible, English art is impossible. Give it up at once. You are wasting time, and money, and energy upon it, and though you exhaust centuries and treasuries, and break hearts for it, you will never raise it above the merest dilettanteism. Think not of it. It is a dangerous vanity, a mere gulph in which genius after genius will be swallowed up, and it will not close. And so it will continue to be, unless the one bold and broad step be taken at the beginning. We shall not manufacture art out of pottery and printed stuffs; we shall not reason out art by our philosophy; we shall not stumble upon art by our experiments, nor create it by our fancies: I do not say that we can even build it out of brick and stone; but there is a chance for us in these, and there is none else; and that chance rests on the bare possibility of obtaining the consent, both of architects and of the public, to choose a style, and to use it universally.

VII. How surely its principles ought at first to be limited, we may easily determine by the consideration of the necessary modes of teaching any other branch of general knowledge. When we begin to teach children writing, we force them to absolute copyism, and require absolute accuracy in the formation of the letters; as they obtain command of the received modes of literal expression, we cannot prevent their falling into such variations as are consistent with their feeling, their circumstances, or their characters. So, when a boy is first taught to write Latin, an authority is required of him for every expression he uses; as he becomes master of the language he may take a license, and feel his right to do so without any authority, and yet write better Latin than when he borrowed every separate expression. In the same way our architects would have to be taught to write the accepted style. We must first determine what buildings are to be considered Augustan in their authority; their modes of construction and laws of proportion are to be studied with the most penetrating care; then the different forms and uses of their decorations are to be classed and catalogued, as a German grammarian classes the powers of prepositions; and under this absolute, irrefragable authority, we are to begin to work; admitting not so much as an alteration in the depth of a cavetto, or the breadth of a fillet. Then, when our sight is once accustomed to the grammatical forms and arrangements, and our thoughts familiar with the expression of them all; when we can speak this dead language naturally, and apply it to whatever ideas we have to render, that is to say, to every practical purpose of life; then, and not till then, a license might be permitted; and individual authority allowed to change or to add to the received forms, always within certain limits; the decorations, especially, might be made subjects of variable fancy, and enriched with ideas either original or taken from other schools. And thus in process of time and by a great national movement, it might come to pass, that a new style should arise, as language itself changes; we might perhaps come to speak Italian instead of Latin, or to speak modern instead of old English; but this would be a matter of entire indifference, and a matter, besides, which no determination or desire could either hasten or prevent. That alone which it is in our power to obtain, and which it is our duty to desire, is an unanimous style of some kind, and such comprehension and practice of it as would enable us to adapt its features to the peculiar character of every several building, large or small, domestic, civil, or ecclesiastical. . . .

VIII. It is almost impossible for us to conceive, in our present state of doubt and ignorance, the sudden dawn of intelligence and fancy, the rapidly increasing sense of power and facility, and, in its *proper sense*, of Freedom, which such wholesome restraint would instantly cause throughout the whole circle of the arts. Freed from the agitation and embarrassment of that liberty of choice which is the cause of half the discomforts of the world; freed from the accompanying necessity of studying all past, present, or even possible styles; and enabled, by concentration of individual, and co-operation of multitudinous energy, to penetrate into the uttermost secrets of the adopted style, the architect would find his whole understanding enlarged, his practical knowledge certain and ready to hand, and his imagination playful and vigorous, as a child's would be within a walled garden, who would sit down and shudder if he were left free in a fenceless plain. How many and how bright would be the results in every direction of interest, not to the arts merely, but to national happiness and virtue, it would be as difficult to preconceive as it would seem extravagant to state: but the first, perhaps the least, of them would be an increased sense of fellowship among ourselves, a cementing of every patriotic bond of union, a proud and happy recognition of our affection for and sympathy with each other, and our willingness in all things to submit ourselves to every law that would advance the interest of the community; a barrier, also, the best conceivable, to the unhappy rivalry of the upper and middle classes, in houses, furniture, and establishments; and even a check to much of what is as vain as it is painful in the oppositions of religious parties respecting matters of ritual. These, I say, would be the first consequences. Economy increased tenfold, as it would be by the simplicity of practice; domestic comforts uninterfered with by the caprice and mistakes of architects ignorant of the capacities of the styles they use, and all the symmetry and sightliness of our harmonized streets and public buildings, are things of slighter account in the catalogue of benefits. . . .

I have paused, not once nor twice, as I wrote, and often have checked the course of what might otherwise have been importunate persuasion, as the thought has crossed me, how soon all Architecture may be vain, except that which is not made with hands. There is something ominous in the light which has enabled us to look back with disdain upon the ages among whose lovely vestiges we have been wandering. I could smile when I hear the hopeful exultation of many, at the new reach of worldly science, and vigor of worldly effort; as if we were again at the beginning of days. There is thunder on the horizon as well as dawn. The sun was risen upon the earth when Lot entered into Zoar.

THE HERO AS DIVINITY
THOMAS CARLYLE
1795-1881

"THE Hero as Divinity" is an extract from the first of the lectures on *Heroes, Hero-Worship, and the Heroic in History*, delivered in the years 1837-40, and published in 1841. Whether or not we agree with Carlyle's philosophy of history, there is no doubt that he is a magnificently stimulating and forcible writer. This essay is given here because it stresses the importance of religion in life. *Sartor Resartus* is an equally powerful presentation of Carlyle's ideas.

WE have undertaken to discourse here for a little on Great Men, their manner of appearance in our world's business, how they have shaped themselves in the world's history, what ideas men formed of them, what work they did; — on Heroes, namely, and on their reception and performance; what I call Hero-worship and the Heroic in human affairs. Too evidently this is a large topic; deserving quite other treatment than we can expect to give it at present. A large topic; indeed, an illimitable one; wide as Universal History itself. For, as I take it, Universal History, the history of what man has accomplished in this world, is at bottom the History of the Great Men who have worked here. They were the leaders of men, these great ones; the modellers, patterns, and in a wide sense creators, of whatsoever the general mass of men contrived to do or to attain; all things that we see standing accomplished in the world are properly the outer material result, the practical realisation and embodiment, of Thoughts that dwelt in the Great Men sent into the world: the soul of the whole world's history, it may justly be considered, were the history of these. Too clearly it is a topic we shall do no justice to in this place!

One comfort is, that Great Men, taken up in any way, are

profitable company. We cannot look, however imperfectly, upon a great man, without gaining something by him. He is the living light-fountain, which it is good and pleasant to be near. The light which enlightens, which has enlightened the darkness of the world; and this not as a kindled lamp only, but rather as a natural luminary shining by the gift of Heaven; a flowing light-fountain, as I say, of native original insight, of manhood and heroic nobleness; — in whose radiance all souls feel that it is well with them. On any terms whatsoever, you will not grudge to wander in such neighbourhood for a while. These Six classes of Heroes, chosen out of widely-distant countries and epochs, and in mere external figure differing altogether, ought, if we look faithfully at them, to illustrate several things for us. Could we see *them* well, we should get some glimpses into the very marrow of the world's history. How happy, could I but, in any measure, in such times as these, make manifest to you the meanings of Heroism; the divine relation (for I may well call it such) which in all times unites a Great Man to other men; and thus, as it were, not exhaust my subject, but so much as break ground on it! At all events, I must make the attempt.

It is well said, in every sense, that a man's religion is the chief fact with regard to him. A man's, or a nation of men's. By religion I do not mean here the church-creed which he professes, the articles of faith which he will sign and, in words or otherwise, assert; not this wholly, in many cases not this at all. We see men of all kinds of professed creeds attain to almost all degrees of worth or worthlessness under each or any of them. This is not what I call religion, this profession and assertion; which is often only a profession and assertion from the outworks of the man, from the mere argumentative region of him, if even so deep as that.

But the thing a man does practically believe (and this is often enough *without* asserting it even to himself, much less to others); the thing a man does practically lay to heart, and know for certain, concerning his vital relations to this mysterious Universe, and his duty and destiny there, that is in all cases the primary thing for him, and creatively determines all the rest. That is his *religion;* or, it may be, his mere scepticism and *no-religion:* the manner it is in which he feels himself to be spiritually related to the Unseen World or No-World; and I say, if you tell me what that is, you tell me to a very great extent what the man is, what the kind of things he will do is. Of a man or of a nation we inquire, therefore, first of all, What religion they had? Was it Heathenism, — plurality of gods, mere sensuous representation of this Mystery of Life, and for chief recognised element therein Physical Force? Was it Christianism; faith in an Invisible, not as real only, but as the only reality; Time, through every meanest moment of it, resting on Eternity; Pagan empire of Force displaced by a nobler supremacy, that of Holiness? Was it Scepticism, uncertainty and inquiry whether there was an Unseen World, any Mystery of Life except a mad one; — doubt as to all this, or perhaps unbelief and flat denial? Answering of this question is giving us the soul of the history of the man or nation. The thoughts they had were the parents of the actions they did; their feelings were parents of their thoughts: it was the unseen and spiritual in them that determined the outward and actual; — their religion, as I say, was the great fact about them. In these Discourses, limited as we are, it will be good to direct our survey chiefly to that religious phasis of the matter. That once known well, all is known. We have chosen as the first Hero in our series, Odin, the central figure of Scandinavian Paganism; an emblem to us of a most extensive province of things. Let us look for a little at the Hero as Divinity, the oldest primary form of Heroism.

Surely it seems a very strange-looking thing this Paganism; almost inconceivable to us in these days. A bewildering, inextricable jungle of delusions, confusions, falsehoods, and absurdities, covering the whole field of Life! A thing that fills us with astonishment, almost, if it were possible, with incredulity, — for truly it is not easy to understand that sane men could ever calmly, with their eyes open, believe and live by such a set of doctrines. That men should have worshipped their poor fellow-man as a God, and not him only, but stocks and stones, and all manner of animate and inanimate objects; and fashioned for themselves such a distracted chaos of hallucinations by way of Theory of the Universe: all this looks like an incredible fable. Nevertheless, it is a clear fact that they did it. Such hideous inextricable jungle of misworships, misbeliefs, men, made as we are, did actually hold by, and live at home in. This is strange. Yes, we may pause in sorrow and silence over the depths of darkness that are in man; if we rejoice in the heights of purer vision he has attained to. Such things were and are in man; in all men; in us too.

Some speculators have a short way of accounting for the Pagan religion: mere quackery, priestcraft, and dupery, say they; no sane man ever did believe it, — merely contrived to persuade other men, not worthy of the name of sane, to believe it! It will be often our duty to protest against this sort of hypothesis about men's doings and history; and I here, on the very threshold, protest against it in reference to Paganism, and to all other *isms* by which man has ever for a length of time striven to walk in this world. They have all had a truth in them, or men would not have taken them up. Quackery and dupery do abound; in religions, above all in the more advanced decaying stages of religions, they have

THE HERO AS DIVINITY

fearfully abounded; but quackery was never the originating influence in such things; it was not the health and life of such things, but their disease, the sure precursor of their being about to die! Let us never forget this. It seems to me a most mournful hypothesis, that of quackery giving birth to any faith even in savage men. Quackery gives birth to nothing; gives death to all things. We shall not see into the true heart of anything, if we look merely at the quackeries of it; if we do not reject the quackeries altogether; as mere diseases, corruptions, with which our and all men's sole duty is to have done with them, to sweep them out of our thoughts as out of our practice. Man everywhere is the born enemy of lies. I find Grand Lamaism [1] itself to have a kind of truth in it. Read the candid, clear-sighted, rather sceptical Mr. Turner's *Account of his Embassy* to that country, and see. They have their belief, these poor Thibet people, that Providence sends down always an Incarnation of Himself into every generation. At bottom some belief in a kind of Pope! At bottom still better, belief that there is a *Greatest* Man; that *he* is discoverable; that, once discovered, we ought to treat him with an obedience which knows no bounds! This is the truth of Grand Lamaism; the 'discoverability' is the only error here. The Thibet priests have methods of their own of discovering what Man is Greatest, fit to be supreme over them. Bad methods: but are they so much worse than our methods, — of understanding him to be always the eldest-born of a certain genealogy? Alas, it is a difficult thing to find good methods for! — We shall begin to have a chance of understanding Paganism, when we first admit that to its followers it was, at one time, earnestly

[1] *Lamaism* is a form of Buddhism. Buddha is supposed to be incarnate in the grand lamas, the priest-gods, of whom the Dalai Lama at Lhassa is the most important. On the death of a grand lama, the spirit passes to another incarnation, either telling before death or indicating afterward by a sign in what young child it is to be found.

true. Let us consider it very certain that men did believe in Paganism; men with open eyes, sound senses, men made altogether like ourselves; that we, had we been there, should have believed in it. Ask now, What Paganism could have been?

Another theory, somewhat more respectable, attributes such things to Allegory. It was a play of poetic minds, say these theorists; a shadowing-forth, in allegorical fable, in personification and visual form, of what such poetic minds had known and felt of this Universe. Which agrees, add they, with a primary law of human nature, still everywhere observably at work, though in less important things. That what a man feels intensely, he struggles to speak-out of him, to see represented before him in visual shape, and as if with a kind of life and historical reality in it. Now doubtless there is such a law, and it is one of the deepest in human nature; neither need we doubt that it did operate fundamentally in this business. The hypothesis which ascribes Paganism wholly or mostly to this agency, I call a little more respectable; but I cannot yet call it the true hypothesis. Think, would *we* believe, and take with us as our life-guidance, an allegory, a poetic sport? Not sport but earnest is what we should require. It is a most earnest thing to be alive in this world; to die is not sport for a man. Man's life never was a sport to him; it was a stern reality, altogether a serious matter to be alive!

I find, therefore, that though these Allegory theorists are on the way towards truth in this matter, they have not reached it either. Pagan Religion is indeed an Allegory, a Symbol of what men felt and knew about the Universe; and all Religions are Symbols of that, altering always as that alters: but it seems to me a radical perversion, and even *in*version, of the business, to put that forward as the origin and moving cause, when it was rather the result and termination. To get beautiful allegories, a perfect poetic symbol, was not the want of men; but to know what they were to believe about this Universe, what course they were to steer in it; what, in this mysterious Life of theirs, they had to hope and to fear, to do and to forbear doing. The *Pilgrim's Progress* is an Allegory, and a beautiful, just and serious one: but consider whether Bunyan's Allegory could have *preceded* the Faith it symbolises! The Faith had to be already there, standing believed by everybody; — of which the Allegory could *then* become a shadow; and, with all its seriousness, we may say a *sportful* shadow, a mere play of the Fancy, in comparison with that awful Fact and scientific certainty which it poetically strives to emblem. The Allegory is the product of the certainty, not the producer of it; not in Bunyan's nor in any other case. For Paganism, therefore, we have still to inquire, Whence came that scientific certainty, the parent of such a bewildered heap of allegories, errors and confusions? How was it, what was it?

Surely it were a foolish attempt to pretend 'explaining,' in this place, or in any place, such a phenomenon as that far-distant distracted cloudy imbroglio of Paganism, — more like a cloudfield than a distant continent of firm land and facts! It is no longer a reality, yet it was one. We ought to understand that this seeming cloudfield was once a reality; that not poetic allegory, least of all that dupery and deception was the origin of it. Men, I say, never did believe idle songs, never risked their soul's life on allegories: men in all times, especially in early earnest times, have had an instinct for detecting quacks, for detesting quacks. Let us try if, leaving out both the quack theory and the allegory one, and listening with affectionate attention to that far-off confused rumour of the Pagan ages, we cannot ascertain so much as this at least, That there was a kind of fact at the heart of them; that they too were not mendacious and distracted, but in their own poor way true and sane!

You remember that fancy of Plato's, of a man who had grown to maturity in some dark distance, and was brought on a sudden into the upper air to see the sun rise. What would his wonder be, his rapt astonishment at the sight we daily witness with indifference! With the free open sense of a child, yet with the ripe faculty of a man, his whole heart would be kindled by that sight, he would discern it well to be Godlike, his soul would fall down in worship before it. Now, just such a childlike greatness was in the primitive nations. The first Pagan Thinker among rude men, the first man that began to think, was precisely this child-man of Plato's. Simple, open as a child, yet with the depth and strength of a man. Nature had as yet no name to him; he had not yet united under a name the infinite variety of sights, sounds, shapes and motions, which we now collectively name Universe, Nature, or the like, — and so with a name dismiss it from us. To the wild deep-hearted man all was yet new, not veiled under names or formulas; it stood naked, flashing-in on him there, beautiful, awful, unspeakable. Nature was to this man, what to the Thinker and Prophet it for ever is, *preter*natural. This green flowery rock-built earth, the trees, the mountains, rivers, many-sounding seas; — that great deep sea of azure that swims overhead; the winds sweeping through it; the black cloud fashioning itself together, now pouring out fire, now hail and rain; what *is* it? Ay, what? At bottom we do not yet know; we can never know at all. It is not by our superior insight that we escape the difficulty; it is by our superior levity, our inattention, our *want* of insight. It is by *not* thinking that we cease to wonder at it. Hardened round us, encasing wholly every notion we form, is a wrappage of traditions,

THE HERO AS DIVINITY

hearsays, mere *words*. We call that fire of the black thunder-cloud 'electricity,' and lecture learnedly about it, and grind the like of it out of glass and silk: but *what* is it? What made it? Whence comes it? Whither goes it? Science has done much for us; but it is a poor science that would hide from us the great deep sacred infinitude of Nescience, whither we can never penetrate, on which all science swims as a mere superficial film. This world, after all our science and sciences, is still a miracle; wonderful, inscrutable, *magical* and more, to whosoever will *think* of it.

That great mystery of TIME, were there no other; the illimitable, silent, never-resting thing called Time, rolling, rushing on, swift, silent, like an all-embracing ocean-tide, on which we and all the Universe swim like exhalations, like apparitions which *are*, and then *are not:* this is for ever very literally a miracle; a thing to strike us dumb, — for we have no word to speak about it. This Universe, ah me — what could the wild man know of it; what can we yet know? That is a Force, and thousandfold Complexity of Forces; a Force which is *not we*. That is all; it is not we, it is altogether different from *us*. Force, Force, everywhere Force; we ourselves a mysterious Force in the centre of that. 'There is not a leaf rotting on the highway but has Force in it: how else could it rot?' Nay surely, to the Atheistic Thinker, if such a one were possible, it must be a miracle too, this huge illimitable whirlwind of Force, which envelops us here; never-resting whirlwind, high as Immensity, old as Eternity. What is it? God's creation, the religious people answer; it is the Almighty God's! Atheistic science babbles poorly of it, with scientific nomenclatures, experiments and what-not, as if it were a poor dead thing, to be bottled-up in Leyden jars and sold over counters: but the natural sense of man, in all times, if he will honestly apply his sense, proclaims it to be a living thing, — ah, an unspeakable, godlike thing; towards which the best attitude for us, after never so much science, is awe, devout prostration and humility of soul; worship if not in words, then in silence.

But now I remark further: What in such a time as ours it requires a Prophet or Poet to teach us, namely, the stripping-off of those poor undevout wrappages, nomenclatures and scientific hearsays, — this, the ancient earnest soul, as yet unencumbered with these things, did for itself. The world, which is now divine only to the gifted, was then divine to whosoever would turn his eye upon it. He stood bare before it face to face. 'All was Godlike or God':— Jean Paul[1] still finds it so; the giant Jean Paul, who has power to escape out of hearsays: but there then were no hearsays. Canopus shining-down over the desert, with its blue diamond brightness (that wild blue spirit-like brightness, far brighter than we ever witness here), would pierce into the heart of the wild Ishmaelitish man, whom it was guiding through the solitary waste there. To his wild heart, with all feelings in it, with no *speech* for any feeling, it might seem a little eye, that Canopus, glancing-out on him from the great deep Eternity; revealing the inner Splendour to him. Cannot we understand how these men *worshipped* Canopus; became what we call Sabeans worshipping the stars? Such is to me the secret of all forms of Paganism. Worship is transcendent wonder; wonder for which there is now no limit or measure; that is worship. To these primeval men, all things and everything they saw exist beside them were an emblem of the Godlike, of some God.

And look what perennial fibre of truth was in that. To us also, through every star, through every blade of grass, is not a God made visible, if we will open our minds and eyes? We do not worship in that way now: but is it not reckoned

---

[1] Jean Paul Friedrich Richter (1763-1825), the greatest humorist in modern German literature.

still a merit, proof of what we call a 'poetic nature,' that we recognise how every object has a divine beauty in it; how every object still verily is 'a window through which we may look into Infinitude itself'? He that can discern the loveliness of things, we call him Poet, Painter, Man of Genius, gifted, lovable. These poor Sabeans did even what he does, — in their own fashion. That they did it, in what fashion soever, was a merit: better than what the entirely stupid man did, what the horse and camel did, — namely, nothing!

But now if all things whatsoever that we look upon are emblems to us of the Highest God, I add that more so than any of them is man such an emblem. You have heard of St. Chrysostom's celebrated saying in reference to the Shekinah, or Ark of Testimony, visible Revelation of God, among the Hebrews: "The true Shekinah is Man!" Yes, it is even so: this is no vain phrase; it is veritably so. The essence of our being, the mystery in us that calls itself "I," — ah, what words have we for such things? — is a breath of Heaven; the Highest Being reveals himself in man. This body, these faculties, this life of ours, is it not all as a vesture for that Unnamed? 'There is but one Temple in the Universe,' says the devout Novalis, 'and that is the Body of Man. Nothing is holier than that high form. Bending before men is a reverence done to this Revelation in the Flesh. We touch Heaven when we lay our hand on a human body!' This sounds much like a mere flourish of rhetoric; but it is not so. If well meditated, it will turn out to be a scientific fact; the expression, in such words as can be had, of the actual truth of the thing. *We* are the miracle of miracles, — the great inscrutable mystery of God. We cannot understand it, we know not how to speak of it; but we may feel and know, if we like, that it is verily so.

Well; these truths were once more readily felt than now. The young generations of the world, who had in them the freshness of young children, and yet the depth of earnest men, who did not think they had finished-off all things in Heaven and Earth by merely giving them scientific names, but had to gaze direct at them there, with awe and wonder: they felt better what of divinity is in man and Nature; — they, without being mad, could *worship* Nature, and man more than anything else in Nature. Worship, that is, as I said above, admire without limit: this, in the full use of their faculties, with all sincerity of heart, they could do. I consider Hero-worship to be the grand modifying element in that ancient system of thought. What I called the perplexed jungle of Paganism sprang, we may say, out of many roots: every admiration, adoration of a star or natural object, was a root or fibre of a root; but Hero-worship is the deepest root of all; the tap-root, from which in a great degree all the rest were nourished and grown.

And now if worship even of a star had some meaning in it, how much more might that of a Hero! Worship of a Hero is transcendent admiration of a Great Man. I say great men are still admirable! I say there is, at the bottom, nothing else admirable! No nobler feeling than this of admiration for one higher than himself dwells in the breast of man. It is to this hour, and at all hours, the vivifying influence in man's life. Religion I find stand upon it; not Paganism only, but far higher and truer religions, — all religion hitherto known. Hero-worship, heartfelt prostrate admiration, submission, burning, boundless, for a noblest godlike Form of Man, — is not that the germ of Christianity itself? The greatest of all Heroes is One — whom we do not name here! Let sacred silence meditate that sacred matter; you will find it the ultimate perfection of a principle extant throughout man's whole history on earth.

Or coming into lower, less *un*speakable provinces, is not all Loyalty akin to religious Faith also? Faith is loyalty to some inspired Teacher, some spiritual Hero. And what therefore is loyalty proper, the life-breath of all society, but an effluence of Hero-worship, submissive admiration for the truly great? Society is founded on Hero-worship. All dignities of rank, on which human association rests, are what we may call a *Hero*archy (Government of Heroes), — or a Hierarchy, for it is 'sacred' enough withal! The Duke means *Dux*, Leader; King is *Kön-ning*, *Kan-ning*, Man that *knows* or *cans*.[1] Society everywhere is some representation, not *in*supportably inaccurate, of a graduated Worship of Heroes; — reverence and obedience done to men really great and wise. Not *in*supportably inaccurate, I say! They are all as bank-notes, these social dignitaries, all representing gold; — and several of them, alas, always are *forged* notes. We can do with some forged false notes; with a good many even; but not with all, or the most of them forged! No: there have to come revolutions then; cries of Democracy, Liberty and Equality, and I know not what: — the notes being all false, and no gold to be had for *them*, people take to crying in their despair that there is no gold, that there never was any! — 'Gold,' Hero-worship, *is* nevertheless, as it was always and everywhere, and cannot cease till man himself ceases.

I am well aware that in these days Hero-worship, the thing I call Hero-worship, professes to have gone out, and finally ceased. This, for reasons which it will be worth while some time to inquire into, is an age that as it were denies the existence of great men; denies the desirableness of great men. Show our critics a great man, a Luther for example, they begin to what they call 'account' for him; not to worship him, but take the dimensions of him, — and bring him out to be a little kind of man! He was the 'crea-

---

[1] King is really O. E. *cyning* (*cynn* + patronymic *ing*) or *cyng* = scion of the (noble) kin, or son (or descendant) of one of (noble) birth.

ture of the Time,' they say; the Time called him forth, the Time did everything, he nothing — but what we the little critic could have done too! This seems to me but melancholy work. The Time call forth? Alas, we have known Times *call* loudly enough for their great man; but not find him when they called! He was not there; Providence had not sent him; the Time, *calling* its loudest, had to go down to confusion and wreck because he would not come when called.

For if we will think of it, no Time need have gone to ruin, could it have *found* a man great enough, a man wise and good enough: wisdom to discern truly what the Time wanted, valour to lead it on the right road thither; these are the salvation of any Time. But I liken common languid Times, with their unbelief, distress, perplexity, with their languid doubting characters and embarrassed circumstances, impotently crumbling down into ever worse distress towards final ruin; — all this I liken to dry dead fuel, waiting for the lightning out of Heaven that shall kindle it. The great man, with his free force direct out of God's own hand, is the lightning. His word is the wise healing word which all can believe in. All blazes round him now, when he has once struck on it, into fire like his own. The dry mouldering sticks are thought to have called him forth. They did want him greatly; but as to calling him forth —! — Those are critics of small vision, I think, who cry: "See, is it not the sticks that made the fire?" No sadder proof can be given by a man of his own littleness than disbelief in great men. There is no sadder symptom of a generation than such general blindness to the spiritual lightning, with faith only in the heap of barren dead fuel. It is the last consummation of unbelief. In all epochs of the world's history, we shall find the Great Man to have been the indispensable saviour of his epoch; — the lightning, without which the fuel never would have burnt. The History of the World, I said already, was the Biography of Great Men.

Such small critics do what they can to promote unbelief and universal spiritual paralysis: but happily they cannot always completely succeed. In all times it is possible for a man to arise great enough to feel that they and their doctrines are chimeras and cobwebs. And what is notable, in no time whatever can they entirely eradicate out of living men's hearts a certain altogether peculiar reverence for Great Men; genuine admiration, loyalty, adoration, however dim and perverted it may be. Hero-worship endures forever while man endures. Boswell venerates his Johnson, right truly even in the Eighteenth century. The unbelieving French believe in their Voltaire; and burst-out round him into very curious Hero-worship, in that last act of his life when they 'stifle him under roses.' It has always seemed to me extremely curious this of Voltaire. Truly, if Christianity be the highest instance of Hero-worship, then we may find here in Voltaireism one of the lowest! He whose life was that of a kind of Antichrist, does again on this side exhibit a curious contrast. No people ever were so little prone to admire at all as those French of Voltaire. *Persiflage* was the character of their whole mind; adoration had nowhere a place in it. Yet see! The old man of Ferney comes up to Paris; an old, tottering, infirm man of eighty-four years. They feel that he too is a kind of Hero; that he has spent his life in opposing error and injustice, delivering Calases, unmasking hypocrites in high places; — in short that *he* too, though in a strange way, has fought like a valiant man. They feel withal that, if *persiflage* be the great thing, there never was such a *persifleur*. He is the realised ideal of every one of them; the thing they are all wanting to be; of all Frenchmen the most French. *He* is properly their god, — such god as they are fit for. Accordingly all persons, from the Queen Antoinette to the Douanier at the Porte St. Denis, do they not worship him? People of quality disguise themselves as tavern-waiters. The Maître de Poste, with a broad oath, orders his Postillion, "*Va bon train;* thou art driving M. de Voltaire." At Paris his carriage is 'the nucleus of a comet, whose train fills whole streets.' The ladies pluck a hair or two from his fur, to keep it as a sacred relic. There was nothing highest, beautifulest, noblest in all France, that did not feel this man to be higher, beautifuler, nobler.

Yes, from Norse Odin to English Samuel Johnson, from the divine Founder of Christianity to the withered Pontiff of Encyclopedism, in all times and places, the Hero has been worshipped. It will ever be so. We all love great men; love, venerate and bow down submissive before great men: nay, can we honestly bow down to anything else? Ah, does not every true man feel that he is himself made higher by doing reverence to what is really above him? No nobler or more blessed feeling dwells in man's heart. And to me it is very cheering to consider that no sceptical logic, or general triviality, insincerity and aridity of any Time and its influences can destroy this noble inborn loyalty and worship that is in man. In times of unbelief, which soon have to become times of revolution, much down-rushing, sorrowful decay and ruin is visible to everybody. For myself, in these days, I seem to see in this indestructibility of Hero-worship the everlasting adamant lower than which the confused wreck of revolutionary things cannot fall. The confused wreck of things crumbling and even crashing and tumbling all round us in these revolutionary ages, will get down so far; *no* farther. It is an eternal corner-stone, from which they can begin to build themselves up again. That man, in some sense or other, worships Heroes; that we all of us reverence and must ever reverence Great Men: this is, to me, the living rock amid all rushings-down whatsoever; — the one fixed point in modern revolutionary history, otherwise as if bottomless and shoreless.

ÆS TRIPLEX [1]

ROBERT LOUIS STEVENSON

PUBLISHED as a magazine article in 1878. Now included in the volume *Virginibus Puerisque.*

THE changes wrought by death are in themselves so sharp and final, and so terrible and melancholy in their cousequences, that the thing stands alone in man's experience, and has no parallel upon earth. It outdoes all other accidents because it is the last of them. Sometimes it leaps suddenly upon its victims, like a Thug; sometimes it lays a regular siege and creeps upon their citadel during a score of years. And when the business is done, there is sore havoc made in other people's lives, and a pin knocked out by which many subsidiary friendships hung together. There are empty chairs, solitary walks, and single beds at night. Again, in taking away our friends, death does not take them away utterly but leaves behind a mocking, tragical, and soon intolerable residue, which must be hurriedly concealed. Hence a whole chapter of sights and customs striking to the mind, from the pyramids of Egypt to the gibbets and dule trees of mediæval Europe. The poorest persons have a bit of pageant going toward the tomb; memorial stones are set up over the least memorable; and, in order to preserve some show of respect for what remains of our old loves and friendships, we must accompany it with much grimly ludicrous ceremonial, and the hired undertaker parades before the door. All this, and much more of the same sort, accompanied by the eloquence of poets, has gone a great way to put humanity in error; nay, in many philosophies the error has been

[1] From *Virginibus Puerisque,* by permission of the publishers, Charles Scribner's Sons.

embodied and laid down with every circumstance of logic; although in real life the bustle and swiftness, in leaving people little time to think, have not left them time enough to go dangerously wrong in practice.

As a matter of fact, although few things are spoken of with more fearful whisperings than this prospect of death, few have less influence on conduct under healthy circumstances. We have all heard of cities in South America built upon the side of fiery mountains, and how, even in this tremendous neighborhood, the inhabitants are not a jot more impressed by the solemnity of mortal conditions than if they were delving gardens in the greenest corner of England. There are serenades and suppers and much gallantry among the myrtles overhead; and meanwhile the foundation shudders underfoot, the bowels of the mountain growl, and at any moment living ruin may leap sky-high into the moonlight, and tumble man and his merry-making in the dust. In the eyes of very young people, and very dull old ones, there is something indescribably reckless and desperate in such a picture. It seems not credible that respectable married people, with umbrellas, should find appetite for a bit of supper within quite a long distance of a fiery mountain; ordinary life begins to smell of high-handed debauch when it is carried on so close to a catastrophe; and even cheese and salad, it seems, could hardly be relished in such circumstances without something like a defiance of the Creator. It should be a place for nobody but hermits dwelling in prayer and maceration, or mere born-devils drowning care in a perpetual carouse.

And yet, when one comes to think upon it calmly, the situation of these South American citizens forms only a very pale figure for the state of ordinary mankind. This world, itself, travelling blindly and swiftly in overcrowded space, among a million other worlds travelling blindly and swiftly in contrary directions, may very well come by a knock that would set it into explosion like a penny squib. And what, pathologically looked at, is the human body with all its organs, but a mere bagful of petards? The least of these is as dangerous to the whole economy as the ship's powder-magazine to the ship; and with every breath we breathe, and every meal we eat, we are putting one or more of them in peril. If we clung as devotedly as some philosophers pretend we do to the abstract idea of life, or were half as frightened as they make out we are, for the subversive accident that ends it all, the trumpets might sound by the hour and no one would follow them into battle — the blue-peter might fly at the truck, but who would climb into a sea-going ship? Think (if these philosophers were right) with what a preparation of spirit we should affront the daily peril of the dinner-table: a deadlier spot than any battle-field in history, where the far greater proportion of our ancestors have miserably left their bones! What woman would ever be lured into marriage, so much more dangerous than the wildest sea? And what would it be to grow old? For, after a certain distance, every step we take in life we find the ice growing thinner below our feet, and all around us and behind us we see our contemporaries going through. By the time a man gets well into the seventies, his continued existence is a mere miracle; and when he lays his old bones in bed for the night, there is an overwhelming probability that he will never see the day. Do the old men mind it, as a matter of fact? Why, no. They were never merrier; they have their grog at night, and tell the raciest stories; they hear of the death of people about their own age, or even younger, not as if it was a grisly warning, but with a simple childlike pleasure at having outlived some one else; and when a draught might puff them out like a guttering candle, or a bit of a stumble shatter them like so much glass, their old hearts keep sound and unaffrighted, and they go on, bubbling with laughter, through years of man's age compared to which the valley at Balaclava was as safe and peaceful as a village cricket-green on Sunday. It may fairly be questioned (if we look to the peril only) whether it was a much more daring feat for Curtius to plunge into the gulf, than for any old gentleman of ninety to doff his clothes and clamber into bed.

Indeed, it is a memorable subject for consideration, with what unconcern and gaiety mankind pricks on along the Valley of the Shadow of Death. The whole way is one wilderness of snares, and the end of it, for those who fear the last pinch, is irrevocable ruin. And yet we go spinning through it all, like a party for the Derby. Perhaps the reader remembers one of the humorous devices of the deified Caligula: how he encouraged a vast concourse of holiday-makers on to his bridge over Baiæ bay; and when they were in the height of their enjoyment, turned loose the Prætorian guards among the company, and had them tossed into the sea. This is no bad miniature of the dealings of nature with the transitory race of man. Only, what a checkered picnic we have of it, even while it lasts! and into what great waters, not to be crossed by any swimmer, God's pale Prætorian throws us over in the end!

We live the time that a match flickers; we pop the cork of a ginger-beer bottle, and the earthquake swallows us on the instant. Is it not odd, is it not incongruous, is it not, in the highest sense of human speech, incredible, that we should think so highly of the ginger-beer, and regard so little the devouring earthquake? The love of Life and the fear of Death are two famous phrases that grow harder to understand the more we think about them. It is a well-known fact that an immense proportion of boat accidents would never happen if people held the sheet in their hands instead of making it fast; and yet, unless it be some martinet of a professional mariner or some landsman with shattered nerves, every one of God's creatures makes it fast. A strange instance of man's unconcern and brazen boldness in the face of death!

We confound ourselves with metaphysical phrases, which we import into daily talk with noble inappropriateness. We have no idea of what death is, apart from its circumstances and some of its consequences to others; and although we have some experience of living, there is not a man on earth who has flown so high into abstraction as to have any practical guess at the meaning of the word *life*. All literature, from Job and Omar Khayyam to Thomas Carlyle or Walt Whitman, is but an attempt to look upon the human state with such largeness of view as shall enable us to rise from the consideration of living to the Definition of Life. And our sages give us about the best satisfaction in their power when they say that it is a vapor, or a show, or made of the same stuff with dreams. Philosophy, in its more rigid sense, has been at the same work for ages; and after a myriad bald heads have wagged over the problem, and piles of words have been heaped one upon another into dry and cloudy volumes without end, philosophy has the honor of laying before us, with modest pride, her contribution toward the subject: that life is a Permanent Possibility of Sensation. Truly a fine result! A man may very well love beef, or hunting, or a woman; but surely, surely, not a Permanent Possibility of Sensation! He may be afraid of a precipice, or a dentist, or a large enemy with a club, or even an undertaker's man; but not certainly of abstract death. We may trick with the word life in its dozen senses until we are weary of tricking; we may argue in terms of all the philosophies on earth, but one fact remains true throughout — that we do not love life, in the sense that we are greatly preoccupied about its conservation; that we do not, properly speaking, love life at all, but living. Into the views of the least careful there will enter some degree of providence; no man's eyes are fixed entirely on the passing hour; but although we have some anticipation of good health, good weather, wine, active employment, love, and self-approval, the sum of these anticipations does not amount to anything like a general view of life's possibilities and issues; nor are those who cherish them most vividly, at all the most scrupulous of their personal safety. To be deeply interested in the accidents of our existence, to enjoy keenly the mixed texture of human experience, rather leads a man to disregard precautions, and risk his neck against a straw. For surely the love of living is stronger in an Alpine climber roping over a peril, or a hunter riding merrily at a stiff fence, than in a creature who lives upon a diet and walks a measured distance in the interest of his constitution.

There is a great deal of very vile nonsense talked upon both sides of the matter: tearing divines reducing life to the dimensions of a mere funeral procession, so short as to be hardly decent; and melancholy unbelievers yearning for the tomb as if it were a world too far away. Both sides must feel a little ashamed of their performances now and again when they draw in their chairs to dinner. Indeed, a good meal and a bottle of wine is an answer to most standard works upon the question. When a man's heart warms to his viands, he forgets a great deal of sophistry, and soars into a rosy zone of contemplation. Death may be knocking at the door, like the Commander's statue; we have something else in hand, thank God, and let him knock. Passing bells are ringing all the world over. All the world over, and every hour, some one is parting company with all his aches and ecstasies. For us also the trap is laid. But we are so fond of life that we have no leisure to entertain the terror of death. It is a honeymoon with us all through, and none of the longest. Small blame to us if we give our whole hearts to this glowing bride of ours, to the appetites, to honor, to the hungry curiosity of the mind, to the pleasure of the eyes in nature, and the pride of our own nimble bodies.

We all of us appreciate the sensations; but as for caring about the Permanence of the Possibility, a man's head is generally very bald, and his senses very dull, before he comes to that. Whether we regard life as a lane leading to a dead wall — a mere bag's end, as the French say — or whether we think of it as a vestibule or gymnasium, where we wait our turn and prepare our faculties for some more noble destiny; whether we thunder in a pulpit, or pule in little atheistic poetry-books, about its vanity and brevity; whether we look justly for years of health and vigor, or are about to mount into a Bath-chair, as a step toward the hearse; in each and all of these views and situations there is but one conclusion possible: that a man should stop his ears against paralyzing terror, and run the race that is set before him with a single mind. No one surely could have recoiled with more heartache and terror from the thought of death than our respected lexicographer; and yet we know how little it affected his conduct, how wisely and boldly he walked, and in what a fresh and lively vein he spoke of life. Already an old man, he ventured on his Highland tour; and his heart, bound with triple brass, did not recoil before twenty-seven individual cups of tea. As courage and intelligence are the two qualities best worth a good man's cultivation, so it is the first part of intelligence to recognize our precarious estate in life, and the first part of courage to be not at all abashed before the fact. A frank and somewhat headlong carriage, not looking too anxiously before, not dallying in maudlin regret over the past, stamps the man who is well armored for this world.

And not only well armored for himself, but a good friend,

and a good citizen to boot. We do not go to cowards for tender dealing; there is nothing so cruel as panic; the man who has least fear for his own carcass, has most time to consider others. That eminent chemist who took his walks abroad in tin shoes, and subsisted wholly upon tepid milk, had all his work cut out for him in considerate dealings with his own digestion. So soon as prudence has begun to grow up in the brain, like a dismal fungus, it finds its first expression in a paralysis of generous acts. The victim begins to shrink spiritually; he develops a fancy for parlors with a regulated temperature, and takes his morality on the principle of tin shoes and tepid milk. The care of one important body or soul becomes so engrossing, that all the noises of the outer world begin to come thin and faint into the parlor with the regulated temperature; and the tin shoes go equably forward over blood and rain. To be overwise is to ossify; and the scruple-monger ends by standing stock-still. Now the man who has his heart on his sleeve, and a good whirling weathercock of a brain, who reckons his life as a thing to be dashingly used and cheerfully hazarded, makes a very different acquaintance of the world, keeps all his pulses going true and fast, and gathers impetus as he runs, until, if he be running toward anything better than wildfire, he may shoot up and become a constellation in the end. Lord, look after his health; Lord, have a care of his soul, says he; and he has at the key of the position, and swashes through incongruity and peril toward his aim. Death is on all sides of him with pointed batteries, as he is on all sides of all of us; unfortunate surprises gird him round; mim-mouthed friends and relations hold up their hands in quite a little elegiacal synod about his path: and what cares he for all this? Being a true lover of living, a fellow with something pushing and spontaneous in his inside, he must, like any other soldier, in any other stirring, deadly warfare, push on at his best pace until he touch the goal. "A peerage or Westminster Abbey!" cried Nelson in his bright, boyish, heroic manner. These are great incentives; not for any of these, but for the plain satisfaction of living, of being about their business in some sort or other, do the brave, serviceable men of every nation tread down the nettle danger, and pass flyingly over all the stumbling-blocks of prudence. Think of the heroism of Johnson, think of that superb indifference to mortal limitation that set him upon his dictionary, and carried him through triumphantly until the end! Who, if he were wisely considerate of things at large, would ever embark upon any work much more considerable than a halfpenny post card? Who would project a serial novel, after Thackeray and Dickens had each fallen in mid-course? Who would find heart enough to begin to live, if he dallied with the consideration of death?

And, after all, what sorry and pitiful quibbling all this is! To forego all the issues of living in a parlor with a regulated temperature — as if that were not to die a hundred times over, and for ten years at a stretch! As if it were not to die in one's own lifetime, and without even the sad immunities of death! As if it were not to die, and yet be the patient spectators of our own pitiable change! The Permanent Possibility is preserved, but the sensations carefully held at arm's length, as if one kept a photographic plate in a dark chamber. It is better to lose health like a spendthrift than to waste it like a miser. It is better to live and be done with it, than to die daily in the sickroom. By all means begin your folio; even if the doctor does not give you a year, even if he hesitates about a month, make one brave push and see what can be accomplished in a week. It is not only in finished undertakings that we ought to honor useful labor. A spirit goes out of the man who means execution, which outlives the most untimely ending. All who have meant good work with their whole hearts, have done good work, although they may die before they have the time to sign it. Every heart that has beat strong and cheerfully has left a hopeful impulse behind it in the world, and bettered the tradition of mankind. And even if death catch people, like an open pitfall, and in mid-career, laying out vast projects, and planning monstrous foundations, flushed with hope, and their mouths full of boastful language, they should be at once tripped up and silenced: is there not something brave and spirited in such a termination? and does not life go down with a better grace, foaming in full body over a precipice, than miserably straggling to an end in sandy deltas? When the Greeks made their fine saying that those whom the gods love die young, I cannot help believing they had this sort of death also in their eye. For surely, at whatever age it overtake the man, this is to die young. Death has not been suffered to take so much as an illusion from his heart. In the hot-fit of life, a-tiptoe on the highest point of being, he passes at a bound on to the other side. The noise of the mallet and chisel is scarcely quenched, the trumpets are hardly done blowing, when, trailing with him clouds of glory, this happy-starred, full-blooded spirit shoots into the spiritual land.

HOW TO OVERCOME THE OBSTACLES TO GOOD CITIZENSHIP [1]

JAMES BRYCE

THE lectures published under the title *The Hindrances to Good Citizenship* were delivered at Yale University in 1909. As hindrances Lord Bryce considered separately — Indolence, Private Self-Interest, Party Spirit. In the final lecture, of which this extract forms the last part, he reviewed the whole series and suggested how to overcome the obstacles. Although these lectures were delivered before the Great War, they apply with equal force to the present period of world reconstruction. There was never a time when it was so necessary to develop in men a sense of civic and national and human responsibility.

To contrive plans by which the interest of the citizen in public affairs shall be aroused and sustained, is far easier than to induce the citizen to use and to go on using, year in and year out, the contrivances and opportunities provided for his benefit. Yet it is from the heart and will of the citizen that all real and lasting improvements must proceed. In the words of the Gospel, it is the inside of the cup and platter that must be made clean. The central problem of civic duty is the ethical problem. Indifference, selfish interests, the excesses of party spirit, will all begin to disappear as civic life is lifted on to a higher plane, and as the number of those who, standing on that higher plane, will apply a strict test to their own conduct and to that of their leaders, realizing and striving to discharge their responsibilities, goes on steadily increasing until they come to form the majority of the people. What we have called "the better conscience" must be grafted on to the "wild stock" of the natural Average Man.

How is this to be done? The difficulty is the same as that

[1] Copyright, 1909, by Yale University Press.

THE OBSTACLES TO GOOD CITIZENSHIP 185

which meets the social reformer or the preacher of religion.

One must try to reach the Will through the Soul. The most obvious way to begin is through the education of those who are to be citizens, moral education combined with and made the foundation for instruction in civic duty. This is a task which the Swiss alone among European nations seem to have seriously undertaken. Here in America it has become doubly important through the recent entrance into your community of a vast mass of immigrants, most of them ignorant of our language, still more of them ignorant, not only of your institutions, but of the general principles and habits of free government. Most of them doubtless belong to races of high natural intelligence, and many of them have the simple virtues of the peasant. You are providing for all of them good schools, and their children will soon become Americans in speech and habits, quite patriotic enough so far as flag-waving goes. But they will not so soon or so completely acquire your intellectual and moral standard, or imbibe your historical and religious traditions. There is no fear but what they will quickly learn to vote. To some Europeans you seem to have been overconfident in intrusting them with a power which most of them cannot yet have learned to use wisely. That however you have done, and as you hold that it cannot now be undone, your task must now be to teach them, if you can, to understand your institutions, to think about the vote they have to give, and to realize the responsibilities which the suffrage implies as these were realized by your New England forefathers when they planted free commonwealths in the wilderness nearly three centuries ago.

Valuable as instruction may be in fitting the citizen to comprehend and judge upon the issues which his vote determines, there must also be the will to apply his knowledge for the public good. What appeal shall be made to him?

We — I say "we" because this is our task in Europe no less than it is yours here — we may appeal to his enlightened self-interest, making self-interest so enlightened that it loses its selfish quality. We can remind him of all the useful work which governments may accomplish when they are conducted by the right men in the right spirit. Take, for instance, the work to be performed in those cities wherein so large and increasing a part of the population now dwell. How much remains to be done to make cities healthier, to secure better dwellings for the poor, to root out nests of crime, to remove the temptations to intemperance and gambling, to bring within the reach of the poorest all possible facilities both for intellectual progress and for enjoying the pleasures of art and music. How much may we do so to adorn the city with parks and public buildings as to make its external aspect instil the sense of beauty into its inhabitants and give them a fine pride in it! These are some of the tasks which cannot be safely intrusted to a municipality unless its government is above suspicion, unless men of probity and capacity are placed in power, unless the whole community extends its sympathy to the work and keeps a vigilant eye upon all the officials. Municipal governments cannot be encouraged to own public utilities so long as there is a risk that somebody may own municipal governments. Have we not here a strong motive for securing purity and efficiency in city administration? Is it not the personal interest of every one of us that the city we dwell in should be such as I have sought to describe? Nothing makes more for happiness than to see others around one happy. The rich residents need not grudge — nor indeed would your rich residents grudge, for there is less grumbling among the rich tax payers here than in Europe — taxation which they could see was being honestly spent for the benefit of the city. The interest each one of us has as a member of a city or a nation in seeing our fellow-citizens healthy, peaceful, and happy is a greater interest, if it be measured in terms of our own real enjoyment of life, than is that interest, of which we so constantly are reminded, which we have in making the State either wealthy by the development of trade, or formidable to foreign countries by its armaments.

We may also appeal to every citizen's sense of dignity and self-respect. We may bid him recollect that he is the heir of rights and privileges which your and our ancestors fought for, and which place him whatever his birth or fortune, among the rulers of his country. He is unworthy of himself, unmindful of what he owes to the Constitution that has given him these functions, if he does not try to discharge them worthily. These considerations are no doubt familiar to us Englishmen and Americans, though we may not always feel their force as deeply as we ought. To the new immigrants of whom I have already spoken they are unfamiliar; yet to the best among these also they have sometimes powerfully appealed. You had, in the last generation, no more high-minded and patriotic citizen than the German exile of 1849, the late Mr. Carl Schurz.

When every motive has been invoked, and every expedient applied that can stimulate the sense of civic duty, one never can feel sure that the desired result will follow. The moral reformer and the preacher of religion have the same experience. The ebbs and flows of ethical life are beyond the reach of scientific prediction. There are times of awakening, "times of refreshing from the presence of the Lord," as your Puritan ancestors said, but we do not know when they will come nor can we explain why they come just when they do. Every man can recall moments in his own life when the sky seemed to open above him, and when his vision was so quickened that all things stood transfigured in a purer and brighter radiance, when duty, and even toil done for the sake of duty, seemed beautiful and full of joy.

You remember Wordsworth's lines

> "Hence, in a season of fair weather,
> Though inland far we be,
> Our souls have sight of that celestial sea
> That brought us hither."

If we survey the wide field of European history, we shall find that something like this happens with nations also. They, too, have moments of exaltation, moments of depression. Their ideals rise and fall. They are for a time filled with a spirit which seeks truth, which loves honour, which is ready for self-sacrifice; and after a time the light begins to fade from the hills and this spirit lingers only among the best souls.

Such a spirit is sometimes evoked by a great national crisis which thrills all hearts. This happened to England or at least to a large part of the people of England, in the seventeenth century. It happened to Germany in the days of the War of Liberation, and to Italy when she was striving to expel the Austrians and the petty princes who ruled by Austria's help. You here felt it during the War of Secession. Sometimes, and usually at one of these crises, a great man stands out who helps to raise the feeling of his people and inspire them with his own lofty thoughts and aims. Such a man was Mazzini, seventy years ago in Italy. Such were Washington and Lincoln, the former more by his example than by his words, the latter by both, yet most by the quiet patience, dignity, and hopefulness which he showed in the darkest hours. Nations respond to the appeal which such a man makes to their best instincts. He typifies for the moment whatever is highest in them.

Unhappily, with nations as with individuals, there is apt to be a relapse from these loftier moods into the old common ways when selfish interest and trivial pleasures resume their sway. There comes a sort of reaction from the stress of virtue and strenuous high soaring effort. Everything looks gray and dull. The divine light has died out of the sky. This, too, is an oft-repeated lesson of European history. Yet the reaction and decline are not inevitable. When an individual man has been raised above himself by some spiritual impulse, he is sometimes able to hold the ground he has won. His will may have been strengthened. He has learnt to control the meaner desires. The impulse that stirred him is not wholly spent, because the nobler thoughts and acts which it prompted have become a habit with him. So, too, with a nation. What habits are to the individual man, that, to a nation, are its Traditions. They are the memories of the Past turned into the standards of the Present. High traditions go to form a code of honour, which speaks with authority to the sense of honour. Whoever transgresses that code is felt to be unworthy of the nation, unfit to hold that place in its respect and confidence which the great ones of the days of old have held. Pride in the glorious foretime of the race and in its heroes sustains in the individual man who is called to public duty, the personal pride which makes him feel that all his affections and all his emotions stand rooted in the sense of honour, which is, for the man and for the nation, the foundation of all virtue.

We have seen in our own time, in the people of Japan, a striking example of what the passionate attachment to a national ideal can do in war to intensify the sense of duty and self-sacrifice. A similar example is held up to us by those who have recorded the earlier annals of Rome. The deepest moral they teach is the splendid power which the love of Rome and the idea of what her children owed to her exercised over her great citizens, enabling them to set shining examples of devotion to the city which the world has admired ever since. Each example evoked later examples in later generations, till at last in a changed community, its upper class demoralized by wealth and power even more than it was torn by discord, its lower classes corrupted by the upper and looking on their suffrage as a means of gain, the ancient traditions died out. Whoever, studying the conditions of modern European democracies, sees the infinite facilities which popular government in large countries full of rich men and of opportunities for acquiring riches, offers for the perversion of government to private selfish ends, will often feel that those European states which have maintained the highest standard of civic purity have done it in respect of their Traditions. Were these to be weakened, the fabric might crumble into dust.

Every new generation as it comes up can make the traditions which it finds better or worse. If its imagination is touched and its emotions stirred by all that is finest in the history of its country, it learns to live up to the ideals set before it, and thus it strengthens the best standards of conduct it has inherited and prolongs the reverence felt for them.

The responsibility for forming ideals and fixing standards does not belong to statesmen alone. It belongs, and now perhaps more largely than ever before, to the intellectual leaders of the nation, and especially to those who address the people in the Universities and through the press. Teachers, writers, journalists, are forming the mind of modern nations to an extent previously unknown. Here they have opportunities such as have existed never before, nor in any other country, for trying to inspire the nation with a love of truth and honour, with a sense of the high obligations of citizenship, and especially of those who hold public office.

Of the power which the daily press exerts upon the thoughts and the tastes of the people through the matter it scatters among them, and of the grave import of the choice it has always and everywhere to make between the serious treatment of public issues and that cheap cynicism which so many readers find amusing, there is no need to speak here. You know better than I do how far those who direct the press realize and try to discharge the responsibilities which attach to their power.

The observer who seeks to discern and estimate the forces working for good or evil that mark the spirit and tendencies of an age, finds it easiest to do this by noting the changes which have occurred within his own memory. To-day everyone seems to dwell upon the growth not only of luxury, but of the passion for amusement, and most of those who can look back thirty or forty years find in this growth grounds for discouragement. I deny neither the fact nor the significance of the auguries that it suggests. But let us also note a hopeful sign manifest during the last twenty years both here and in England. It is the diffusion among the educated and richer classes of a warmer feeling of sympathy and a stronger feeling of responsibility for the less fortunate sections of the community. There is more of a sense of brotherhood, more of a desire to help, more of a discontent with those arrangements of society which press hardly on the common man than there was forty years ago. This altruistic spirit which is now everywhere visible in the field of private philanthropic work, seems likely to spread into the field of civic action also, and may there become a new motive power. It has already become a more efficient force in legislation than it ever was before. We may well hope that it will draw more and more of those who love and seek to help their fellow-men into that legislative and administrative work whose opportunities for grappling with economic and social problems become every day greater.

Here in America I am told in nearly every city I visit that the young men are more and more caring for and bestirring themselves to discharge their civic duties. That is the best news one can hear. Surely no country makes so clear a call upon her citizens to work for her as yours does. Think of the wide-spreading results which good solid work produces on so vast a community, where everything achieved for good in one place is quickly known and may be quickly imitated in another. Think of the advantages for the development of the highest civilization which the boundless resources of your territory provide. Think of that principle of the Sovereignty of the People which you have carried further than it was ever carried before and which requires and inspires and, indeed, compels you to endeavour to make the whole people fit to bear a weight and discharge a task such as no other multitude of men ever yet undertook. Think of the sense of fraternity, also without precedent in any other great nation, which binds all Americans together and makes it easier here than elsewhere for each citizen to meet every other citizen as an equal upon a common ground. One who, coming from the Old World, remembers the greater difficulties the Old World has to face, rejoices to think how much, with all these advantages, the youth of America, such youth as I see here to-night in this venerable University, may accomplish for the future of your country. Nature has done her best to provide a foundation whereon the fabric of an enlightened and steadily advancing civilization may be reared. It is for you to build upon that foundation. Free from many of the dangers that surround the states of Europe, you have unequalled opportunities for showing what a high spirit of citizenship — zealous, intelligent, disinterested — may do for the happiness and dignity of a mighty nation, enabling it to become what its founders hoped it might be — a model for other peoples more lately emerged into the sunlight of freedom.

ABRAHAM LINCOLN [1]

RALPH WALDO EMERSON

WE meet under the gloom of a calamity which darkens down over the minds of good men in all civil society, as the fearful tidings travel over sea, over land, from country to country, like the shadow of an uncalculated eclipse over the planet. Old as history is, and manifold as are its tragedies, I doubt if any death has caused so much pain to mankind as this has caused, or will cause, on its announcement; and this, not so much because nations are by modern arts brought so closely together, as because of the mysterious hopes and fears which, in the present day, are connected with the name and institutions of America.

In this country, on Saturday, every one was struck dumb, and saw at first only deep below deep, as he meditated on the ghastly blow. And perhaps, at this hour, when the coffin which contains the dust of the President sets forward on its long march through mourning States, on its way to his home in Illinois, we might well be silent, and suffer the awful voices of the time to thunder to us. Yes, but that first despair was brief: the man was not so to be mourned. He was the most active and hopeful of men; and his work had not perished: but acclamations of praise for the task he had accomplished burst out into a song of triumph, which even tears for his death cannot keep down.

The President stood before us as a man of the people. He was thoroughly American, had never crossed the sea, had never been spoiled by English insularity or French dissipa-

[1] Spoken at the funeral services held in Concord, Massachusetts, April 19, 1865. Reprinted by arrangement with Houghton Mifflin Company.

tion; a quite native, aboriginal man, as an acorn from the oak; no aping of foreigners, no frivolous accomplishments, Kentuckian born, working on a farm, a flatboatman, a captain in the Black Hawk war, a country lawyer, a representative in the rural Legislature of Illinois; — on such modest foundations the broad structure of his fame was laid. How slowly, and yet by happily prepared steps, he came to his place. All of us remember — it is only a history of five or six years — the surprise and the disappointment of the country at his first nomination by the Convention at Chicago. Mr. Seward, then in the culmination of his good fame, was the favorite of the Eastern States. And when the new and comparatively unknown name of Lincoln was announced, (notwithstanding the report of the acclamations of that Convention,) we heard the result coldly and sadly. It seemed too rash, on a purely local reputation, to build so grave a trust in such anxious times; and men naturally talked of the chances in politics as incalculable. But it turned out not to be chance. The profound good opinion which the people of Illinois and of the West had conceived of him, and which they had imparted to their colleagues that they also might justify themselves to their constituents at home, was not rash, though they did not begin to know the riches of his worth.

A plain man of the people, an extraordinary fortune attended him. He offered no shining qualities at the first encounter; he did not offend by superiority. He had a face and manner which disarmed suspicion, which inspired confidence, which confirmed good-will. He was a man without vices. He had a strong sense of duty, which it was very easy for him to obey. Then, he had what farmers call a long head; was excellent in working out the sum for himself; in arguing his case and convincing you fairly and firmly. Then, it turned out that he was a great worker; had prodigious faculty of performance; worked easily. A good worker is so rare; everybody has some disabling quality. In a host of young men that start together and promise so many brilliant leaders for the next age, each fails on trial; one by bad health, one by conceit, or by love of pleasure, or lethargy, or an ugly temper, — each has some disqualifying fault that throws him out of the career. But this man was sound to the core, cheerful, persistent, all right for labor, and liked nothing so well.

Then, he had a vast good-nature, which made him tolerant and accessible to all; fair-minded, leaning to the claim of the petitioner; affable, and not sensible to the affliction which the innumerable visits paid to him when President would have brought to any one else. And how this good-nature became a noble humanity, in many a tragic case which the events of the war brought to him, every one will remember; and with what increasing tenderness he dealt when a whole race was thrown on his compassion. The poor negro said of him, on an impressive occasion, "Massa Linkum am eberywhere."

Then his broad good-humor, running easily into jocular talk, in which he delighted and in which he excelled, was a rich gift to this wise man. It enabled him to keep his secret; to meet every kind of man and every rank in society; to take off the edge of the severest decisions; to mask his own purpose and sound his companion; and to catch with true instinct the temper of every company he addressed. And, more than all, it is to a man of severe labor, in anxious and exhausting crises, the natural restorative, good as sleep, and is the protection of the overdriven brain against rancor and insanity.

He is the author of a multitude of good sayings, so disguised as pleasantries that it is certain they had no reputation at first but as jests; and only later, by the very acceptance and adoption they find in the mouths of millions, turn out to be the wisdom of the hour. I am sure if this man had ruled in a period of less facility of printing, he would have become mythological in a very few years, like Æsop or Pilpay, or one of the Seven Wise Masters, by his fables and proverbs. But the weight and penetration of many passages in his letters, messages and speeches, hidden now by the very closeness of their application to the moment, are destined hereafter to wide fame. What pregnant definitions; what unerring common sense; what foresight; and, on great occasion, what lofty, and more than national, what humane tone! His brief speech at Gettysburg will not easily be surpassed by words on any recorded occasion. This, and one other American speech, that of John Brown to the court that tried him, and a part of Kossuth's speech at Birmingham, can only be compared with each other, and with no fourth.

His occupying the chair of State was a triumph of the good-sense of mankind, and of the public conscience. This middle-class country had got a middle-class President, at last. Yes, in manners and sympathies, but not in powers, for his powers were superior. This man grew according to the need. His mind mastered the problem of the day; and, as the problem grew, so did his comprehension of it. Rarely was man so fitted to the event. In the midst of fears and jealousies, in the Babel of counsels and parties, this man wrought incessantly with all his might and all his honesty, laboring to find what the people wanted, and how to obtain that. It cannot be said there is any exaggeration of his worth. If ever a man was fairly tested, he was. There was no lack of resistance, nor of slander, nor of ridicule. The times have allowed no state secrets; the nation has been in such ferment, such multitudes had to be trusted, that no secret could be kept. Every door was ajar, and we know all that befell.

Then, what an occasion was the whirlwind of the war. Here was place for no holiday magistrate, no fair-weather sailor; the new pilot was hurried to the helm in a tornado. In four years — four years of battle-days — his endurance, his fertility of resources, his magnanimity, were sorely tried and never found wanting. There, by his courage, his justice, his even temper, his fertile counsel, his humanity, he stood a heroic figure in the centre of a heroic epoch. He is the true history of the American people in his time. Step by step he walked before them; slow with their slowness, quickening his march by theirs, the true representative of this continent; an entirely public man; father of his country, the pulse of twenty millions throbbing in his heart, the thought of their minds articulated by his tongue.

Adam Smith remarks that the axe, which in Houbraken's portraits of British kings and worthies is engraved under those who have suffered at the block, adds a certain lofty charm to the picture. And who does not see, even in this tragedy so recent, how fast the terror and ruin of the massacre are already burning into glory around the victim? Far happier this fate than to have lived to be wished away; to have watched the decay of his own faculties; to have seen — perhaps even he — the proverbial ingratitude of statesmen; to have seen mean men preferred. Had he not lived long enough to keep the greatest promise that ever man made to his fellow-men — the practical abolition of slavery? He had seen Tennessee, Missouri and Maryland emancipate their slaves. He had seen Savannah, Charleston and Richmond surrendered; had seen the main army of the rebellion lay down its arms. He had conquered the public opinion of Canada, England and France. Only Washington can compare with him in fortune.

And what if it should turn out, in the unfolding of the web, that he had reached the term; that this heroic deliverer could no longer serve us; that the rebellion had touched its natural conclusion, and what remained to be done required new and uncommitted hands, — a new spirit born out of the ashes of the war; and that Heaven, wishing to show the world a completed benefactor, shall make him serve his country even more by his death than by his life? Nations, like kings, are not good by facility and complaisance. "The kindness of kings consists in justice and strength." Easy good-nature has been the dangerous foible of the Republic, and it was necessary that its enemies should outrage it, and drive us to unwonted firmness, to secure the salvation of this country in the next ages.

The ancients believed in a serene and beautiful Genius which ruled in the affairs of nations; which, with a slow but stern justice, carried forward the fortunes of certain chosen houses, weeding out single offenders or offending families, and securing at last the firm prosperity of the favorites of Heaven. It was too narrow a view of the Eternal Nemesis. There is a serene Providence which rules the fate of nations, which makes little account of time, little of one generation or race, makes no account of disasters, conquers alike by what is called defeat or by what is called victory, thrusts aside enemy and obstruction, crushes everything immoral as inhuman, and obtains the ultimate triumph of the best race by the sacrifice of everything which resists the moral laws of the world. It makes its own instruments, creates the man for the time, trains him in poverty, inspires his genius, and arms him for his task. It has given every race its own talent, and ordains that only that race which combines perfectly with the virtues of all shall endure.

A DEFINITION OF A GENTLEMAN[1]
JOHN HENRY NEWMAN

HENCE it is that it is almost a definition of a gentleman to say he is one who never inflicts pain. This description is both refined and, as far as it goes, accurate. He is mainly occupied in merely removing the obstacles which hinder the free and unembarrassed action of those about him; and he concurs with their movements rather than takes the initiative himself. His benefits may be considered as parallel to what are called comforts or conveniences in arrangements of a personal nature: like an easy chair or a good fire, which do their part in dispelling cold and fatigue, though nature provides both means of rest and animal heat without them. The true gentleman in like manner carefully avoids whatever may cause a jar or a jolt in the minds of those with whom he is cast; — all clashing of opinion, or collision of feeling, all restraint, or suspicion, or gloom, or resentment; his great concern being to make every one at their ease and at home. He has his eyes on all his company; he is tender towards the bashful, gentle towards the distant, and merciful towards the absurd; he can recollect to whom he is speaking; he guards against unseasonable allusions, or topics which may irritate; he is seldom prominent in conversation, and never wearisome. He makes light of favours while he does them, and seems to be receiving when he is conferring. He never speaks of himself except when compelled, never defends himself by a mere retort, he has no ears for slander or gossip, is scrupulous in imputing motives to those who interfere with him, and interprets every thing

[1] From *The Idea of a University*, Discourse VIII, "University Teaching."

for the best. He is never mean or little in his disputes, never takes unfair advantage, never mistakes personalities or sharp sayings for arguments, or insinuates evil which he dare not say out. From a long-sighted prudence, he observes the maxim of the ancient sage, that we should ever conduct ourselves towards our enemy as if he were one day to be our friend. He has too much good sense to be affronted at insults, he is too well employed to remember injuries, and too indolent to bear malice. He is patient, forbearing, and resigned, on philosophical principles; he submits to pain, because it is inevitable, to bereavement, because it is irreparable, and to death, because it is his destiny. If he engages in controversy of any kind, his disciplined intellect preserves him from the blundering discourtesy of better, perhaps, but less educated minds; who, like blunt weapons, tear and hack instead of cutting clean, who mistake the point in argument, waste their strength on trifles, misconceive their adversary, and leave the question more involved than they find it. He may be right or wrong in his opinion, but he is too clear-headed to be unjust; he is as simple as he is forcible, and as brief as he is decisive. Nowhere shall we find greater candour, consideration, indulgence: he throws himself into the minds of his opponents, he accounts for their mistakes. He knows the weakness of human reason as well as its strength, its province and its limits. If he be an unbeliever, he will be too profound and large-minded to ridicule religion or to act against it; he is too wise to be a dogmatist or fanatic in his infidelity. He respects piety and devotion; he even supports institutions as venerable, beautiful, or useful, to which he does not assent; he honours the ministers of religion, and it contents him to decline its mysteries without assailing or denouncing them. He is a friend of religious toleration, and that, not only because his philosophy has taught him to look on all forms

A DEFINITION OF A GENTLEMAN

of faith with an impartial eye, but also from the gentleness and effeminacy of feeling, which is the attendant on civilization.

Not that he may not hold a religion too, in his own way, even when he is not a Christian. In that case his religion is one of imagination and sentiment; it is the embodiment of those ideas of the sublime, majestic, and beautiful, without which there can be no large philosophy. Sometimes he acknowledges the being of God, sometimes he invests an unknown principle or quality with the attributes of perfection. And this deduction of his reason, or creation of his fancy, he makes the occasion of such excellent thoughts, and the starting-point of so varied and systematic a teaching, that he even seems like a disciple of Christianity itself. From the very accuracy and steadiness of his logical powers, he is able to see what sentiments are consistent in those who hold any religious doctrine at all, and he appears to others to feel and to hold a whole circle of theological truths, which exist in his mind no otherwise than as a number of deductions.

THE SKY[1]

JOHN RUSKIN

It is a strange thing how little in general people know about the sky. It is the part of creation in which nature has done more for the sake of pleasing man, more for the sole and evident purpose of talking to him and teaching him, than in any other of her works, and it is just the part in which we least attend to her. There are not many of her other works in which some more material or essential purpose than the mere pleasing of man is not answered by every part of their organization; but every essential purpose of the sky might, so far as we know, be answered, if once in three days, or thereabouts, a great ugly black rain cloud were brought up over the blue, and everything well watered, and so all left blue again till next time, with perhaps a film of morning and evening mist for dew. And instead of this, there is not a moment of any day of our lives, when nature is not producing scene after scene, picture after picture, glory after glory, and working still upon such exquisite and constant principles of the most perfect beauty, that it is quite certain it is all done for us, and intended for our perpetual pleasure. And every man, wherever placed, however far from other sources of interest or of beauty, has this doing for him constantly. The noblest scenes of the earth can be seen and known but by few; it is not intended that man should live always in the midst of them, he injures them by his presence, he ceases to feel them if he be always with them; but the sky is for all; bright as it is, it is not "too bright, nor good, for human nature's daily food"; it is fitted in all its func-

[1] From *Modern Painters.* Vol. I. 1843.

tions for the perpetual comfort and exalting of the heart, for the soothing it and purifying it from its dross and dust. Sometimes gentle, sometimes capricious, sometimes awful, never the same for two moments together; almost human in its passions, almost spiritual in its tenderness, almost divine in its infinity, its appeal to what is immortal in us, is as distinct, as its ministry of chastisement or of blessing to what is mortal is essential. And yet we never attend to it, we never make it a subject of thought, but as it has to do with our animal sensations; we look upon all by which it speaks to us more clearly than to brutes, upon all which bears witness to the intention of the Supreme, that we are to receive more from the covering vault than the light and the dew which we share with the weed and the worm, only as a succession of meaningless and monotonous accident, too common and too vain to be worthy of a moment of watchfulness, or a glance of admiration. If in our moments of utter idleness and insipidity, we turn to the sky as a last resource, which of its phenomena do we speak of? One says it has been wet, and another it has been windy, and another it has been warm. Who, among the whole chattering crowd, can tell me of the forms and the precipices of the chain of tall white mountains that girded the horizon at noon yesterday? Who saw the narrow sunbeam that came out of the south and smote upon their summits until they melted and mouldered away in a dust of blue rain? Who saw the dance of the dead clouds when the sunlight left them last night, and the west wind blew them before it like withered leaves? All has passed, unregretted as unseen; or if the apathy be ever shaken off, even for an instant, it is only by what is gross, or what is extraordinary; and yet it is not in the broad and fierce manifestations of the elemental energies, not in the clash of the hail, nor the drift of the whirlwind, that the highest characters of the sublime are developed. God is not in the earthquake, nor in the fire, but in the still small voice. They are but the blunt and low faculties of our nature, which can only be addressed through lampblack and lightning. It is in quiet and subdued passages of unobtrusive majesty, the deep, and the calm, and the perpetual, — that which must be sought ere it is seen, and loved ere it is understood, — things which the angels work out for us daily, and yet vary eternally, which are never wanting, and never repeated, which are to be found always yet each found but once; it is through these that the lesson of devotion is chiefly taught, and the blessing of beauty given. These are what the artist of highest aim must study; it is these, by the combination of which his ideal is to be created; these, of which so little notice is ordinarily taken by common observers, that I fully believe, little as people in general are concerned with art, more of their ideas of sky are derived from pictures than from reality, and that if we could examine the conception formed in the minds of most educated persons when we talk of clouds, it would frequently be found composed of fragments of blue and white reminiscences of the old masters.

"The chasm of sky above my head
Is Heaven's profoundest azure. No domain
For fickle, short-lived clouds, to occupy,
Or to pass through; but rather an *abyss*
In which the everlasting stars abide,
And whose soft gloom, and boundless depth, might tempt
The curious eye to look for them by day."

And, in his American Notes, I remember Dickens notices the same truth, describing himself as lying drowsily on the barge deck, looking not at, but *through* the sky. And if you look intensely at the pure blue of a serene sky, you will see that there is a variety and fulness in its very repose. It is not flat dead color, but a deep, quivering, transparent body of penetrable air, in which you trace or imagine short, falling spots of deceiving light, and dim shades, faint, veiled vestiges of dark vapor.

ON GOING A JOURNEY
WILLIAM HAZLITT
1778-1830

THIS essay is from the volume *Table Talk* published in 1822. Hazlitt was one of the keenest and most suggestive of critics. He was a man of philosophic interests, but of a passionate temperament, with a great gusto for life, nature, and books. The strongly personal element in his writing makes him a companionable essayist.

ONE of the pleasantest things in the world is going a journey; but I like to go by myself. I can enjoy society in a room; but out of doors, nature is company enough for me. I am then never less alone than when alone.

"The fields his study, nature was his book."

I cannot see the wit of walking and talking at the same time. When I am in the country, I wish to vegetate like the country. I am not for criticising hedge-rows and black cattle. I go out of town in order to forget the town and all that is in it. There are those who for this purpose go to watering-places, and carry the metropolis with them. I like more elbow-room, and fewer incumbrances. I like solitude, when I give myself up to it, for the sake of solitude; nor do I ask for

"—— a friend in my retreat,
Whom I may whisper solitude is sweet."

The soul of a journey is liberty, perfect liberty, to think, feel, do just as one pleases. We go a journey chiefly to be free of all impediments and of all inconveniences; to leave ourselves behind, much more to get rid of others. It is because I want a little breathing-space to muse on indifferent matters, where Contemplation

"May plume her feathers and let grow her wings,
That in the various bustle of resort
Were all too ruffled, and sometimes impair'd,"

that I absent myself from the town for awhile, without feeling at a loss the moment I am left by myself. Instead of a friend in a post-chaise or in a Tilbury, to exchange good things with, and vary the same stale topics over again, for once let me have a truce with impertinence. Give me the clear blue sky over my head, and the green turf beneath my feet, a winding road before me, and a three hours' march to dinner — and then to thinking! It is hard if I cannot start some game on these lone heaths. I laugh, I run, I leap, I sing for joy. From the point of yonder rolling cloud, I plunge into my past being, and revel there, as the sun-burnt Indian plunges headlong into the wave that wafts him to his native shore. Then long-forgotten things, like "sunken wrack and sumless treasuries," burst upon my eager sight, and I begin to feel, think, and be myself again. Instead of an awkward silence, broken by attempts at wit or dull common-places, mine is that undisturbed silence of the heart which alone is perfect eloquence. No one likes puns, alliterations, antitheses, argument, and analysis better than I do; but I sometimes had rather be without them. "Leave, oh, leave me to my repose!" I have just now other business in hand, which would seem idle to you, but is with me "very stuff of the conscience." Is not this wild rose sweet without a comment? Does not this daisy leap to my heart set in its coat of emerald? Yet if I were to explain to you the circumstance that has so endeared it to me, you would only smile. Had I not better then keep it to myself, and let it serve me to brood over, from here to yonder craggy point, and from thence onward to the far distant horizon? I should be but bad company all that way, and therefore prefer being alone. I have heard it said that you may, when the moody fit comes on, walk or ride on by yourself, and indulge your reveries. But this looks like a breach of manners, a neglect of others, and you are thinking all the time that you ought to rejoin your party. "Out upon such half-faced fellowship," say I. I like to be either entirely to myself, or entirely at the disposal of others; to talk or be silent, to walk or sit still, to be sociable or solitary. I was pleased with an observation of Mr. Cobbett's, that "he thought it a bad French custom to drink our wine with our meals, and that an Englishman ought to do only one thing at a time." So I cannot talk and think, or indulge in melancholy musing and lively conversation by fits and starts. "Let me have a companion of my way," says Sterne, "were it but to remark how the shadows lengthen as the sun declines." It is beautifully said: but in my opinion, this continual comparing of notes interferes with the involuntary impression of things upon the mind, and hurts the sentiment. If you only hint what you feel in a kind of dumb show, it is insipid: if you have to explain it, it is making a toil of a pleasure. You cannot read the book of nature, without being perpetually put to the trouble of translating it for the benefit of others. I am for the synthetical method on a journey, in preference to the analytical. I am content to lay in a stock of ideas then, and to examine and anatomise them afterwards. I want to see my vague notions float like the down of the thistle before the breeze, and not to have them entangled in the briars and thorns of controversy. For once, I like to have it all my own way; and this is impossible unless you are alone, or in such company as I do not covet. I have no objection to argue a point with any one for twenty miles of measured road, but not for pleasure. If you remark the scent of a bean-field crossing the road, perhaps your fellow-traveller has no smell. If you point to a distant object, perhaps he is short-sighted, and has to take out his glass to look at it. There is a feeling in the air, a tone in the colour of a cloud which hits your fancy, but the effect of which you are unable to account for. There is then no sympathy, but an uneasy craving after it, and a dissatisfaction which pursues you on the way, and in the end probably produces ill humour. Now I never quarrel with myself, and take all my own conclusions for granted till I find it necessary to defend them against objections. It is not merely that you may not be of accord on the objects and circumstances that present themselves before you — these may recall a number of objects, and lead to associations too delicate and refined to be possibly communicated to others. Yet these I love to cherish, and sometimes still fondly clutch them, when I can escape from the throng to do so. To give way to our feelings before company, seems extravagance or affectation; and on the other hand, to have to unravel this mystery of our being at every turn, and to make others take an equal interest in it (otherwise the end is not answered) is a task to which few are competent. We must "give it an understanding, but no tongue." My old friend Coleridge, however, could do both. He could go on in the most delightful explanatory way over hill and dale, a summer's day, and convert a landscape into a didactic poem or a Pindaric ode. "He talked far above singing." If I could so clothe my ideas in sounding and flowing words, I might perhaps wish to have some one with me to admire the swelling theme; or I could be more content, were it possible for me still to hear his echoing voice in the woods of All-Foxden. They had "that fine madness in them which our first poets had"; and if they could have been caught by some rare instrument, would have breathed such strains as the following:

> "— Here be woods as green
> As any, air likewise as fresh and sweet
> As when smooth Zephyrus plays on the fleet

>   Face of the curled stream, with flow'rs as many
>   As the young spring gives, and as choice as any;
>   Here be all new delights, cool streams and wells,
>   Arbours o'ergrown with woodbine, caves and dells;
>   Choose where thou wilt, while I sit by and sing,
>   Or gather rushes to make many a ring
>   For thy long fingers; tell thee tales of love,
>   How the pale Phœbe, hunting in a grove,
>   First saw the boy Endymion, from whose eyes
>   She took eternal fire that never dies;
>   How she convey'd him softly in a sleep,
>   His temples bound with poppy, to the steep
>   Head of old Latmos, where she stoops each night,
>   Gilding the mountain with her brother's light,
>   To kiss her sweetest."—
>   FAITHFUL SHEPHERDESS.

Had I words and images at command like these, I would attempt to wake the thoughts that lie slumbering on golden ridges in the evening clouds: but at the sight of nature my fancy, poor as it is, droops and closes up its leaves, like flowers at sunset. I can make nothing out on the spot: — I must have time to collect myself. —

In general, a good thing spoils out-of-door prospects: it should be reserved for Table-talk. Lamb is for this reason, I take it, the worst company in the world out of doors; because he is the best within. I grant, there is one subject on which it is pleasant to talk on a journey; and that is, what one shall have for supper when we get to our inn at night. The open air improves this sort of conversation or friendly altercation, by setting a keener edge on appetite. Every mile of the road heightens the flavour of the viands we expect at the end of it. How fine it is to enter some old town, walled and turreted just at the approach of night-fall, or to come to some straggling village, with the lights streaming through the surrounding gloom; and then after inquiring for the best entertainment that the place affords, to "take one's ease at one's inn!" These eventful moments in our lives' history are too precious, too full of solid, heart-felt happiness to be frittered and dribbled away in imperfect sympathy. I would have them all to myself, and drain them to the last drop: they will do to talk of or to write about afterwards. What a delicate speculation it is, after drinking whole goblets of tea,

"The cups that cheer, but not inebriate,"

and letting the fumes ascend into the brain, to sit considering what we shall have for supper — eggs and a rasher, a rabbit smothered in onions, or an excellent veal-cutlet! Sancho in such a situation once fixed upon cow-heel; and his choice, though he could not help it, is not to be disparaged. Then in the intervals of pictured scenery and Shandean contemplation, to catch the preparation and the stir in the kitchen — *Procul, O procul este profani!* These hours are sacred to silence and to musing, to be treasured up in the memory, and to feed the source of smiling thoughts hereafter. I would not waste them in idle talk; or if I must have the integrity of fancy broken in upon, I would rather it were by a stranger than a friend. A stranger takes his hue and character from the time and place; he is a part of the furniture and costume of an inn. If he is a Quaker, or from the West Riding of Yorkshire, so much the better. I do not even try to sympathise with him, and he breaks no squares. I associate nothing with my travelling companion but present objects and passing events. In his ignorance of me and my affairs, I in a manner forget myself. But a friend reminds one of other things, rips up old grievances, and destroys the abstraction of the scene. He comes in ungraciously between us and our imaginary character. Something is dropped in the course of conversation that gives a hint of your profession and pursuits; or from having some one with you that knows the less sublime portions of your history, it seems that other people do. You are no longer a citizen of the world: but your "unhoused free condition is put into circumscription and confine." The *incognito* of an inn is one of its striking privileges — "lord of one's-self, uncumber'd with a name." Oh! it is great to shake off the trammels of the world and of public opinion — to lose our importunate, tormenting, everlasting personal identity in the elements of nature, and become the creature of the moment, clear of all ties — to hold to the universe only by a dish of sweet-breads, and to owe nothing but the score of the evening — and no longer seeking for applause and meeting with contempt, to be known by no other title than *the Gentleman in the parlour!* One may take one's choice of all characters in this romantic state of uncertainty as to one's real pretensions, and become indefinitely respectable and negatively right-worshipful. We baffle prejudice and disappoint conjecture; and from being so to others, begin to be objects of curiosity and wonder even to ourselves. We are no more those hackneyed commonplaces that we appear in the world: an inn restores us to the level of nature, and quits scores with society! I have certainly spent some enviable hours at inns — sometimes when I have been left entirely to myself, and have tried to solve some metaphysical problem, as once at Witham-common, where I found out the proof that likeness is not a case of the association of ideas — at other times, when there have been pictures in the room, as at St. Neot's (I think it was), where I first met with Gribelin's engravings of the Cartoons, into which I entered at once, and at a little inn on the borders of Wales, where there happened to be hanging some of Westall's drawings, which I compared triumphantly (for a theory that I had, not for the admired artist) with the figure of a girl who had ferried me over the Severn, standing up in the boat between me and the twilight — at other times I might mention luxuriating in books, with a peculiar interest in this way, as I remember sitting up half the night to read *Paul and Virginia*, which I picked up at an inn at Bridgewater, after being drenched in the rain all day; and at the same place I got through two volumes of Madame D'Arblay's *Camilla*. It was on the tenth of April, 1798, that I sat down to a volume of the *New Eloise*, at the inn at Llangollen, over a bottle of sherry and a cold chicken. The letter I chose was that in which St. Preux describes his feelings as he first caught a glimpse from the heights of the Jura of the Pays de Vaud, which I had brought with me as a *bon bouche* to crown the evening with. It was my birth-day, and I had for the first time come from a place in the neighbourhood to visit this delightful spot. The road to Llangollen turns off between Chirk and Wrexham; and on passing a certain point, you come all at once upon the valley, which opens like an amphitheatre, broad, barren hills rising in majestic state on either side, with "green upland swells that echo to the bleat of flocks" below, and the river Dee babbling over its stony bed in the midst of them. The valley at this time "glittered green with sunny showers," and a budding ash-tree dipped its tender branches in the chiding stream. How proud, how glad I was to walk along the high road that overlooks the delicious prospect, repeating the lines which I have just quoted from Mr. Coleridge's poems. But besides the prospect which opened beneath my feet, another also opened to my inward sight, a heavenly vision, on which were written, in letters large as Hope could make them, these four words, LIBERTY, GENIUS, LOVE, VIRTUE; which have since faded into the light of common day, or mock my idle gaze.

"The beautiful is vanished, and returns not."

Still I would return some time or other to this enchanted spot; but I would return to it alone. What other self could I find to share that influx of thoughts, of regret, and delight, the fragments of which I could hardly conjure up to myself, so much have they been broken and defaced! I could stand on some tall rock, and overlook the precipice of years that separates me from what I then was! I was at that time going shortly to visit the poet whom I have above named. Where is he now? Not only I myself have changed; the world, which was then new to me, has become old and incorrigible. Yet will I turn to thee in thought, O sylvan Dee, in joy, in youth and gladness as thou then wert; and thou shalt always be to me the river of Paradise, where I will drink of the waters of life freely!

There is hardly any thing that shows the short-sightedness or capriciousness of the imagination more than travelling does. With change of place we change our ideas; nay, our opinions and feelings. We can by an effort indeed transport ourselves to old and long-forgotten scenes, and then the picture of the mind revives again; but we forget those that we have just left. It seems that we can think but of one place at a time. The canvas of the fancy is but of a certain extent, and if we paint one set of objects upon it, they immediately efface every other. We cannot enlarge our conceptions, we only shift our point of view. The landscape bares its bosom to the enraptured eye, we take our fill of it, and seem as if we could form no other image of beauty or grandeur. We pass on, and think no more of it: the horizon that shuts it from our sight, also blots it from our memory like a dream. In travelling through a wild barren country, I can form no idea of a woody and cultivated one. It appears to me that all the world must be barren, like what I see of it. In the country we forget the town, and in town we despise the country. "Beyond Hyde Park," says Sir Fopling Flutter, "all is a desert." All that part of the map that we do not see before us is a blank. The world in our conceit of it is not much bigger than a nutshell. It is not one prospect expanded into another, county joined to county, kingdom to kingdom, lands to seas, making an image voluminous and vast; — the mind can form no larger idea of space than the eye can take in at a single glance. The rest is a name written in a map, a calculation of arithmetic. For instance, what is the true signification of that immense mass of territory and population, known by the name of China to us? An inch of paste-board on a wooden globe, of no more account than a China orange! Things near us are seen of the size of life: things at a distance are diminished to the size of the understanding. We measure the universe by ourselves, and even comprehend the texture of our own being only piece-meal. In this way, however, we remember an infinity of things and places. The mind is like a mechanical instrument that plays a great variety of tunes, but it must play them in succession. One idea recalls another, but it at the same time excludes all others. In trying to renew old recollections, we cannot as it were unfold the whole web of our existence; we must pick out the single threads. So in coming to a place where we have formerly lived and with which we have intimate associations, every one must have found that the feeling grows more vivid the nearer we approach the spot, from the mere anticipation of the actual impression: we remember circumstances, feelings, persons, faces, names, that we had not thought of for years; but for the time all the rest of the world is forgotten! — To return to the question I have quitted above.

I have no objection to go to see ruins, aqueducts, pictures, in company with a friend or a party, but rather the contrary, for the former reason reversed. They are intelligible matters, and will bear talking about. The sentiment here is not tacit, but communicable and overt. Salisbury Plain is barren of criticism, but Stonehenge will bear a discussion antiquarian, picturesque, and philosophical. In setting out on a party of pleasure, the first consideration always is where we shall go to: in taking a solitary ramble, the question is what we shall meet with by the way. "The mind is its own place"; nor are we anxious to arrive at the end of our journey. I can myself do the honours indifferently well to works of art and curiosity. I once took a party to Oxford with no mean *éclat* — shewed them that seat of the Muses at a distance,

"With glistering spires and pinnacles adorn'd"—

descanted on the learned air that breathes from the grassy quadrangles and stone walls of halls and colleges — was at home in the Bodleian; and at Blenheim quite superseded the powdered Ciceroni that attended us, and that pointed in vain with his wand to common-place beauties in matchless pictures. — As another exception to the above reasoning, I should not feel confident in venturing on a journey in a foreign country without a companion. I should want at intervals to hear the sound of my own language. There is an involuntary antipathy in the mind of an Englishman to foreign manners and notions that requires the assistance of social sympathy to carry it off. As the distance from home increases, this relief, which was at first a luxury, becomes a passion and an appetite. A person would almost feel stifled to find himself in the deserts of Arabia without friends and countrymen: there must be allowed to be something in the view of Athens or old Rome that claims the utterance of speech; and I own that the Pyramids are too mighty for any simple contemplation. In such situations, so opposite to all one's ordinary train of ideas, one seems a species by one's-self, a limb torn off from society, unless one can meet with instant fellowship and support. — Yet I did not feel this want or craving very pressing once, when I first set my foot on the laughing shores of France. Calais was peopled with novelty and delight. The confused, busy murmur of the place was like oil and wine poured into my ears; nor did the mariners' hymn, which was sung from the top of an old crazy vessel in the harbour, as the sun went down, send an alien sound into my soul. I only breathe the air of general humanity. I walked over "the vine-covered hills and gay regions of France," erect and satisfied; for the image of man was not cast down and chained to the foot of arbitrary thrones: I was at no loss for language, for that of all the great schools of painting was open to me. The whole is vanished like a shade. Pictures, heroes, glory, freedom, all are fled: nothing remains but the Bourbons and the French people! — There is undoubtedly a sensation in travelling into foreign parts that is to be had nowhere else: but it is more pleasing at the time than lasting. It is too remote from our habitual associations to be a common topic of discourse or reference, and, like a dream or another state of existence, does not piece into our daily modes of life. It is an animated but a momentary hallucination. It demands an effort to exchange our actual for our ideal identity; and to feel the pulse of our old transports revive very keenly, we must "jump" all our present comforts and connexions. Our romantic and itinerant character is not to be domesticated. Dr. Johnson remarked how little foreign travel added to the facilities of conversation in those who had been abroad. In fact, the time we have spent there is both delightful and in one sense instructive; but it appears to be cut out of our substantial, downright existence, and never to join kindly on to it. We are not the same, but another, and perhaps more enviable individual, all the time we are out of our own country. We are lost to ourselves, as well as our friends. So the poet somewhat quaintly sings,

"Out of my country and myself I go."

Those who wish to forget painful thoughts, do well to absent themselves for a while from the ties and objects that recall them: but we can be said only to fulfil our destiny in the place that gave us birth. I should on this account like well enough to spend the whole of my life in travelling abroad, if I could any where borrow another life to spend afterwards at home!

PHASES OF FARM LIFE [1]

JOHN BURROUGHS

1837–1921

"PHASES of Farm Life" is from that book of outdoor essays *Signs and Seasons*. The simplicity and sincerity with which Burroughs writes of nature or common life, give quality to his style. He was more influential than any other American writer of his time in awakening a healthy interest in outdoor things. Among his best books are *Wake Robin*, *Locusts and Wild Honey*, *Pepacton*, *Riverby*, *Winter Sunshine*.

... IT is not of country life in general that I am to speak, but of some phases of farm life, and of farm life in my native State.

Many of the early settlers of New York were from New England, Connecticut perhaps sending out the most. My own ancestors were from the latter State. The Connecticut emigrant usually made his first stop in our river counties, Putnam, Dutchess, or Columbia. If he failed to find his place there, he made another flight to Orange, to Delaware, or to Schoharie County, where he generally stuck. But the State early had one element introduced into its rural and farm life not found farther East, namely, the Holland Dutch. These gave features more or less picturesque to the country that are not observable in New England. The Dutch took root at various points along the Hudson, and about Albany and in the Mohawk valley, and remnants of their rural and domestic architecture may still be seen in these sections of the State. A Dutch barn became proverbial. "As broad as a Dutch barn" was a phrase that, when applied to the person of a man or woman, left room for little more to be said. The main feature of these barns was their enormous expansion of roof. It was a comfort to look at them, they

[1] Reprinted by arrangement with Houghton Mifflin Company.

suggested such shelter and protection. The eaves were very low and the ridge-pole very high. Long rafters and short posts gave them a quaint, short-waisted, grandmotherly look. They were nearly square, and stood very broad upon the ground. Their form was doubtless suggested by the damper climate of the Old World, where the grain and hay, instead of being packed in deep solid mows, used to be spread upon poles and exposed to the currents of air under the roof. Surface and not cubic capacity is more important in these matters in Holland than in this country. Our farmers have found that, in a climate where there is so much weather as with us, the less roof you have the better. Roofs will leak, and cured hay will keep sweet in a mow of any depth and size in our dry atmosphere.

The Dutch barn was the most picturesque barn that has been built, especially when thatched with straw, as they nearly all were, and forming one side of an inclosure of lower roofs or sheds also covered with straw, beneath which the cattle took refuge from the winter storms. Its immense, unpainted gable, cut with holes for the swallows, was like a section of a respectable-sized hill, and its roof like its slope. Its great doors always had a hood projecting over them, and the doors themselves were divided horizontally into upper and lower halves; the upper halves very frequently being left open, through which you caught a glimpse of the mows of hay, or the twinkle of flails when the grain was being threshed.

The old Dutch farmhouses, too, were always pleasing to look upon. They were low, often made of stone, with deep window-jambs and great family fireplaces. The outside door, like that of the barn, was always divided into upper and lower halves. When the weather permitted, the upper half could stand open, giving light and air without the cold draught over the floor where the children were playing that our wide-swung doors admit. This feature of the Dutch house and barn certainly merits preservation in our modern buildings.

The large, unpainted timber barns that succeeded the first Yankee settlers' log stables were also picturesque, especially when a lean-to for the cow-stable was added, and the roof carried down with a long sweep over it; or when the barn was flanked by an open shed with a hayloft above it, where the hens cackled and hid their nests, and from the open window of which the hay was always hanging.

Then the great timbers of these barns and the Dutch barn, hewn from maple or birch or oak trees from the primitive woods, and put in place by the combined strength of all the brawny arms in the neighborhood when the barn was raised, — timbers strong enough and heavy enough for docks and quays, and that have absorbed the odors of the hay and grain until they look ripe and mellow and full of the pleasing sentiment of the great, sturdy, bountiful interior! The "big beam" has become smooth and polished from the hay that has been pitched over it, and the sweaty, sturdy forms that have crossed it. One feels that he would like a piece of furniture — a chair, or a table, or a writing-desk, a bedstead, or a wainscoting — made from these long-seasoned, long-tried, richly-toned timbers of the old barn. But the smart-painted, natty barn that follows the humbler structure, with its glazed windows, its ornamented ventilator and gilded weather vane, — who cares to contemplate it? The wise human eye loves modesty and humility; loves plain, simple structures; loves the unpainted barn that took no thought of itself, or the dwelling that looks inward and not outward; is offended when the farm-buildings get above their business and aspire to be something on their own account, suggesting, not cattle and crops and plain living, but the vanities of the town and the pride of dress and equipage.

Indeed, the picturesque in human affairs and occupations is always born of love and humility, as it is in art or literature; and it quickly takes to itself wings and flies away at the advent of pride, or any selfish or unworthy motive. The more directly the farm savors of the farmer, the more the fields and buildings are redolent of human care and toil, without any thought of the passer-by, the more we delight in the contemplation of it.

It is unquestionably true that farm life and farm scenes in this country are less picturesque than they were fifty or one hundred years ago. This is owing partly to the advent of machinery, which enables the farmer to do so much of his work by proxy, and hence removes him farther from the soil, and partly to the growing distaste for the occupation among our people. The old settlers — our fathers and grandfathers — loved the farm, and had no thoughts above it; but the later generations are looking to the town and its fashions, and only waiting for a chance to flee thither. Then pioneer life is always more or less picturesque; there is no room for vain and foolish thoughts; it is a hard battle, and the people have no time to think about appearances. When my grandfather and grandmother came into the country where they reared their family and passed their days, they cut a road through the woods and brought all their worldly gear on a sled drawn by a yoke of oxen. Their neighbors helped them build a house of logs, with a roof of black-ash bark and floor of hewn white-ash plank. A great stone chimney and fireplace — the mortar of red clay — gave light and warmth, and cooked the meat and baked the bread, when there was any to cook or to bake. Here they lived and reared their family, and found life sweet. Their unworthy descendant, yielding to the inherited love of the soil, flees the city and its artificial ways, and gets a few acres in the country, where he proposes to engage in the pursuit supposed to be free to every American citizen, — the pursuit of happiness. The humble old farmhouse is discarded, and a smart, modern country-house put up. Walks and roads are made and graveled; trees and hedges are planted; the rustic old barn is rehabilitated; and, after it is all fixed, the uneasy proprietor stands off and looks, and calculates by how much he has missed the picturesque, at which he aimed. Our new houses undoubtedly have greater comforts and conveniences than the old; and, if we could keep our pride and vanity in abeyance and forget that all the world is looking on, they might have beauty also.

The man that forgets himself, he is the man we like; and the dwelling that forgets itself, in its purpose to shelter and protect its inmates and make them feel at home in it, is the dwelling that fills the eye. When you see one of the great cathedrals, you know that it was not pride that animated these builders, but fear and worship; but when you see the house of the rich farmer, or of the millionaire from the city, you see the pride of money and the insolence of social power.

Machinery, I say, has taken away some of the picturesque features of farm life. How much soever we may admire machinery and the faculty of mechanical invention, there is no machine like a man; and the work done directly by his hands, the things made or fashioned by them, have a virtue and a quality that cannot be imparted by machinery. The line of mowers in the meadows, with the straight swaths behind them, are more picturesque than the "Clipper" or "Buckeye" mower, with its team and driver. So are the flails of the threshers, chasing each other through the air, more pleasing to the eye and the ear than the machine, with its uproar, its choking clouds of dust, and its general hurly-burly.

Sometimes the threshing was done in the open air, upon a broad rock, or a smooth, dry plat of greensward; and it is occasionally done there yet, especially the threshing of the buckwheat crop by a farmer who has not a good barn floor, or who cannot afford to hire the machine. The flail makes a louder *thud* in the fields than you would imagine; and in the splendid October weather it is a pleasing spectacle to behold the gathering of the ruddy crop, and three or four lithe figures beating out the grain with their flails in some sheltered nook, or some grassy lane lined with cedars. When there are three flails beating together it makes lively music; and when there are four they follow each other so fast that it is a continuous roll of sound, and it requires a very steady stroke not to hit or get hit by the others. There is just room and time to get your blow in, and that is all. When one flail is upon the straw, another has just left it, another is half-way down, and the fourth is high and straight in the air. It is like a swiftly revolving wheel that delivers four blows at each revolution. Threshing, like mowing, goes much easier in company than when alone; yet many a farmer or laborer spends nearly all the late fall and winter days shut in the barn, pounding doggedly upon the endless sheaves of oats and rye.

When the farmers made "bees," as they did a generation or two ago much more than they do now, a picturesque element was added. There was the stone bee, the husking bee, the "raising," the "moving," etc. When the carpenters had got the timbers of the house or barn ready, and the foundation was prepared, then the neighbors for miles about were invited to come to the "raisin'." The afternoon was the time chosen. The forenoon was occupied by the carpenter and farm hands in putting the sills and "sleepers" in place ("sleepers," what a good name for those rude hewn timbers that lie under the floor in the darkness and silence!). When the hands arrived, the great beams and posts and joists and braces were carried to their place on the platform, and the first "bent," as it was called, was put together and pinned by oak pins that the boys brought. Then pike poles are distributed, the men, fifteen or twenty of them, arranged in a line abreast of the bent; the boss carpenter steadies and guides the corner post and gives the word of command, — "Take holt, boys!" "Now, set her up!" "Up with her!" "Up she goes!" When it gets shoulder high it becomes heavy, and there is a pause. The pikes are brought into requisition; every man gets a good hold and braces himself, and waits for the words. "All together now"; shouts the captain, "Heave her up!" "He-o-he!" (heave all, — heave), "he-o-he," at the top of his voice, every man doing his best. Slowly the great timbers go up; louder grows the word of command, till the bent is up. Then it is plumbed and stay-lathed, and another is put together and raised in the same way, till they are all up. Then comes the putting on the great plates, — timbers that run lengthwise of the building and match the sills below. Then, if there is time, the putting up of the rafters. In every neighborhood there was always some man who was especially useful at "raisin's." He was bold and strong and quick. He helped guide and superintend the work. He was the first one up on the bent, catching a pin or a brace and putting it in place. He walked the lofty and perilous plate, with the great beetle in hand; put the pins in the holes, and, swinging the heavy instrument through the air, drove the pins home. He was as much at home up there as a squirrel.

Now that balloon frames are mainly used for houses, and lighter sawed timbers for barns, the old-fashioned raising is rarely witnessed.

Then the moving was an event, too. A farmer had a barn to move, or wanted to build a new house on the site of the old one, and the latter must be drawn to one side. Now this work is done with pulleys and rollers by a few men and a horse; then the building was drawn by sheer bovine strength. Every man that had a yoke of cattle in the country round about was invited to assist. The barn or house was pried up and great runners, cut in the woods, placed under it, and under the runners were placed skids. To these runners it was securely chained and pinned; then the cattle — stags, steers, and oxen, in two long lines, one at each runner — were hitched fast, and, while men and boys aided with great levers, the word to go was given. Slowly the two lines of bulky cattle straightened and settled into their bows; the big chains that wrapped the runners tightened, a dozen or more "gads" were flourished, a dozen or more lusty throats urged their teams at the top of their voices, when there was a creak or a groan as the building stirred. Then the drivers redoubled their efforts; there was a perfect Babel of discordant sounds; the oxen bent to the work, their eyes bulged, their nostrils distended; the lookers-on cheered, and away went the old house or barn as nimbly as a boy on a handsled. Not always, however; sometimes the chains would break, or one runner strike a rock, or bury itself in the earth. There were generally enough mishaps or delays to make it interesting.

In the section of the State of which I write, flax used to be grown, and cloth for shirts and trousers, and towels and sheets, etc., woven from it. It was no laughing matter for the farm-boy to break in his shirt or trousers those days. The hair shirts in which the old monks used to mortify the flesh could not have been much before them in this mortifying particular. But after the bits of shives and sticks were subdued, and the knots humbled by use and the washboard, they were good garments. If you lost your hold in a tree and your shirt caught on a knot or limb, it would save you.

But when has any one seen a crackle, or a swingling-knife, or a hetchel, or a distaff, and where can one get some tow for strings or for gun-wadding, or some swingling-tow for a bonfire? The quill-wheel, and the spinning-wheel, and the loom are heard no more among us. The last I knew of a certain hetchel, it was nailed up behind the old sheep that did the churning; and when he was disposed to shirk or hang back and stop the machine, it was always ready to spur him up in no uncertain manner. The old loom became a hen-roost in an out-building; and the crackle upon which the flax was broken, — where, oh, where is it?

When the produce of the farm was taken a long distance to market, — that was an event, too; the carrying away of the butter in the fall, for instance, to the river, a journey that occupied both ways four days. Then the family marketing was done in a few groceries. Some cloth, new caps and boots for the boys, and a dress, or a shawl, or a cloak for the girls were brought back, besides news and adventure, and strange tidings of the distant world. The farmer was days in getting ready to start; food was prepared and put in a box to stand him on the journey, so as to lessen the hotel expenses, and oats put up for the horses. The butter was loaded up overnight, and in the cold November morning, long before it was light, he was up and off. I seem to hear the wagon yet, its slow rattle over the frozen ground diminishing in the distance. On the fourth day toward night all grew expectant of his return, but it was usually dark before his wagon was heard coming down the hill, or his voice from before the door summoning a light. When the boys got big enough, one after the other accompanied him each year, until all had made the famous journey and seen the great river and the steamboats, and the thousand and one marvels of the far-away town. When it came my turn to go, I was in a great state of excitement for a week beforehand, for fear my clothes would not be ready, or else that it would be too cold, or else that the world would come to an end before the time fixed for starting. The day previous I roamed the woods in quest of game to supply my bill of fare on the way, and was lucky enough to shoot a partridge and an owl, though the latter I did not take. Perched high on a "springboard" I made the journey, and saw more sights and wonders than I have ever seen on a journey since, or ever expect to again.

But now all this is changed. The railroad has found its way through or near every settlement, and marvels and wonders are cheap. Still, the essential charm of the farm remains and always will remain: the care of crops, and of cattle, and of orchards, bees, and fowls; the clearing and improving of the ground; the building of barns and houses; the direct contact with the soil and with the elements; the watching of the clouds and of the weather; the privacies with nature, with bird, beast, and plant; and the close acquaintance with the heart and virtue of the world. The farmer should be the true naturalist; the book in which it is all written is open before him night and day, and how sweet and wholesome all his knowledge is!

The predominant feature of farm life in New York, as in other States, is always given by some local industry of one kind or another. In many of the high cold counties in the eastern centre of the State, this ruling industry is hop-growing; in the western, it is grain and fruit growing; in sections along the Hudson, it is small-fruit growing, as berries, currants, grapes; in other counties, it is milk and butter; in others, quarrying flagging-stone. I recently visited a section of Ulster County, where everybody seemed getting out hoop-poles and making hoops. The only talk was of hoops, hoops! Every team that went by had a load or was going for a load of hoops. The principal fuel was hoop-shavings or discarded hoop-poles. No man had any money until he sold his hoops. When a farmer went to town to get some grain, or a pair of boots, or a dress for his wife, he took a load of hoops. People stole hoops and poached for hoops, and bought, and sold, and speculated in hoops. If there was a corner it was in hoops; big hoops, little hoops, hoops for kegs, and firkins, and barrels, and hogsheads, and pipes; hickory hoops, birch hoops, ash hoops, chestnut hoops, hoops enough to go around the world. Another place it was shingle, shingle; everybody was shaving hemlock shingle.

In most of the eastern counties of the State, the interest and profit of the farm revolve about the cow. The dairy is the one great matter, — for milk, when milk can be shipped to the New York market, and for butter when it cannot. Great barns and stables and milking-sheds, and immense meadows and cattle on a thousand hills, are the prominent agricultural features of these sections of the country. Good grass and good water are the two indispensables to successful dairying. And the two generally go together. Where there are plenty of copious cold springs, there is no dearth of grass. When the cattle are compelled to browse upon weeds and various wild growths, the milk and butter will betray it in the flavor. Tender, juicy grass, the ruddy blossoming clover, or the fragrant, well-cured hay, make the delicious milk and the sweet butter. Then there is a charm about a natural pastoral country that belongs to no other. Go through Orange County in May and see the vivid emerald of the smooth fields and hills. It is a new experience of the beauty and effectiveness of simple grass. And this grass has rare virtues, too, and imparts a flavor to the milk and butter that has made them famous.

Along all the sources of the Delaware the land flows with milk, if not with honey. The grass is excellent, except in times of protracted drought, and then the browsings in the beech and birch woods are good substitute. Butter is the staple product. Every housewife is or wants to be a famous butter-maker, and Delaware County butter rivals Orange in market. It is a high, cool grazing country. The farms lie tilted up against the sides of the mountain or lapping over the hills, striped or checked with stone wall, and presenting to the eye long stretches of pasture and meadow land, alternating with plowed fields and patches of waving grain. Few of their features are picturesque; they are bare, broad, and simple. The farmhouse gets itself a coat of white paint, and green blinds to the windows, and the barn and wagonhouse a coat of red paint with white trimmings, as soon as possible. A penstock flows by the doorway, rows of tin pans sun themselves in the yard, and the great wheel of the churning machine flanks the milk-house, or rattles behind it. The winters are severe, the snow deep. The principal fuel is still wood, — beech, birch, and maple. It is hauled off the mountain in great logs when the first November or December snows come, and cut up and piled in the woodhouses and under a shed. Here the axe still rules the winter, and it may be heard all day and every day upon the woodpile, or echoing through the frost-bound wood, the coat of the chopper hanging to a limb, and his white chips strewing the snow.

Many cattle need much hay; hence in dairy sections haying is the period of "storm and stress" in the farmer's year. To get the hay in, in good condition, and before the grass gets too ripe, is a great matter. All the energies and resources of the farm are bent to this purpose. It is a thirty or forty day war, in which the farmer and his "hands" are pitted against the heat and the rain and the legions of timothy and clover. Everything about it has the urge, the hurry, the excitement of a battle. Outside help is procured; men flock in from adjoining counties, where the ruling industry is something else and is less imperative; coopers, blacksmiths, and laborers of various kinds drop their tools, and take down their scythes and go in quest of a job in haying. Every man is expected to pitch his endeavors in a little higher key than at any other kind of work. The wages are extra, and the work must correspond. The men are in the meadow by half-past four or five in the morning, and mow an hour or two before breakfast. A good mower is proud of his skill. He does not "lop in," and his "pointing out" is perfect, and you can hardly see the ribs of his swath. He stands up to his grass and strikes level and sure. He will turn a double down through the stoutest grass, and when the hay is raked away you will not find a spear left standing. The Americans are — or were — the best mowers. A foreigner could never quite give the masterly touch. The hayfield has its code. One man must not take another's swath unless he expects to be crowded. Each expects to take his turn leading the band. The scythe may be so whet as to ring out a saucy challenge to the rest. It is not good manners to mow up too close to your neighbor, unless you are trying to keep out of the way of the man behind you. Many a race has been brought on by some one being a little indiscreet in this respect. Two men may mow all day together under the impression that each is trying to put the other through. The one that leads strikes out briskly, and the other, not to be outdone, follows close. Thus the blood of each is soon up; a little heat begets more heat, and it is fairly a race before long. It is a great ignominy to be mowed out of your swath. Hay-gathering is clean, manly work all through. Young fellows work in haying who do not do another stroke on the farm the whole year. It is a gymnasium in the meadows and under the summer sky. How full of pictures, too! — the smooth slopes dotted with cocks with lengthening shadows; the great, broad-backed, soft-cheeked loads, moving along the lanes and brushing under the trees; the unfinished stack with forkfuls of hay being handed up its sides to the builder, and when finished the shape of a great pear, with a pole in the top for the stem. Maybe in the fall and winter the calves and yearlings will hover around it and gnaw its base until it overhangs them and shelters them from the storm. Or the farmer will "fodder" his cows there, — one of the most picturesque scenes to be witnessed on the farm, — twenty or thirty or forty milchers filing along toward the stack in the field, or clustered about it, waiting the promised bite. In great, green flakes the hay is rolled off, and distributed about in small heaps upon the unspotted snow. After the cattle have eaten, the birds — snow buntings and red polls — come and pick up the crumbs, the seeds of the grasses and weeds. At night the fox and the owl come for mice.

What a beautiful path the cows make through the snow to the stack or to the spring under the hill! — always more or less wayward, but broad and firm, and carved and indented by a multitude of rounded hoofs.

In fact, the cow is the true pathfinder and pathmaker. She has the leisurely, deliberate movement that insures an easy and a safe way. Follow her trail through the woods, and you have the best, if not the shortest, course. How she beats down the brush and briers and wears away even the roots of the trees! A herd of cows left to themselves fall naturally into single file, and a hundred or more hoofs are not long in smoothing and compacting almost any surface.

Indeed, all the ways and doings of cattle are pleasant to look upon, whether grazing in the pasture, or browsing in the woods, or ruminating under the trees, or feeding in the stall, or reposing upon the knolls. There is virtue in the cow; she is full of goodness; a wholesome odor exhales from her; the whole landscape looks out of her soft eyes; the quality and the aroma of miles of meadow and pasture lands are in her presence and products. I had rather have the care of cattle than be the keeper of the great seal of the nation. Where the cow is, there is Arcadia; so far as her influence prevails, there is contentment, humility, and sweet, homely life!

Blessed is he whose youth was passed upon the farm, and if it was a dairy farm his memories will be all the more fragrant. The driving of the cows to and from the pasture, every day and every season for years, — how much of summer and of nature he got into him on these journeys! What rambles and excursions did this errand furnish the excuse for! The birds and birds' nests, the berries, the squirrels, the woodchucks, the beech woods with their treasures into which the cows loved so to wander and to browse, the fragrant wintergreens and a hundred nameless adventures, all strung upon that brief journey of half a mile to and from the remote pastures. Sometimes one cow or two will be missing when the herd is brought home at night; then to hunt them up is another adventure. My grandfather went out one night to look up an absentee from the yard, when he heard something in the brush, and out stepped a bear into the path before him.

Every Sunday morning the cows were salted. The farm-boy would take a pail with three or four quarts of coarse salt, and, followed by the eager herd, go to the field and deposit the salt in handfuls upon smooth stones and rocks and upon clean places on the turf. If you want to know how good salt is, see a cow eat it. She gives the true saline smack. How she dwells upon it, and gnaws the sward and licks the stones where it has been deposited! The cow is the most delightful feeder among animals. It makes one's mouth water to see her eat pumpkins, and to see her at a pile of apples is distracting. How she sweeps off the delectable grass! The sound of her grazing is appetizing; the grass betrays all its sweetness and succulency in parting under her sickle.

The region of which I write abounds in sheep also. Sheep love high, cool, breezy lands. Their range is generally much above that of cattle. Their sharp noses will find picking where a cow would fare poorly indeed. Hence most farmers utilize their high, wild, and mountain lands by keeping a small flock of sheep. But they are the outlaws of the farm and are seldom within bounds. They make many lively expeditions for the farm-boy — driving them out of mischief, hunting them up in the mountains, or salting them on the breezy hills. Then there is the annual sheep-washing, when on a warm day in May or early June the whole herd is driven a mile or more to a suitable pool in the creek, and one by one doused and washed and rinsed in the water. We used to wash below an old grist-mill, and it was a pleasing spectacle — the mill, the dam, the overhanging rocks and trees, the round, deep pool, and the huddled and frightened sheep.

One of the features of farm life peculiar to this country, and one of the most picturesque of them all, is sugar-making in the maple woods in spring. This is the first work of the season, and to the boys is more play than work. In the Old World, and in more simple and imaginative times, how such an occupation as this would have got into literature, and how many legends and associations would have clustered around it! It is woodsy, and savors of the trees; it is an encampment among the maples. Before the bud swells, before the grass springs, before the plow is started, comes the sugar harvest. It is the sequel of the bitter frost; a sap-run is the sweet good-by of winter. It denotes a certain equipoise of the season; the heat of the day fully balances the frost of the night. In New York and New England the time of the sap hovers about the vernal equinox, beginning a week or ten days before, and continuing a week or ten days after. As the days and nights get equal, the heat and cold get equal, and the sap mounts. A day that brings the bees out of the hive will bring the sap out of the maple-tree. It is the fruit of the equal marriage of the sun and frost. When the frost is all out of the ground, and all the snow gone from its surface, the flow stops. The thermometer must not rise above 38° or 40° by day, or sink below 24° or 25° at night, with wind in the northwest; a relaxing south wind, and the run is over for the present. Sugar weather is crisp weather. How the tin buckets glisten in the gray woods; how the robins laugh; how the nuthatches call; how lightly the thin blue smoke rises among the trees! The squirrels are out of their dens; the migrating water-fowls are streaming northward; the sheep and cattle look wistfully toward the bare fields; the tide of the season, in fact, is just beginning to rise.

Sap-letting does not seem to be an exhaustive process to the trees, as the trees of a sugar-bush appear to be as thrifty and as long-lived as other trees. They come to have a maternal, large-waisted look, from the wounds of the axe or the auger, and that is about all.

In my sugar-making days, the sap was carried to the boiling-place in pails by the aid of a neck-yoke and stored in hogsheads, and boiled or evaporated in immense kettles or caldrons set in huge stone arches; now, the hogshead goes to the trees hauled upon a sled by a team, and the sap is evaporated in broad, shallow, sheet-iron pans, — a great saving of fuel and of labor.

Many a farmer sits up all night boiling his sap, when the run has been an extra good one, and a lonely vigil he has of it amid the silent trees and beside his wild hearth. If he has a sap-house, as is now so common, he may make himself fairly comfortable; and if a companion, he may have a good time or a glorious wake.

Maple-sugar in its perfection is rarely seen, perhaps never seen, in the market. When made in large quantities and indifferently, it is dark and coarse; but when made in small quantities — that is, quickly from the first run of sap and properly treated — it has a wild delicacy of flavor that no other sweet can match. What you smell in freshly cut maple-wood, or taste in the blossom of the tree, is in it. It is then, indeed, the distilled essence of the tree. Made into syrup, it is white and clear as clover-honey; and crystallized into sugar, it is pure as the wax. The way to attain this result is to evaporate the sap under cover in an enameled kettle; when reduced about twelve times, allow it to settle half a day or more; then clarify with milk or the white of an egg. The product is virgin syrup, or sugar worthy the table of the gods.

Perhaps the most heavy and laborious work of the farm in the section of the State of which I write is fence-building. But it is not unproductive labor, as in the South or West, for the fence is of stone, and the capacity of the soil for grass or grain is, of course, increased by its construction. It is killing two birds with one stone: a fence is had, the best in the world, while the available area of the field is enlarged. In fact, if there are ever sermons in stones, it is when they are built into a stone wall, — turning your hindrances into helps, shielding your crops behind the obstacles to your husbandry, making the enemies of the plow stand guard over its products. This is the kind of farming worth imitating. A stone wall with a good rock bottom will stand as long as a man lasts. Its only enemy is the frost, and it works so gently that it is not till after many years that its effect is perceptible. An old farmer will walk with you through his fields and say, "This wall I built at such and such a time, or the first year I came on the farm, or when I owned such and such a span of horses," indicating a period thirty, forty, or fifty years back. "This other, we built the summer so and so worked for me," and he relates some incident, or mishap, or comical adventures that the memory calls up. Every line of fence has a history; the mark of his plow or his crowbar is upon the stones; the sweat of his early manhood put them in place; in fact, the long black line covered with lichens and in places tottering to the fall revives long-gone scenes and events in the life of the farm.

The time for fence-building is usually between seed-time and harvest, May and June; or in fall after the crops are gathered. The work has its picturesque features — the prying of rocks; supple forms climbing or swinging from the end of the great levers, or the blasting of the rocks with powder; the hauling of them into position with oxen or horses, or with both; the picking of the stone from the greensward; the bending, athletic form of the wall-layers; the snug new fence creeping slowly up the hill or across the field, absorbing the windrow of loose stones; and, when the work is done, much ground reclaimed to the plow and the grass, and a strong barrier erected.

It is a common complaint that the farm and farm life are not appreciated by our people. We long for the more elegant pursuits, or the ways and fashions of the town. But the farmer has the most sane and natural occupation, and ought to find life sweeter, if less highly seasoned, than any other. He alone, strictly speaking, has a home. How can a man take root and thrive without land? He writes his history upon his field. How many ties, how many resources, he has — his friendships with his cattle, his team, his dog, his trees, the satisfaction in his growing crops, in his improved fields; his intimacy with nature, with bird and beast, and with the quickening elemental forces; his co-operations with the cloud, the sun, the seasons, heat, wind, rain, frost! Nothing will take the various social distempers which the city and artificial life breed out of a man like farming, like direct and loving contact with the soil. It draws out the poison. It humbles him, teaches him patience and reverence, and restores the proper tone to his system.

Cling to the farm, make much of it, put yourself into it, bestow your heart and your brain upon it, so that it shall savor of you and radiate your virtue after your day's work is done!

"Be thou diligent to know the state of thy flocks, and look well to thy herds.

"For riches are not forever; and doth the crown endure to every generation?

"The hay appeareth, and the tender grass showeth itself, and herbs of the mountains are gathered.

"The lambs are for thy clothing, and the goats are the price of the field.

"And thou shalt have goat's milk enough for thy food, for the food of thy household, and for the maintenance for thy maidens."

THE INITIATION[1]

JOSEPH CONRAD
1857–

JOSEPH CONRAD, though by birth a Pole, is one of the greatest of present-day writers in English. His novels and tales picture with singular fascination the Sea and the East. This selection is from a book called *The Mirror of the Sea*. Other good books by him are *Youth, Lord Jim, The Nigger of the Narcissus, Nostromo, Typhoon, Victory*.

THE love that is given to ships is profoundly different from the love men feel for every other work of their hands — the love they bear to their houses, for instance — because it is untainted by the pride of possession. The pride of skill, the pride of responsibility, the pride of endurance there may be, but otherwise it is a disinterested sentiment. No seaman ever cherished a ship, even if she belonged to him, merely because of the profit she put in his pocket. No one, I think, ever did; for a ship-owner, even of the best, has always been outside the pale of that sentiment embracing in a feeling of intimate, equal fellowship the ship and the man, backing each other against the implacable, if sometimes dissembled, hostility of their world of waters. The sea — this truth must be confessed — has no generosity. No display of manly qualities — courage, hardihood, endurance, faithfulness — has ever been known to touch its irresponsible consciousness of power. The ocean has the conscienceless temper of a savage autocrat spoiled by much adulation. He cannot brook the slightest appearance of defiance, and has remained the irreconcilable enemy of ships and men ever since ships and men had the unheard of audacity to go afloat

[1] From *The Mirror of the Sea*. Reprinted by permission of Doubleday, Page & Co., the owners of the copyright.

together in the face of his frown. From that day he has gone on swallowing up fleets and men without his resentment being glutted by the number of victims — by so many wrecked ships and wrecked lives. To-day, as ever, he is ready to beguile and betray, to smash and to drown the incorrigible optimism of men who, backed by the fidelity of ships, are trying to wrest from him the fortune of their house, the dominion of their world, or only a dole of food for their hunger. If not always in the hot mood to smash, he is always stealthily ready for a drowning. The most amazing wonder of the deep is its unfathomable cruelty.

I felt its dread for the first time in mid-Atlantic one day, many years ago, when we took off the crew of a Danish brig homeward-bound from the West Indies. A thin, silvery mist softened the calm and majestic splendor of light without shadows — seemed to render the sky less remote and the ocean less immense. It was one of the days when the might of the sea appears indeed lovable, like the nature of a strong man in moments of quiet intimacy. At sunrise we had made out a black speck to the westward, apparently suspended high up in the void behind a stirring, shimmering veil of silvery blue gauze that seemed at times to stir and float in the breeze which fanned us slowly along. The peace of that enchanting forenoon was so profound, so untroubled, that it seemed that every word pronounced loudly on our deck would penetrate to the very heart of that infinite mystery born from the conjunction of water and sky. We did not raise our voices. "A water-logged derelict, I think, sir," said the second officer, quietly, coming down from aloft with the binoculars in their case slung across his shoulders; and our captain, without a word, signed to the helmsman to steer for the black speck. Presently we made out a low, jagged stump sticking up forward — all that remained of her departed masts.

The captain was expatiating in a low, conversational tone to the chief mate upon the danger of these derelicts, and upon his dread of coming upon them at night, when suddenly a man forward screamed out, "There's people on board of her, sir! I see them!" in a most extraordinary voice — a voice never heard before in our ship; the amazing voice of a stranger. It gave the signal for a sudden tumult of shouts. The watch below ran up the forecastle head in a body, the cook dashed out of the galley. Everybody saw the poor fellows now. They were there. And all at once our ship, which had the well-earned name of being without a rival for speed in light winds, seemed to us to have lost the power of motion, as if the sea, becoming viscous, had clung to her sides. And yet she moved. Immensity the inseparable companion of a ship's life, chose that day to breathe upon her as gently as a sleeping child. The clamor of our excitement had died out, and our living ship, famous for never losing steerage way as long as there was air enough to float a feather, stole, without a ripple, silent and white as a ghost, towards her mutilated and wounded sister, come upon at the point of death in the sunlit haze of a calm day at sea.

With binoculars glued to his eyes, the captain said in a quavering tone: "They are waving to us with something aft there." He put down the glasses on the skylight brusquely, and began to walk about the poop. "A shirt or a flag," he ejaculated, irritably. "Can't make it out . . . Some damn rag or other!" He took a few more turns on the poop, glancing down over the rail now and then to see how fast we were moving. His nervous footsteps rang sharply in the quiet of the ship, where the other men, all looking the same way, had forgotten themselves in a staring immobility. "This will never do!" he cried out, suddenly. "Lower the boats at once! Down with them!"

Before I jumped into mine he took me aside, as being an inexperienced junior, for a word of warning.

"You look out as you come alongside that she does n't take you down with her. You understand?"

He murmured this confidentially, so that none of the men at the falls should overhear, and I was shocked. "Heavens! as if in such an emergency one stopped to think of danger!" I exclaimed to myself mentally, in scorn of such cold-blooded caution.

It takes many lessons to make a real seaman, and I got my rebuke at once. My experienced commander seemed in one searching glance to read my thoughts on my ingenuous face.

"What you 're going for is to save life, not to drown your boat's crew for nothing," he growled severely in my ear. But as we shoved off he leaned over and cried out: "It all rests on the power of your arms, men. Give way for life!"

We made a race of it, and I would never have believed that a common boat's crew of a merchantman could keep up so much determined fierceness in the regular swing of their stroke. What our captain had clearly perceived before we left had become plain to all of us since. The issue of our enterprise hung on a hair above that abyss of waters which will not give up its dead till the Day of Judgment. It was a race of two ship's boats matched against Death for a prize of nine men's lives, and Death had a long start. We saw the crew of the brig from afar working at the pumps — still pumping on that wreck, which already had settled so far down that the gentle, low swell, over which our boats rose and fell easily without a check to their speed, welling up almost level with her head-rails, plucked at the ends of broken gear swinging desolately under her naked bowsprit.

We could not, in all conscience, have picked out a better

day for our regatta had we had the free choice of all the days that ever dawned upon the lonely struggles and solitary agonies of ships since the Norse rovers first steered to the westward against the run of Atlantic waves. It was a very good race. At the finish there was not an oar's-length between the first and second boat, with Death coming in a good third on the top of the very next smooth swell, for all one knew to the contrary. The scuppers of the brig gurgled softly all together when the water rising against her sides subsided sleepily with a low wash, as if playing about an immovable rock. Her bulwarks were gone fore-and-aft, and one saw her bare deck low-lying like a raft and swept clean of boats, spars, houses — of everything except the ring-bolts and the heads of the pumps. I had one dismal glimpse of it as I braced myself up to receive upon my breast the last man to leave her, the captain, who literally let himself fall into my arms.

It had been a weirdly silent rescue — a rescue without a hail, without a single uttered word, without a gesture or a sign, without a conscious exchange of glances. Up to the very last moment those on board stuck to their pumps, which spouted two clear streams of water upon their bare feet. Their brown skin showed through the rents of their shirts; and the two small bunches of half-naked, tattered men went on bowing from the waist to one another in their back-breaking labor, up and down, absorbed, with no time for a glance over the shoulder at the help that was coming to them. As we dashed, unregarded, alongside, a voice let out one, only one hoarse howl of command, and then, just as they stood, without caps, with the salt drying gray in the wrinkles and folds of their hairy, haggard faces, blinking stupidly at us their red eyelids, they made a bolt away from the handles, tottering and jostling against one another, and positively flung themselves over upon our very heads. The clatter they made tumbling into the boats had an extraordinarily destructive effect upon the illusion of tragic dignity our self-esteem had thrown over the contests of mankind with the sea. On that exquisite day of gently breathing peace and veiled sunshine perished my romantic love to what men's imagination had proclaimed the most august aspect of nature. The cynical indifference of the sea to the merits of human suffering and courage, laid bare in this ridiculous, panic-tainted performance extorted from the dire extremity of nine good and honorable seamen, revolted me. I saw the duplicity of the sea's most tender mood. It was so because it could not help itself, but the awed respect of the early days was gone. I felt ready to smile bitterly at its enchanting charm and glare viciously at its furies. In a moment before we shoved off, I had looked coolly at the life of my choice. Its illusions were gone, but its fascinations remained. I had become a seaman at last.

We pulled hard for a quarter of an hour, then laid on our oars waiting for our ship. She was coming down on us with swelling sails, looking delicately tall and exquisitely noble through the mist. The captain of the brig, who sat in the stern-sheets by my side with his face in his hands, raised his head and began to speak with a sort of sombre volubility. They had lost their masts and sprung a leak in a hurricane; drifted for weeks, always at the pumps, met more bad weather; the ships they sighted failed to make them out, the leak gained upon them slowly, and the seas had left them nothing to make a raft of. It was very hard to see ship after ship pass by at a distance, "as if everybody had agreed that we must be left to drown," he added. But they went on trying to keep the brig afloat as long as possible, and working the pumps constantly on insufficient food, mostly raw, till "yesterday evening," he continued, monotonously, "just as the sun went down, the men's hearts broke."

He made an almost imperceptible pause here, and went on again with exactly the same intonation:

"They told me the brig could not be saved, and they thought they had done enough for themselves. I said nothing to that. It was true. It was no mutiny. I had nothing to say to them. They lay about aft all night, as still as so many dead men. I did not lie down. I kept a lookout. When the first light came I saw your ship at once. I waited for more light; the breeze began to fail on my face. Then I shouted out as loud as I was able, 'Look at that ship!' but only two men got up very slowly and came to me. At first only we three stood alone, for a long time, watching you coming down to us, and feeling the breeze drop to a calm almost; but afterwards others, too, rose, one after another, and by-and-by I had all my crew behind me. I turned round and said to them that they could see the ship was coming our way, but in this small breeze she might come too late after all, unless we turned to and tried to keep the brig afloat long enough to give you time to save us all. I spoke like that to them, and then I gave the command to man the pumps."

He gave the command, and gave the example, too, by going himself to the handles, but it seems that these men did actually hang back for a moment, looking at one another dubiously before they followed him. "He! he! he!" He broke out into a most unexpected, imbecile, pathetic, nervous little giggle. "Their hearts were broken so! They had been played with too long," he explained apologetically, lowering his eyes, and became silent.

Twenty-five years is a long time — a quarter of a century is a dim and distant past; but to this day I remember the dark-brown feet, hands, and faces of two of these men whose hearts had been broken by the sea. They were lying very still on their sides on the bottom boards between the thwarts, curled up like dogs. My boat's crew, leaning over the looms of their oars, stared and listened as if at the play. The master of the brig looked up suddenly to ask me what day it was.

They had lost the date. When I told him it was Sunday, the 22d, he frowned, making some mental calculation, then nodded twice sadly to himself, staring at nothing.

His aspect was miserably unkempt and wildly sorrowful. Had it not been for the unquenchable candor of his blue eyes, whose unhappy, tired glance every moment sought his abandoned, sinking brig, as if it could find rest nowhere else, he would have appeared mad. But he was too simple to go mad, too simple with that manly simplicity which alone can bear men unscathed in mind and body through an encounter with the deadly playfulness of the sea or with its less abominable fury.

Neither angry nor playful nor smiling, it enveloped our distant ship growing bigger as she neared us, our boats with the rescued men and the dismantled hull of the brig we were leaving behind, in the large and placid embrace of its quietness, half-lost in the fair haze, as if in a dream of infinite and faithful clemency. There was no frown, no wrinkle on its face, not a ripple. And the run of the slight swell was so smooth that it resembled the graceful undulation of a piece of shimmering gray silk shot with tender green. We pulled an easy stroke; but when the master of the brig, after a glance over his shoulder, stood up with a low exclamation, my men feathered their oars instinctively, without an order, and the boat lost her way.

He was steadying himself on my shoulder with a strong grip, while his other arm, flung up rigidly, pointed a denunciatory finger at the immense tranquillity of the ocean. After his first exclamation, which stopped the swing of our oars, he made no sound, but his whole attitude seemed to cry out an indignant "Behold!" ... I could not imagine what vision of evil had come to him. I was startled, and the amazing energy of his immobilized gesture made my heart beat faster with the anticipation of something monstrous and unsuspected. The stillness around us became crushing.

For a moment the succession of silky undulations ran on innocently. I saw each of them swell up the misty line of the horizon, far, far away beyond the derelict brig, and the next moment, with a slight, friendly toss of our boat, it had passed under us and was gone. The lulling cadence of the rise and fall, the invariable gentleness of this irresistible force, the great charm of the deep waters, warmed my breast deliciously, like the subtle poison of a love-potion. But all this lasted only a few soothing seconds before I jumped up, too, making the boat roll like the veriest landlubber.

Something startling, mysterious, hastily confused, was taking place. I watched it with incredulous and fascinated awe, as one watches the confused, swift movements of some deed of violence done in the dark. As if at a given signal, the run of the smooth undulations seemed checked suddenly around the brig. By a strange optical delusion the whole sea appeared to rise upon her in one overwhelming heave of its silky surface, where in one spot a smother of foam broke out ferociously. And then the effort subsided. It was all over, and the smooth swell ran on as before from the horizon in uninterrupted cadence of motion, passing under us with a slight, friendly toss of our boat. Far away, where the brig had been, an angry white stain undulating on the surface of steely-gray waters, shot with gleams of green, diminished swiftly, without a hiss, like a patch of pure snow melting in the sun. And the great stillness after this initiation into the sea's implacable hate seemed full of dread thoughts and shadows of disaster.

A NIGHT AMONG THE PINES [1]
ROBERT LOUIS STEVENSON

THIS is a chapter from *Travels with a Donkey* — 1879, a small book of great distinction which deals delightfully with the author's wanderings in the mountains of central France.

FROM Bleymard after dinner, although it was already late, I set out to scale a portion of the Lozère. An ill-marked stony drove-road guided me forward; and I met nearly half-a-dozen bullock-carts descending from the woods, each laden with a whole pine-tree for the winter's firing. At the top of the woods, which do not climb very high upon this cold ridge, I struck leftward by a path among the pines, until I hit on a dell of green turf, where a streamlet made a little spout over some stones to serve me for a water-tap. 'In a more sacred or sequestered bower . . . nor nymph nor faunus haunted.' The trees were not old, but they grew thickly round the glade: there was no outlook, except north-eastward upon distant hill-tops, or straight upward to the sky; and the encampment felt secure and private like a room. By the time I had made my arrangements and fed Modestine, the day was already beginning to decline. I buckled myself to the knees into my sack and made a hearty meal; and as soon as the sun went down, I pulled my cap over my eyes and fell asleep.

Night is a dead monotonous period under a roof; but in the open world it passes lightly, with its stars and dews and perfumes, and the hours are marked by changes in the face of Nature. What seems a kind of temporal death to people choked between walls and curtains, is only a light and living

[1] Reprinted from *Travels with a Donkey* by permission of the publishers, Charles Scribner's Sons.

slumber to the man who sleeps afield. All night long he can hear Nature breathing deeply and freely; even as she takes her rest, she turns and smiles; and there is one stirring hour unknown to those who dwell in houses, when a wakeful influence goes abroad over the sleeping hemisphere, and all the outdoor world are on their feet. It is then that the cock first crows, not this time to announce the dawn, but like a cheerful watchman speeding the course of night. Cattle awake on the meadows; sheep break their fast on dewy hillsides, and change to a new lair among the ferns; and houseless men, who have lain down with the fowls, open their dim eyes and behold the beauty of the night.

At what inaudible summons, at what gentle touch of Nature, are all these sleepers thus recalled in the same hour to life? Do the stars rain down an influence, or do we share some thrill of mother earth below our resting bodies? Even shepherds and old country-folk, who are the deepest read in these arcana, have not a guess as to the means or purpose of this nightly resurrection. Towards two in the morning they declare the thing takes place; and neither know nor inquire further. And at least it is a pleasant incident. We are disturbed in our slumber only, like the luxurious Montaigne, 'that we may the better and more sensibly relish it.' We have a moment to look upon the stars. And there is a special pleasure for some minds in the reflection that we share the impulse with all outdoor creatures in our neighborhood, that we have escaped out of the Bastille of civilisation, and are become, for the time being, a mere kindly animal and a sheep of Nature's flock.

When that hour came to me among the pines, I wakened thirsty. My tin was standing by me half full of water. I emptied it at a draught; and feeling broad awake after this internal cold aspersion, sat upright to make a cigarette. The stars were clear, coloured, and jewel-like, but not frosty.

A faint silvery vapour stood for the Milky Way. All around me the black fir-points stood upright and stock-still. By the whiteness of the pack-saddle, I could see Modestine walking round and round at the length of her tether; I could hear her steadily munching at the sward; but there was not another sound, save the indescribable quiet talk of the runnel over the stones. I lay lazily smoking and studying the colour of the sky, as we call the void of space, from where it showed a reddish grey behind the pines to where it showed a glossy blue-black between the stars. As if to be more like a pedlar, I wear a silver ring. This I could see faintly shining as I raised or lowered the cigarette; and at each whiff the inside of my hand was illuminated, and became for a second the highest light in the landscape.

A faint wind, more like a moving coolness than a stream of air, passed down the glade from time to time; so that even in my great chamber the air was being renewed all night long. I thought with horror of the inn at Chasseradès and the congregated nightcaps; with horror of the nocturnal prowesses of clerks and students, of hot theatres and pass-keys and close rooms. I have not often enjoyed a more serene possession of myself, nor felt more independent of material aids. The outer world, from which we cower into our houses, seemed after all a gentle habitable place; and night after night a man's bed, it seemed, was laid and waiting for him in the fields, where God keeps an open house. I thought I had rediscovered one of those truths which are revealed to savages and hid from political economists; at the least, I had discovered a new pleasure for myself. And yet even while I was exulting in my solitude I became aware of a strange lack. I wished a companion to lie near me in the starlight, silent and not moving, but ever within touch. For there is a fellowship more quiet even than solitude, and which, rightly understood, is solitude made perfect. And to live out of doors with the woman a man loves is of all lives the most complete and free.

As I thus lay, between content and longing, a faint noise stole towards me through the pines. I thought, at first, it was the crowing of cocks or the barking of dogs at some very distant farm; but steadily and gradually it took articulate shape in my ears, until I became aware that a passenger was going by upon the high-road in the valley, and singing loudly as he went. There was more of good-will than grace in his performance; but he trolled with ample lungs; and the sound of his voice took hold upon the hillside and set the air shaking in the leafy glens. I have heard people passing by night in sleeping cities; some of them sang; one, I remember, played loudly on the bagpipes. I have heard the rattle of a cart or carriage spring up suddenly after hours of stillness, and pass, for some minutes, within the range of my hearing as I lay abed. There is a romance about all who are abroad in the black hours, and with something of a thrill we try to guess their business. But here the romance was double: first, this glad passenger, lit internally with wine, who sent up his voice in music through the night; and then I, on the other hand, buckled into my sack, and smoking alone in the pine-woods between four and five thousand feet towards the stars.

When I awoke again (Sunday, 29th September), many of the stars had disappeared; only the stronger companions of the night still burned visibly overhead; and away towards the east I saw a faint haze of light upon the horizon, such as had been the Milky Way when I was last awake. Day was at hand. I lit my lantern, and by its glow-worm light put on my boots and gaiters; then I broke up some bread for Modestine, filled my can at the water-tap, and lit my spirit-lamp to boil myself some chocolate. The blue darkness lay long in the glade where I had so sweetly slumbered; but soon there was a broad streak of orange melting into gold along the mountain-tops of Vivarais. A solemn glee possessed my mind at this gradual and lovely coming in of day. I heard the runnel with delight; I looked round me for something beautiful and unexpected; but the still black pine-trees, the hollow glade, the munching ass, remained unchanged in figure. Nothing had altered but the light, and that, indeed, shed over all a spirit of life and of breathing peace, and moved me to a strange exhilaration.

I drank my water-chocolate, which was hot if it was not rich, and strolled here and there, and up and down about the glade. While I was thus delaying, a gush of steady wind, as long as a heavy sigh, poured direct out of the quarter of the morning. It was cold, and set me sneezing. The trees near at hand tossed their black plumes in its passage; and I could see the thin distant spires of pine along the edge of the hill rock slightly to and fro against the golden east. Ten minutes after, the sunlight spread at a gallop along the hillside, scattering shadows and sparkles, and the day had come completely.

I hastened to prepare my pack, and tackle the steep ascent that lay before me, but I had something on my mind. It was only a fancy; yet a fancy will sometimes be importunate. I had been most hospitably received and punctually served in my green caravanserai. The room was airy, the water excellent, and the dawn had called me to a moment. I say nothing of the tapestries or the inimitable ceiling, nor yet of the view which I commanded from the windows; but I felt I was in some one's debt for all this liberal entertainment. And so it pleased me, in a half-laughing way, to leave pieces of money on the turf as I went along, until I had left enough for my night's lodging. I trust they did not fall to some rich and churlish drover.

A RIVER REVERIE [1]

LAFCADIO HEARN

1850-1904

A DESCRIPTIVE sketch written in 1882 when Hearn was a reporter in New Orleans, and later published in *Fantastics and Other Fancies*. Hearn's prose is remarkable for its movement and color. His temper and method were particularly adapted to the portrayal of vivid beauty and exotic charm; and he was most at home in the warm South, or in Japan. Of his earlier books *Chita* and *Youma* are notable; among the fruits of a Japanese residence are *Glimpses of Unfamiliar Japan, Out of the East, Gleanings in Buddha-Fields, In Ghostly Japan*.

AN old Western river port, lying in a wrinkle of the hills, — a sharp slope down to the yellow water, glowing under the sun like molten bronze, — a broken hollow square of buildings framing it in, whose basements had been made green by the lipping of water during inundations periodical as the rising of the Nile, — a cannonade-rumble of drays over the boulders, and muffled-drum thumping of cotton bales, — white signs black-lettered with names of steamboat companies, and the green latticework of saloon doors flanked by empty kegs, — above, church spires cutting the blue, — below, on the slope, hogsheads, bales, drays, cases, boxes, barrels, kegs, mules, wagons, policemen, loungers, and roustabouts, whose apparel is at once as picturesque, as ragged, and as colorless as the fronts of their favorite haunts on the water-front. Westward the purple of softly-rolling hills beyond the flood, through a diaphanous veil of golden haze, — a marshaled array of white boats with arabesque lightness of painted woodwork, and a long and irregular line of smoking chimneys. The scene never varied save with the varying tints of weather and season. Sometimes the hills

[1] Reprinted by arrangement with Houghton Mifflin Company.

were gray through an atmosphere of rain, — sometimes they vanished altogether in an autumn fog; but the port never changed. And in summer or spring, at the foot of the iron stairway leading up to a steamboat agency in the great middle building facing the river, there was a folding stool — which no one ever tried to steal — which even the most hardened wharf thieves respected, — and on that stool, at the same hour every day, a pleasant-faced old man with a very long white beard used to sit. If you asked anybody who it was, the invariable reply was: "Oh! that's old Captain ——; used to be in the New Orleans trade; — had to give up the river on account of rheumatism; — comes down every day to look at things."

Wonder whether the old captain still sits there of bright afternoons, to watch the returning steamers panting with their mighty run from the Far South, — or whether he has sailed away upon that other river, silent and colorless as winter's fog, to that vast and shadowy port where much ghostly freight is discharged from vessels that never return? He haunts us sometimes, — even as he must have been haunted by the ghosts of dead years.

When some great white boat came in, uttering its long, wild cry of joy after its giant race of eighteen hundred miles, to be reëchoed by the hundred voices of the rolling hills, — surely the old man must have dreamed upon his folding stool of marvelous nights upon the Mississippi, — nights filled with the perfume of orange blossoms under a milky palpitation of stars in amethystine sky, and witchery of tropical moonlight.

The romance of river-life is not like the romance of the sea, — that romance memory evokes for us in the midst of the city by the simple exhalations of an asphalt pavement under the sun, — divine saltiness, celestial freshness, the wild joy of wind-kissed waves, the hum of rigging and crackling of cordage, the rocking as of a mighty cradle. But it is perhaps sweeter. There is no perceptible motion of the river vessel; it is like the movement of a balloon, so steady that not we but the world only seems to move. Under the stars there seems to unroll its endlessness like an immeasurable ribbon of silver-purple. There is a noiseless ripple in it, as of watered silk. There is a heavy, sweet smell of nature, of luxuriant verdure; the feminine outlines of the hills, dotted with the chrome-yellow of window-lights, are blue-black; the vast arch of stars blossoms overhead; there is no sound but the colossal breathing of the laboring engines; the stream widens; the banks lessen; the heavens seem to grow deeper, the stars whiter, the blue bluer. Under the night it is all a blue world, as in a planet illuminated by a colored sun. The calls of the passing boats, sonorous as the music of vast silver trumpets, ring out clear but echoless; — there are no hills to give ghostly answer. Days are born in gold and die in rose-color; and the stream widens, widens, broadens toward the eternity of the sea under the eternity of the sky. We sail out of Northern frosts into Southern lukewarmness, into the luxuriant and somnolent smell of magnolias and lemon-blossoms, — the sugar-country exhales its incense of welcome. And the giant crescent of lights, the stream-song of joyous boats, the world of chimneys, the forests of spars, the burst of morning glory over New Orleans, viewed from the deck of a pilot-house. . . .

These may never be wholly forgotten; after the lapse of fifty years in some dusty and dreary inland city, an odor, an echo, a printed name may resurrect their recollection, fresh as one of those Gulf winds that leave sweet odors after them, like coquettish women, like Talmudic angels.

So that we beheld all these things yesterday and heard all these dead voices once more; saw the old Western port with its water-beslimed warehouses, and the Kentucky hills beyond the river, and the old captain on his folding stool, gazing wistfully at the boats; so that we heard once more the steam whistles of vessels that have long ceased to be, or that, changed into floating wharves, rise and fall with the flood, like corpses.

And all because there came an illustrious visitor to us, who reminded us of all these things; having once himself turned the pilot's wheel, through weird starlight or magical moonshine, gray rain or ghostly fog, golden sun or purple light, — down the great river from Northern frosts to tepid Southern winds, — and up the mighty stream into the misty North again.

To-day his name is a household word in the English-speaking world; his thoughts have been translated into other tongues; his written wit creates mirth at once in Paris salons and in New Zealand homes. Fortune has also extended to him her stairway of gold; and he has hobnobbed much with the great ones of the world. But there is still something of the pilot's cheery manner in his greeting, and the keenness of the pilot's glance in his eyes, and a looking out and afar off, as of the man who of old was wont to peer into the darkness of starless nights, with the care of a hundred lives on his hands.

He has seen many strange cities since that day, — sailed upon many seas, — studied many peoples, — written many wonderful books.

Yet, now that he is in New Orleans again, one cannot help wondering whether his heart does not sometimes prompt him to go to the river, like that old captain of the far Northwestern port, to watch the white boats panting at the wharves, and listen to their cries of welcome or farewell, and dream of nights beautiful, silver-blue, and silent, — and the great Southern moon peering into a pilot-house.

OF TRAVEL
FRANCIS BACON

TRAVEL, in the younger sort, is a part of education; in the elder, a part of experience. He that travelleth into a country before he hath some entrance into the language, goeth to school, and not to travel. That young men travel under some tutor, or grave servant, I allow well; so that he be such a one that hath the language and hath been in the country before; whereby he may be able to tell them what things are worthy to be seen in the country where they go; what acquaintances they are to seek; what exercises or discipline the place yieldeth. For else young men shall go hooded, and look abroad little. It is a strange thing that in sea-voyages, where there is nothing to be seen but sky and sea, men should make diaries; but in land-travel, wherein so much is to be observed, for the most part they omit it; as if chance were fitter to be registered than observation. Let diaries, therefore, be brought in use. The things to be seen and observed are: the courts of princes, specially when they give audience to ambassadors; the courts of justice, while they sit and hear causes; and so of consistories ecclesiastic; the churches and monasteries, with the monuments which are therein extant; the walls and fortifications of cities and towns, and so the havens and harbours; antiquities and ruins; libraries; colleges, disputations, and lectures, where any are; shipping and navies; houses and gardens of state and pleasure, near great cities; armories; arsenals; magazines; exchanges; burses; warehouses; exercises of horsemanship, fencing, training of soldiers, and the like; comedies, such whereunto the better sort of persons do resort; treasuries of jewels and robes; cabinets and rarities; and, to conclude, whatsoever is memorable in the places where they go. After all which the tutors or servants ought to make diligent enquiry. As for triumphs, masques, feasts, weddings, funerals, capital executions, and such shews, men need not to be put in mind of them; yet are they not to be neglected. If you will have a young man to put his travel into a little room, and in short time to gather much, this you must do. First, as was said, he must have some entrance into the language before he goeth. Then he must have such a servant or tutor, as knoweth the country, as was likewise said. Let him carry with him also some card or book describing the country where he travelleth; which will be a good key to his enquiry. Let him keep also a diary. Let him not stay long in one city or town; more or less as the place deserveth, but not long; nay, when he stayeth in one city or town, let him change his lodging from one end and part of the town to another; which is a great adamant of acquaintance. Let him sequester himself from the company of his countrymen, and diet in such places where there is good company of the nation where he travelleth. Let him, upon his removes from one place to another, procure recommendation to some person of quality residing in the place whither he removeth; that he may use his favour in those things he desireth to see or know. Thus he may abridge his travel with much profit. As for the acquaintance which is to be sought in travel; that which is most of all profitable is acquaintance with the secretaries and employed men of ambassadors; for so in travelling in one country he shall suck the experience of many. Let him also see and visit eminent persons in all kinds, which are of great name abroad; that he may be able to tell how the life agreeth with the fame. For quarrels, they are with care and discretion to be avoided: they are commonly for mistresses, healths, place, and words. And let a man beware how he keepeth company with choleric and quarrelsome persons; for they will engage him into their own quarrels. When a traveller returneth home, let him not leave the countries where he hath travelled altogether behind him, but maintain a correspondence by letters with those of his acquaintance which are of most worth. And let his travel appear rather in his discourse than in his apparel or gesture; and in his discourse, let him be rather advised in his answers than forwards to tell stories; and let it appear that he doth not change his country manners for those of foreign parts, but only prick in some flowers of that he hath learned abroad into the customs of his own country.

AN ENGLISH VILLAGE[1]

TICKNER EDWARDES

1865–

THIS extract is from *Lift-Luck on Southern Roads*, a very entertaining and sympathetic account of a walking tour through the southern counties of England. Mr. Edwardes has also written *The Lore of the Honey-bee*, *Neighborhood*, and *The Honey-Star*.

To spend an hour in Winterslow, and never once think of Hazlitt, or the Lambs, must seem little short of a crime to the literary reader. But that is what happened to me, and will probably happen again, if ever I retrace that day's tortuous route. The truth is that Winterslow puts the wayfarer under an immediate and all-sufficing spell of its own. There is a present-day enchantment in the place that annihilates all thought of times foregone. The living people there are so engrossingly attractive, that it never occurs to you to ponder over the dead ones, famous or obscure. It is a vortex of rural peace and quiet, or rather a dimple in the pool, just serving to mark the vital difference between progress and stagnation

I came into the beautiful, old-world settlement of Winterslow well prepared, as the overture prepares one for grand opera. In a field not far from the village, some sheep were folded; and, stopping to listen to the bells, I was immediately struck by the pureness of their tone. The ordinary sheep-bell is a kind of inverted brazen can, but the bells of this fold were real bells, both in shape and quality. The bells on a farm usually belong to the shepherd, and are handed down from father to son in the common calling. Some sets

[1] From *Lift-Luck on Southern Roads*. Reprinted by arrangement with The Macmillan Company.

are of great age, as I judged these to be. But there was no shepherd to inquire of. The fold was in charge of a shaggy grey dog, who, though he looked as if he were full of information, failed to enlighten me, mainly because I could not understand his thunderous speech. However, I made out that he warned me to come no nearer, so I contented myself with leaning over the gate, and listening to the wayward melody of the fold.

Silvery and slow in the noontide sun, the sound crept over to me, and I thought I had never heard a sweeter strain. The notes ran through a full octave, up and down; now in clanging peals of a score together, and now in single tones like bells moved at random by the inconstant breeze. And there was a sort of rhythm through it all, almost a meaning. There were sudden, clear harmonies, and pell-mell discords following them. Once, and for a long time, it seemed, all the bells stopped together, while one of the deepest tolled as regularly as if the sexton himself were at his rope. And then all the bells came swinging in together, the rich quiet notes overreaching one another like floodtide ripples on a sandy shore. I turned at last, and went on to the village. But the soft pealing stayed in my ears: in fancy it returned to me all through the day. And again, in fancy, I heard it far off, as silvery and slow as ever, when I woke in the night, walled up in the queerest, cosiest nesting-place that ever poor vagrant chanced upon. But of that in its place.

My first impression of Winterslow was as of a wide-spreading flower-garden dotted over with gigantic brown toadstools, and here and there a bee-hive fancifully shaped like a house. But, on a nearer view, the toy-houses became veritable human dwellings, and the toadstools real cottages hiding under their thatch. Yet my early conception of the place as a garden remained to the end. In the hour I spent there, I saw more and finer flowers than I looked upon at any other spot in the five counties. Every cottage stood in its patch of rich-hued autumn blossom. The sprawling scarlet of virginia-creeper decked the walls. Ruddy apples shone aloft in the trees. The favourite pampas-grass lit many a nook with its cool silver. Roses met the eye at every turn in make-believe of June. Before I had been there five minutes, I set Winterslow down as a place where it never snowed, nor gloomed, nor blew cold. I give it eternal sunshine unquestioningly, just as surely as I know that the sky above it is always of the same cloudless blue.

That was a busy hour. When I was tired of looking over garden-gates at the lavished treasure beyond, I had the smithy to inquire into. To note the changing clang of the iron as it cooled under the hammer, and learn the true voice of temper; watch the sparks flying out of the shadow, through the slant of sunshine, into shadow again; hearken to the wheezy bellows, the growl of the fire, the competition of uxorious sparrows on the roof.

Then there was a little red house, half private dwelling, half work-shop. The shop was carpeted in shavings, full of a green light from ivy-cumbered window-panes, and pervaded by a serious old man, who quietly hammered at a bench. He was not in the least perturbed when I came and silently looked in upon him like a village urchin. I said, after a while, by way of greeting, that it was good work, this — the contriving and fashioning in wood; and he replied that it was indeed so, provided that a man could get enough of it whereby to live. Then we went partnership in a full five minutes of congenial silence, broken only by the tap of his hammer as he fed it with slender, shining brass-brads. It was a work-box, or some such woman's trifle, that he was engaged upon. I watched it grow together under his deft fingers, helping him with mute commendation until he had got it into final shape. And then he conveyed to me that he was glad of my assistance, by reaching me down a rose from a glass on the window-sill. "I never like to have them out of mind," said he, polishing busily.

I looked in at cottage-doors, with discreet and private eye, in passing; and browsed a while on the labels in the windows of the village shop. There were few men about, these being at their labour in the fields; but the women abounded, all the older ones wearing the print sun-bonnet, last vestige of the national peasant costume. I have often wondered at the strange coincidence, yet it is nevertheless a fact that I never come into a village but I hit upon the one precious half-hour of the day, when the women lay by work for a chat at the cottage-door, or flying interchange of news across the street. So it again happened in Winterslow.

They were all merrily at it as I sauntered through, leaning out of window or door, or gathered in little companies by the garden-gates. And while I stood listening to the murmur of voices, soft or shrill, the school-door burst open like a dam, and a rush of pinafores, pink and white and blue, all but swept me off my feet. I turned eastward from Winterslow at last, with my rose nodding from my buttonhole, and in my ears a medley of music — bells and hammer, the chippering of sparrows and children, the sugared indolence of Wiltshire country-speech.

MY FIRST DAY IN THE ORIENT [1]
LAFCADIO HEARN

... THE first charm of Japan is intangible and volatile as a perfume. It began for me with my first kuruma-ride out of the European quarter of Yokohama into the Japanese town; and so much as I can recall of it is hereafter set down.

It is with the delicious surprise of the first journey through Japanese streets — unable to make one's kuruma-runner understand anything but gestures, frantic gestures to roll on anywhere, everywhere, since all is unspeakably pleasurable and new — that one first receives the real sensation of being in the Orient, in this Far East so much read of, so long dreamed of, yet, as the eyes bear witness, heretofore all unknown. There is a romance even in the first full consciousness of this rather commonplace fact; but for me this consciousness is transfigured inexpressibly by the divine beauty of the day. There is some charm unutterable in the morning air, cool with the coolness of Japanese spring and wind-waves from the snowy cone of Fuji; a charm perhaps due rather to softest lucidity than to any positive tone,— an atmospheric limpidity extraordinary, with only a suggestion of blue in it, through which the most distant objects appear focussed with amazing sharpness. The sun is only pleasantly warm; the jinrikisha, or kuruma, is the most cosy little vehicle imaginable; and the street-vistas, as seen above the dancing white mushroom-shaped hat of my sandalled runner, have an allurement of which I fancy that I could never weary.

[1] From *Glimpses of Unfamiliar Japan*. Reprinted by arrangement with Houghton Mifflin Company.

Elfish everything seems; for everything as well as everybody is small, and queer, and mysterious: the little houses under their blue roofs, the little shop-fronts hung with blue, and the smiling little people in their blue costumes. The illusion is only broken by the occasional passing of a tall foreigner, and by divers shop-signs bearing announcements in absurd attempts at English. Nevertheless such discords only serve to emphasize reality; they never materially lessen the fascination of the funny little streets.

'T is at first a delightfully odd confusion only, as you look down one of them, through an interminable flutter of flags and swaying of dark blue drapery, all made beautiful and mysterious with Japanese or Chinese lettering. For there are no immediately discernible laws of construction or decoration: each building seems to have a fantastic prettiness of its own; nothing is exactly like anything else, and all is bewilderingly novel. But gradually, after an hour passed in the quarter, the eye begins to recognise in a vague way some general plan in the construction of these low, light, queerly-gabled wooden houses, mostly unpainted, with their first storeys all open to the street, and thin strips of roofing sloping above each shop-front, like awnings, back to the miniature balconies of paper-screened second storeys. You begin to understand the common plan of the tiny shops, with their matted floors well raised above the street level, and the general perpendicular arrangement of sign-lettering, whether undulating on drapery or glimmering on gilded and lacquered sign-boards. You observe that the same rich dark blue which dominates in popular costume rules also in shop draperies, though there is a sprinkling of other tints, — bright blue and white and red (no greens or yellows). And then you note also that the dresses of the labourers are lettered with the same wonderful lettering as the shop draperies. No arabesques could produce such an effect. As modified for decorative purposes, these ideographs have a speaking symmetry which no design without a meaning could possess. As they appear on the back of a workman's frock — pure white on dark blue — and large enough to be easily read at a great distance (indicating some guild or company of which the wearer is a member or employee), they give to the poor cheap garment a factitious appearance of splendour.

And finally, while you are still puzzling over the mystery of things, there will come to you like a revelation the knowledge that most of the amazing picturesqueness of these streets is simply due to the profusion of Chinese and Japanese characters in white, black, blue, or gold, decorating everything, — even surfaces of doorposts and paper screens. Perhaps, then, for one moment, you will imagine the effect of English lettering substituted for those magical characters; and the mere idea will give to whatever æsthetic sentiment you may possess a brutal shock, and you will become, as I have become, an enemy of the Romaji-Kwai, — that society founded for the ugly utilitarian purpose of introducing the use of English letters in writing Japanese.

. . . .

My kurumaya calls himself "Cha." He has a white hat which looks like the top of an enormous mushroom; a short blue wide-sleeved jacket; blue drawers, close-fitting as "tights," and reaching to his ankles; and light straw sandals bound upon his bare feet with cords of palmetto-fibre. Doubtless he typifies all the patience, endurance, and insidious coaxing powers of his class. He has already manifested his power to make me give him more than the law allows; and I have been warned against him in vain. For the first sensation of having a human being for a horse, trotting between shafts, unwearyingly bobbing up and down before you for hours, is alone enough to evoke a feeling of compassion. And when this human being, thus trotting between shafts with all his hopes, memories, sentiments, and comprehensions, happens to have the gentlest smile, and the power to return the least favour by an apparent display of infinite gratitude, this compassion becomes sympathy, and provokes unreasoning impulses to self-sacrifice. I think the sight of the profuse perspiration has also something to do with the feeling, for it makes one think of the cost of heart-beats and muscle-contractions, likewise of chills, congestions, and pleurisy. Cha's clothing is drenched; and he mops his face with a small sky-blue towel, with figures of bamboo-sprays and sparrows in white upon it, which towel he carries wrapped about his wrist as he runs.

That, however, which attracts me in Cha — Cha considered not as a motive power at all, but as a personality — I am rapidly learning to discern in the multitudes of faces turned toward us as we roll through these miniature streets. And perhaps the supremely pleasurable impression of this morning is that produced by the singular gentleness of popular scrutiny. Everybody looks at you curiously; but there is never anything disagreeable, much less hostile in the gaze: most commonly it is accompanied by a smile or half smile. And the ultimate consequence of all these kindly curious looks and smiles is that the stranger finds himself thinking of fairyland. Hackneyed to the degree of provocation this statement no doubt is: everybody describing the sensations of his first Japanese day talks of the land as fairyland, and of its people as fairyfolk. Yet there is a natural reason for this unanimity in choice of terms to describe what is almost impossible to describe more accurately at the first essay. To find oneself suddenly in a world where everything is upon a smaller and daintier scale than with us, — a world of lesser and seemingly kindlier beings, all smiling at you as if to wish you well, — a world where all movement is slow and soft, and voices are hushed, — a world where land, life, and

MY FIRST DAY IN THE ORIENT

sky are unlike all that one has known elsewhere, — this is surely the realisation, for imaginations nourished with English folklore, of the old dream of a World of Elves.

The traveller who enters suddenly into a period of social change — especially change from a feudal past to a democratic present — is likely to regret the decay of things beautiful and the ugliness of things new. What of both I may yet discover in Japan I know not; but to-day, in these exotic streets, the old and the new mingle so well that one seems to set off the other. The line of tiny white telegraph poles carrying the world's news to papers printed in a mixture of Chinese and Japanese characters; an electric bell in some tea-house with an Oriental riddle of text pasted beside the ivory button; a shop of American sewing-machines next to the shop of a maker of Buddhist images; the establishment of a photographer beside the establishment of a manufacturer of straw sandals; all these present no striking incongruities, for each sample of Occidental innovation is set into an Oriental frame that seems adaptable to any picture. But on the first day, at least, the Old alone is new for the stranger, and suffices to absorb his attention. It then appears to him that everything Japanese is delicate, exquisite, admirable, — even a pair of common wooden chopsticks in a paper bag with a little drawing upon it; even a package of toothpicks of cherrywood, bound with a paper wrapper wonderfully lettered in three different colours; even the little sky-blue towel, with designs of flying sparrows upon it, which the jinrikisha man uses to wipe his face. The bank bills, the commonest copper coins, are things of beauty. Even the piece of plaited coloured string used by the shopkeeper in tying up your last purchase is a pretty curiosity. Curiosities and dainty objects bewilder you by their very multitude: on either side of you, wherever you turn your eyes, are countless wonderful things as yet incomprehensible.

But it is perilous to look at them. Every time you dare to look, something obliges you to buy it, — unless, as may often happen, the smiling vender invites your inspection of so many varieties of one article, each specially and all unspeakably desirable, that you flee away out of mere terror at your own impulses. The shopkeeper never asks you to buy; but his wares are enchanted, and if you once begin buying you are lost. Cheapness means only a temptation to commit bankruptcy; for the resources of irresistible artistic cheapness are inexhaustible. The largest steamer that crosses the Pacific could not contain what you wish to purchase. For, although you may not, perhaps, confess the fact to yourself, what you really want to buy is not the contents of a shop; you want the shop and the shopkeeper, and streets of shops with their draperies and their inhabitants, the whole city and the bay and the mountains begirdling it, and Fujiyama's white witchery overhanging it in the speckless sky, all Japan, in very truth, with all its magical trees and luminous atmosphere, with all its cities and towns and temples, and forty millions of the most lovable people in the universe.

TOURS [1]

HENRY JAMES
1843–1916

A Little Tour in France (1884), a book of travels, from which the following description of a French provincial city is taken, is in Henry James's most urbane and delightful manner. His great distinction was as a writer of fiction. Among his best-known books are *Roderick Hudson, The American, Daisy Miller, The Portrait of a Lady, The Ambassadors.*

I AM ashamed to begin with saying that Touraine is the garden of France; that remark has long ago lost its bloom. The town of Tours, however, has something sweet and bright, which suggests that it is surrounded by a land of fruits. It is a very agreeable little city; few towns of its size are more ripe, more complete, or, I should suppose, in better humor with themselves and less disposed to envy the responsibilities of bigger places. It is truly the capital of its smiling province; a region of easy abundance, of good living, of genial, comfortable, optimistic, rather indolent opinions. Balzac says in one of his tales that the real Tourangeau will not make an effort, or displace himself even, to go in search of a pleasure; and it is not difficult to understand the sources of this amiable cynicism. He must have a vague conviction that he can only lose by almost any change. Fortune has been kind to him; he lives in a temperate, reasonable, sociable climate, on the banks of a river which, it is true, sometimes floods the country around it, but of which the ravages appear to be so easily repaired that its aggressions may perhaps be regarded (in a region where so many good things are certain) merely as an occasion for healthy suspense. He is surrounded by fine old traditions, religious,

[1] Reprinted by arrangement with Houghton Mifflin Company.

social, architectural, culinary; and he may have the satisfaction of feeling that he is French to the core. No part of his admirable country is more characteristically national. Normandy is Normandy, Burgundy is Burgundy, Provence is Provence; but Touraine is essentially France. It is the land of Rabelais, of Descartes, of Balzac, of good books and good company, as well as good dinners and good houses. George Sand has somewhere a charming passage about the mildness, the convenient quality, of the physical conditions of central France, — "son climat souple et chaud, ses pluies abondantes et courtes." In the Autumn of 1882 the rains perhaps were less short than abundant, but when the days were fine it was impossible that anything in the way of weather could be more charming. The vineyards and orchards looked rich in the fresh, gay light; cultivation was everywhere, but everywhere it seemed to be easy. There was no visible poverty; thrift and success presented themselves as matters of good taste. The white caps of the women glittered in the sunshine and their well-made sabots clicked cheerfully on the hard, clean roads. Touraine is a land of old châteaux, — a gallery of architectural specimens and of large hereditary properties. The peasantry have less of the luxury of ownership than in most other parts of France; though they have enough of it to give them quite their share of that shrewdly conservative look which, in the little chaffering *place* of the market-town, the stranger observes so often in the wrinkled brown masks that surmount the agricultural blouse. This is, moreover, the heart of the old French monarchy; and as that monarchy was splendid and picturesque, a reflection of the splendor still glitters in the current of Loire. Some of the most striking events of French history have occurred on the banks of that river, and the soil it waters bloomed for a while with the flowering of the Renaissance. The Loire gives a great "style" to a landscape of which the features are not, as the phrase is, prominent, and carries the eye to distances even more poetic than the green horizons of Touraine. It is a very fitful stream, and is sometimes observed to run thin and expose all the crudities of its channel, — a great defect certainly in a river which is so much depended upon to give an air to the places it waters. But I speak of it as I saw it last; full, tranquil, powerful, bending in large slow curves and sending back half the light of the sky. Nothing can be finer than the view of its course which you get from the battlements and terraces of Amboise. As I looked down on it from that elevation one lovely Sunday morning, through a mild glitter of autumn sunshine, it seemed the very model of a generous beneficent stream. The most charming part of Tours is naturally the shaded quay that overlooks it, and looks across too, at the friendly faubourg of Saint Symphorien and at the terraced heights which rise above this. Indeed, throughout Touraine, it is half the charm of the Loire that you can travel beside it. The great dyke which protects it, or protects the country from it, from Blois to Angers, is an admirable road; and on the other side, as well, the highway constantly keeps it company. A wide river, as you follow a wide road, is excellent company; it heightens and shortens the way.

The inns at Tours are in another quarter, and one of them, which is midway between the town and the station, is very good. It is worth mentioning for the fact that every one belonging to it is extraordinarily polite, — so unnaturally polite as at first to excite your suspicion that the hotel has some hidden vice, so that the waiters and chambermaids are trying to pacify you in advance. There was one waiter in especial who was the most accomplished social being I have ever encountered; from morning till night he kept up an inarticulate murmur of urbanity; like the hum of a spinning-top. I may add that I discovered no dark secrets at the Hôtel de l'Univers; for it is not a secret to any traveller to-day that the obligation to partake of a lukewarm dinner in an overheated room is as imperative as it is detestable. For the rest, at Tours, there is a certain Rue Royale which has pretensions to the monumental; it was constructed a hundred years ago, and the houses, all alike, have on a moderate scale a pompous eighteenth-century look. It connects the Palais de Justice, the most important secular building in the town, with the long bridge which spans the Loire, — the spacious, solid bridge pronounced by Balzac, in "Le Curé de Tours," "one of the finest monuments of French architecture."

... The most interesting fact, to my mind, about the high-street of Tours was that as you walked toward the bridge on the right-hand *trottoir* you can look up at the house, on the other side of the way, in which Honoré de Balzac first saw the light. That violent and complicated genius was a child of the good-humored and succulent Touraine. There is something anomalous in this fact, though, if one thinks about it a little, one may discover certain correspondences between his character and that of his native province. Strenuous, laborious, constantly infelicitous in spite of his great successes, he suggests at times a very different set of influences. But he had his jovial, full-feeding side, — the side that comes out in the "Contes Drolatiques," which are the romantic and epicurean chronicle of the old manors and abbeys of this region. And he was, moreover, the product of a soil into which a great deal of history had been trodden. Balzac was genuinely as well as affectedly monarchical, and he was saturated with a sense of the past. Number 39 Rue Royale — of which the basement, like all the basements in the Rue Royale, is occupied by a shop — is not shown to the public; and I know not whether tradition designates the chamber in which the author of "Le Lys dans la Vallée" opened his eyes into the world in which he was to see and imagine such extraordinary things. If this were the case, I would willingly have crossed its threshold; not for the sake of any relic of the great novelist which it may possibly contain, nor even for that of any mystic virtue which may be supposed to reside within its walls, but simply because to look at those four modest walls can hardly fail to give one a strong impression of the force of human endeavor. Balzac, in the maturity of his vision, took in more of human life than any one, since Shakespeare, who has attempted to tell us stories about it; and the very small scene on which his consciousness dawned is one end of the immense scale that he traversed. I confess it shocked me a little to find that he was born in a house "in a row," — a house, moreover, which at the date of his birth must have been only about twenty years old. All that is contradictory. If the tenement selected for this honor could not be ancient and embrowned, it should at least have been detached.

... Tours has a garrison of five regiments, and the little red-legged soldiers light up the town. You see them stroll upon the clean, uncommercial quay, where there are no signs of navigation, not even by oar, no barrels nor bales, no loading or un-loading, no masts against the sky nor booming of steam in the air. The most active business that goes on there is that patient and fruitless angling in which the French, as the votaries of art for art, excel all other people. The little soldiers, weighed down by the contents of their enormous pockets, pass with respect from one of these masters of the rod to the other, as he sits soaking an indefinite bait in the large, indifferent stream.

A VERANDA IN THE ALCAZARIA[1]

F. HOPKINSON SMITH
1838-1915

THIS picturesque little sketch is from *Well-worn Roads of Spain, Holland, and Italy*. Besides being a painter and a traveler, Hopkinson Smith was successful as a story-writer. Other of his interesting travel books are *A White Umbrella in Mexico*, and *A Day at Laguerre's:* among his good novels are *Colonel Carter of Cartersville, Oliver Horn*, and *Kennedy Square*.

To really understand and appreciate Spanish life you must live in the streets. Not lounge through them, but sit down somewhere and keep still long enough for the ants to crawl over you, and so contemplate the people at your leisure. If you are a painter you will have every facility given you. The balconies over your head will be full of señoritas fanning lazily and peering at you through the iron gratings; the barber across the way will lay aside his half-moon basin and cross over to your side of the street and chat with you about the bull-fight of yesterday and the fiesta to-morrow, and give you all the scandal of the neighborhood before noon. The sombrerero, whose awnings are hung with great strings of black hats of all shapes and sizes, will leave his shop and watch you by the hour; and the fat, good-natured priest will stand quietly at your elbow and encourage you with such appreciative criticisms as "Muy bien." "Bonita, señor." "Bonisima."

If you keep your eyes about you, you will catch Figaro casting furtive glances at a shaded window above you, and later on a scrap of paper will come fluttering down at your feet, which the quick-witted barber covers with his foot, slyly picks up, and afterwards reads and kisses behind the

[1] Reprinted by arrangement with Houghton Mifflin Company.

half-closed curtains of his shop. So much of this sort of thing will go on during the day that you wonder what the night may bring forth.

The Alcazaria in Seville, upon the broad flags of which I spent the greater part of three days, is just such a street. It is a narrow, winding, crooked thoroughfare, shaded by great awnings stretched between the overhanging roofs, and filled with balconies holding great tropical plants, strings of black hats, festoons of gay-colored stuffs, sly peeping señoritas, fruit sellers, aguadores, donkeys, beggars, and the thousand and one things that make up Spanish life.

Before I finished my picture I had become quite an old settler, and knew what time the doctor came in, and who was sick over the way, and the name of the boy with the crutch, and the picador who lived in the rear and who strutted about on the flagging in his buckskin leggings, padded with steel springs, on the day of the bull-fight, and the story about the sad-faced girl in the window over the wine shop, whose lover was in prison.

But of course one cannot know a street at one sitting. The Alcazaria, on the morning of the first day, was to me only a Spanish street; on the morning of the second day I began to realize that it contained a window over my shoulder opening on a small veranda half hidden in flowers and palms; and on the morning of the third day I knew just the hour at which its occupant returned from mass, the shape of her head and mantilla, and could recognize her duenna at sight.

This charming Spanish beauty greatly interested me. If I accidentally caught her eye through the leaves and flowers, she would drop her lashes so quickly, and with such a half-frightened, timid look, that I immediately looked the other way for full five minutes in lieu of an apology; and I must confess that after studying her movements for three days I should as soon have thought of kissing my hand to the

Mother Superior of the convent as to this modest little maiden. I must also confess that no other señorita led me to any such conclusion in any of the other balconies about me.

On the afternoon of the third day I began final preparations for my departure, and as everybody wanted to see the picture, it was displayed in the shop of the barber because he had a good light. Then I sent his small boy for my big umbrella and for a large, unused canvas which I had stored in the wine shop at the corner, and which, with my smaller traps, he agreed to take to my lodgings; and then there was a general hand-shaking and some slight waving of white hands and handkerchiefs from the balconies over the way, in which my timid señorita did not join; and so, lighting my cigarette, I made my adios and strolled down the street to the church.

It was the hour for vespers, and the streets were filling rapidly with penitents on their way to prayers. With no definite object in view except to see the people and watch their movements, and with that sense of relief which comes over one after his day's work is done, I mingled in the throng and passed between the great swinging doors and into the wide incense-laden interior, and sat down near the door to watch the service. The dim light sifted in through the stained-glass windows and rested on the clouds of incense swung from the censers. Every now and then I heard the tinkling of the altar-bell, and the deep tones of the organ. Around me were the bowed heads of the penitents, silently telling their beads, and next me the upturned face and streaming eyes of a grief-stricken woman, whispering her sorrow to the Virgin. To the left of where I knelt was a small chapel, and, dividing me from this, an iron grating of delicate workmanship, behind which were grouped a number of people praying before a picture of the Christ. Suddenly another figure came in, kneeled, and prayed silently. It was my timid señorita, and before I was through wondering how she could come so quickly, a young priest entered and knelt immediately behind her. He was the same I had seen in the Alcazaria glancing at her window as he passed.

Fearing that I should frighten her, as I had often done before, I moved a few steps away; but she was so lovely and Madonna-like with her mantilla shading her eyes and her fan fluttering slowly like a butterfly, — now poising, now balancing, then waving and settling, — that I instinctively sought for my sketch-book to catch an outline of her pose, feeling assured that I should not be discovered. Before I had half finished she arose, slowly passed the priest, half covered him with her mantilla, and quick as thought slipped a white envelope under his prayer-book!

It was done so neatly and quickly and with such self-possession that it was some time before I recovered my equilibrium. Had I made any mistake? Could it possibly be the same demure, modest, shy señorita of the veranda, or was it not some one resembling her? All these Spanish beauties have black eyes, I thought, carry the colors of their favorite matador on their fans, and look alike. Perhaps, after all, I was mistaken.

I determined to find out.

Before she had reached the outer step of the church I had overtaken her, but her mantilla was too closely drawn for me to see her face. The duenna, however, was unmistakable, for she wore great silver hoops in her ears and an enormously high comb, and once seen was not easily forgotten; but to be quite sure, I followed along until she entered the Alcazaria, and so on to the step of her house. If she touched the old Moorish knocker and rapped, it would end it.

She lingered for a few minutes at the iron gate, chatted with her duenna, watched me across the street, kept her eyes upon me with her old saintly look, patted her attendant on the back, gently closed the gate upon the good woman, leaving her on the inside, then bent her own pretty head, pushed back her mantilla, showing her white throat, and flashing upon me from the corner of her eye the most coquettish, daring, and mischievous of glances, touched her fingertips to her lips, and vanished!

I had made no mistake except in human nature. Surely Murillo must have gone to Italy for his Madonnas. They were not in Seville, if the times have not changed.

I crossed over and had a parting chat with the barber. What about the señorita opposite who had just entered her gate? "Ah, señor! She is most lovely. She is called The Pious; but you need not look that way. She is the betrothed of the olive merchant who lives at San Juan, and who visits her every Sunday. The wedding takes place next month."

Figaro believed it. I could see it in his face. So, perhaps, did the olive merchant.

I did not.

FIFTH AVENUE[1]
FREDERICK M. SMITH

THE world is adorned with cities; and the imagination faring farther, is tempted to linger on the shining half-circle of the Boulevards, on the green and jolly Prater, in the narrow Corso, or in the orange golden Sierpes in Seville. These are all fascinating thoroughfares, full of allurements, and if some have less of the historic, they all have a great deal of the picturesque. But fine as it is to saunter in deeply storied streets, one has not to journey so far from home, and, for myself, I will place beside the best of them a ramble up Fifth Avenue on a warm day in April, or in some mellow, ripening October. The Strand, let us say, is like red Burgundy, or stout brown ale, while our own Street is golden Rüdesheimer or, at its top moments, a vintage even more sparkling from the fields of Northern France.

For a picture where is its equal? The shops — and such shops! — with fine ladies going in and out of them — and some who are not so fine; the great stream of motor vehicles; the errand boys and the clerks; the hopeful young artists with portfolios; dandies with spats and *boutonnières;* blonde, full-bosomed females, with striking clothes and flinty, watchful eyes; an occasional English-looking gentleman in loud tweeds; father, mother, and the girls from Steubenville or Kokomo; and an untold number of persons of an Israelitish cast.

Now and then you will mark a spruce oldish gentleman with white hair and moustache, and you fancy a real New

[1] From "The Pleasant Ways of Sauntering" in *The Unpopular Review*, October–December, 1918. Reprinted by the courtesy of Henry Holt.

Yorker who lives somewhere near Gramercy Park, or Washington Square, or wherever real New Yorkers do live now.

Again, have you ever noticed how, at certain happy afternoon hours, and in certain up-town precincts, bevies of young girls suddenly debouch upon the Avenue? — misses of fourteen and sixteen, wide-eyed, milk-and-rose damsels, all awake to the wonder of living! They are from the private schools in side streets; and they always walk arm in arm, some very lively and titillated, others very superior to a world that is soon to be their oyster. And always they are shepherded carefully under the eye of an oldish young woman with pince-nez. Youth is always inspiriting, and a little more so when it is feminine and innocent with a promise of beauty, and with an air of good breeding.

Another adventure that often happens on the Avenue is the seeing of a familiar face — familiar because you have seen it in the picture magazines or on the stage. With a thrill you discover that you can recognize Julia Marlowe in street clothes, or Miss Marie Tempest without grease paint. Or perhaps you see Mr. Winston Churchill leading a little boy by the hand. It is almost as if you had begun to know these celebrities personally; and you may even go the length of buying Mr. Churchill's next novel because you have once seen him peering into a shop-window.

Men and women, yes; but buildings too! — impressive shops — hotels magnificent — clubs that seem forbidding until you become a member — the gray pile of St. Patrick's; and, most beautiful architectural sight of all, the lacey white tower of St. Thomas's!

Hotels and shops! the first quite beyond most of us; the second, in part at least, for everybody.

Only the saunterer can appraise the wealth of shop-windows — the displays at the great dry-goods stores, and the florists, where the coming seasons are colored forth, whether in bunches of pale yellow primroses and broad-brimmed rose-wreathed hats, or in the flaring chrysanthemums and the soft pelts of the black fox and the lowly skunk. Such windows make patches of color to delight the eye; but it is before others that the loiterer pauses to enjoy by inspection what he usually cannot afford in reality. I do not speak of the displays of diamond merchants; the saunterer cares little for such hard stones. It is the book and print-shops that hold him longest, for here are the rare and precious things that he cannot own — the birds of Audubon, a first edition of "Boswell," the sporting pictures of John Leech.

In the art stores he finds a pretty portrait in oil done in the manner of Romney; or a group of rural characters by George Morland; or a color-print showing some high green valley with its wayside cross in the Tyrol. I am not sure but that to see pictures in this casual, very-much-by-chance fashion is not better than to own them. The eye soon fails to see that to which it is accustomed; but the idler on the Avenue has always a changing feast. And then, if he sees a print which particularly pleases him, he can go that way again and again, making a little pilgrimage, as it were, to worship at a shrine which is not continuing.

In a little less degree — it is wholly a matter of taste — he enjoys the riches of the oriental and antique shops. Here one person will delight in silk shawls embroidered with marvellous birds and golden dragons, and another in spindle-legged chairs, and another in bowls of blue porcelain; and still another in kindling jewels — topaz and emerald, or in clouded turquoise and gray-green jade. He can even play at a rapturous game that he remembers from boyhood, and choose fit ornaments for a real or an imagined sweetheart.

Speaking of America and the Orient — Grant Avenue in San Francisco is not a bad field for the saunterer. It is conventional enough not to worry the idler by demanding too sharp a look-out; but it has an atmosphere very romantic, even edging the mysterious; a savor of its own compounded of sandal-wood and musty interiors; it is gaudy and splendid and dingy by turns; the children are as sweet as the dolls in a toy-shop; the slant-eyed maidens, with their clear, faintly tinted, porcelain skins, have a certain reticent beauty and provocation; the men partake of the inward serenity of the East.

And what of Royal Street, New Orleans — place of romantic balconies? In fact, we have so many thoroughfares which make an especial appeal to the saunterer that one does not willingly leave off talking of them.

If life is a great book in which to read, then a stroll in the street of a world's city is a lively chapter; or, better, it is a sort of preface, foretelling a large part of the varied contents. And, since nowadays we must show that everything we praise has a use — or be set down as thoughtless cumberers of the ground — I contend that the educational value of sauntering is to be reckoned on. To the inquiring mind it suggests many delectable bypaths and gives a nice stimulus to the fancy. I can imagine a man seeing a copy of a Nicolas Maes or a Jan Steen in a window, and so getting curious about Dutch art. Or, who can note the cover designs of certain French masterpieces, bound in paper, without a desire to make an immediate acquaintance?

Does all this sound as if the saunterer were occupied merely with the iridescent surface of life? That is, perhaps, in the main, very true. But any thinking idler in the world's lively thoroughfares will find a great deal that sobers thought. The moralist in Fifth Avenue cannot escape knowing that its beauty and color are but inadequate cloaks for some of the seven deadly sins. He will find vanity and sinful extravagance and much wisdom about the lusts of the flesh. He will see that Mammon is the god of many, and that pleasure is their selfish aim. They pursue it regardless of the future, or of others. They are grasshoppers wasting the sunny season. They have time only for acquaintances, and do not know how to make friends. They do not relish or understand the quieter and more fundamental joys. In short they have forgotten how to walk, speed and display being their chief concerns. This moralist will see in the sumptuous caravansaries that line the street mere symbols of the evils of our present-day life, — its materiality, its instability, its love of luxury, its wastefulness, the gradual dimming of hearth fires, its lack of the finer culture. Even the hired men in uniforms, who open the doors of limousines, seem to sniff at simple folk and simple things. These hostelries are certainly very tempting, with their palatial foyers and their velvet-floored dining parlors, rich with silver, and shining with glass and white linen. But the people who frequent them — the silken women, nice artificers of beauty and the prodigal men — how much of charity and simplicity is in their hearts?

In the distance, to the East, the moralist glimpses the spider-thread of the Third Avenue El., and he remembers the sort of people who mostly journey on it. The contrast between these avenues cannot but give him pause. Is it right that there should be two such planes of living side by side, the first wilfully ignoring or looking askance at the other? So he asks himself. How specious, moreover, and insincere, seems the first in comparison with the second.

Yet I doubt if the moral contrast is so much in favor of Third Avenue. The rich are not always evil, nor the poor virtuous, as much of our sentimental modern teaching would have us believe. The poor to-day will probably be the prodigals to-morrow; and, if you go deep enough into the hearts of both, there is very little to choose between them. We are all cut from pretty much the same piece of cloth, and a shoddy piece it sometimes seems.

A bad outlook, says the moralist; and then, just as he becomes depressed, if not cynical, the fine, sweet face of a woman, or a happy old gentleman leading a child, makes the thoughtful one spy a kind of hope. Then a man in khaki, young, clean, straight, swings into sight and he must be a very despairing person who does not see that under all the superficiality of the Avenue there is much good blood coursing.

So the saunterer — who is not too stern a moralist, but rather inclined to kindliness in his philosophy, and doubtless, too, at heart a little indolent, — finds that life is, at worst, a mixed business, tragic and humorous, fascinating and inexplicable, but not necessarily desperate; and he goes on calmly, thinking that one may as well trust life as doubt it. Very probably at this stage of his cogitation he will slip into some comfortable and quiet refuge to pay extravagantly for tea or something stronger.

POLK STREET[1]
FRANK NORRIS
1870–1902

This description of a San Francisco street, and the characterization on page 343, are from a Californian story, *McTeague* (1899). Norris, who died at what seemed the beginning of his career, was the author of half a dozen novels. Two, at least — *McTeague*, and *The Octopus* — were important contributions to American fiction.

The street never failed to interest him. It was one of those cross-streets peculiar to Western cities, situated in the heart of the residence quarter, but occupied by small tradespeople who lived in the rooms above their shops. There were corner drug stores with huge jars of red, yellow, and green liquids in their windows, very brave and gay; stationers' stores, where illustrated weeklies were tacked upon bulletin boards; barber shops with cigar stands in their vestibules; sad-looking plumbers' offices; cheap restaurants, in whose windows one saw piles of unopened oysters weighted down by cubes of ice, and china pigs and cows knee deep in layers of white beans. At one end of the street McTeague could see the huge power-house of the cable line. Immediately opposite him was a great market; while farther on, over the chimney stacks of the intervening houses, the glass roof of some huge public baths glittered like crystal in the afternoon sun. Underneath him the branch post-office was opening its doors, as was its custom between two and three o'clock on Sunday afternoons. An acrid odor of ink rose upward to him. Occasionally a cable car passed, trundling heavily, with a strident whirring of jostled glass windows.

On week days the street was very lively. It woke to its

[1] From *McTeague*. Reprinted by permission of Doubleday, Page and Company, the owners of the copyright.

work about seven o'clock, at the time when the newsboys made their appearance together with the day laborers. The laborers went trudging past in a straggling file — plumbers' apprentices, their pockets stuffed with sections of lead pipe, tweezers, and pliers; carpenters, carrying nothing but their little pasteboard lunch baskets painted to imitate leather; gangs of street workers, their overalls soiled with yellow clay, their picks and long-handled shovels over their shoulders; plasterers, spotted with lime from head to foot. This little army of workers, tramping steadily in one direction, met and mingled with other toilers of a different description—conductors and "swing men" of the cable company going on duty; heavy-eyed night clerks from the drug stores on their way home to sleep; roundsmen returning to the precinct police station to make their night report, and Chinese market gardeners teetering past under their heavy baskets. The cable cars began to fill up; all along the street could be seen the shopkeepers taking down their shutters.

Between seven and eight the street breakfasted. Now and then a waiter from one of the cheap restaurants crossed from one sidewalk to the other, balancing on one palm a tray covered with a napkin. Everywhere was the smell of coffee and of frying steaks. A little later, following in the path of the day laborers, came the clerks and shop girls, dressed with a certain cheap smartness, always in a hurry, glancing apprehensively at the power-house clock. Their employers followed an hour or so later — on the cable cars for the most part — whiskered gentlemen with huge stomachs, reading the morning papers with great gravity; bank cashiers and insurance clerks with flowers in their buttonholes.

At the same time the school children invaded the street, filling the air with a clamor of shrill voices, stopping at the stationers' shops, or idling a moment in the doorways of the candy stores. For over half an hour they held possession of the sidewalks, then suddenly disappeared, leaving behind one or two stragglers who hurried along with great strides of their little thin legs, very anxious and preoccupied.

Towards eleven o'clock the ladies from the great avenue a block above Polk Street made their appearance, promenading the sidewalks leisurely, deliberately. They were at their morning's marketing. They were handsome women, beautifully dressed. They knew by name their butchers and grocers and vegetable men. From his window McTeague saw them in front of the stalls, gloved and veiled and daintily shod, the subservient provision-men at their elbows, scribbling hastily in the order books. They all seemed to know one another, these grand ladies from the fashionable avenue. Meetings took place here and there; a conversation was begun; others arrived; groups were formed; little impromptu receptions were held before the chopping blocks of butchers' stalls, or on the sidewalk, around boxes of berries and fruit.

From noon to evening the population of the street was of a mixed character. The street was busiest at that time; a vast and prolonged murmur arose — the mingled shuffling of feet, the rattle of wheels, the heavy trundling of cable cars. At four o'clock the school children once more swarmed the sidewalks, again disappearing with surprising suddenness. At six the great homeward march commenced; the cars were crowded, the laborers thronged the sidewalks, the newsboys chanted the evening papers. Then all at once the street fell quiet; hardly a soul was in sight; the sidewalks were deserted. It was supper hour. Evening began; and one by one a multitude of lights, from the demoniac glare of the druggists' windows to the dazzling blue whiteness of the electric globes, grew thick from street corner to street corner. Once more the street was crowded. Now there was no thought but for amusement. The cable cars were loaded with theatre-goers — men in high hats and young girls in furred opera cloaks. On the sidewalks were groups and couples — the plumbers' apprentices, the girls of the ribbon counters, the little families that lived on the second stories over their shops, the dressmakers, the small doctors, the harness makers — all the various inhabitants of the street were abroad, strolling idly from shop window to shop window, taking the air after the day's work. Groups of girls collected on the corners, talking and laughing very loud, making remarks upon the young men that passed them. The *tamale* men appeared. A band of Salvationists began to sing before a saloon.

Then, little by little, Polk Street dropped back to solitude. Eleven o'clock struck from the power-house clock. Lights were extinguished. At one o'clock the cable stopped, leaving an abrupt silence in the air. All at once it seemed very still. The only noises were the occasional footfalls of a policeman and the persistent calling of ducks and geese in the closed market. The street was asleep.

Day after day, McTeague saw the same panorama unroll itself. The bay window of his "Dental Parlors" was for him a point of vantage from which he watched the world go past.

KNOW THYSELF
SAMUEL JOHNSON
1709–1784

THIS paper — No. 24 of *The Rambler* — was written in 1750. We are so familiar with certain well-known essays *about* Johnson that it may be well to be reminded that he himself was no mean writer; that he had a clear and vigorous style, and knew a great deal about human nature.

AMONG the precepts, or aphorisms, admitted by general consent, and inculcated by frequent repetition, there is none more famous among the masters of ancient wisdom, than that compendious lesson, *Be acquainted with thyself;* ascribed by some to an oracle, and by others to Chilo of Lacedæmon.

This is, indeed, a dictate, which, in the whole extent of its meaning, may be said to comprise all the speculation requisite to a moral agent. For what more can be necessary to the regulation of life, than the knowledge of our original, our end, our duties, and our relation to other beings?

It is however very improbable that the first author, whoever he was, intended to be understood in this unlimited and complicated sense; for of the inquiries, which in so large an acceptation it would seem to recommend, some are too extensive for the powers of man, and some require light from above, which was not yet indulged to the heathen world.

We might have had more satisfaction concerning the original import of this celebrated sentence, if history had informed us, whether it was uttered as a general instruction to mankind, or as a particular caution to some private inquirer; whether it was applied to some single occasion, or laid down as the universal rule of life.

There will occur, upon the slightest consideration, many possible circumstances, in which this monition might very properly be inforced: for every errour in human conduct must arise from ignorance in ourselves, either perpetual or temporary; and happen either because we do not know what is best and fittest, or because our knowledge is at the time of action not present to the mind.

When a man employs himself upon remote and unnecessary subjects, and wastes his life upon questions which cannot be resolved, and of which the solution would conduce very little to the advancement of happiness; when he lavishes his hours in calculating the weight of the terraqueous globe, or in adjusting successive systems of worlds beyond the reach of the telescope; he may be very properly recalled from his excursions by this precept, and reminded, that there is a nearer being with which it is his duty to be more acquainted; and from which his attention has hitherto been withheld by studies to which he has no other motive than vanity or curiosity.

The great praise of Socrates is, that he drew the wits of Greece, by his instruction and example, from the vain pursuit of natural philosophy to moral inquiries, and turned their thoughts from stars and tides, and matter and motion, upon the various modes of virtue, and relations of life. All his lectures were but commentaries upon this saying; if we suppose the knowledge of ourselves recommended by Chilo, in opposition to other inquiries less suitable to the state of man.

The great fault of men of learning is still, that they offend against this rule, and appear willing to study any thing rather than themselves; for which reason they are often despised by those with whom they imagine themselves above comparison; despised, as useless to common purposes, as unable to conduct the most trivial affairs, and unqualified to perform those offices by which the concatenation of society is preserved, and mutual tenderness excited and maintained.

Gelidus is a man of great penetration and deep researches. Having a mind naturally formed for the abstruser sciences, he can comprehend intricate combinations without confusion, and being of a temper naturally cool and equal, he is seldom interrupted by his passions in the pursuit of the longest chain of unexpected consequences. He has, therefore, a long time indulged hopes, that the solution of some problems, by which the professors of science have been hitherto baffled, is reserved for his genius and industry. He spends his time in the highest room of his house, into which none of his family are suffered to enter; and when he comes down to his dinner or his rest, he walks about like a stranger that is there only for a day, without any tokens of regard or tenderness. He has totally divested himself of all human sensations; he has neither eye for beauty, nor ear for complaint; he neither rejoices at the good fortune of his nearest friend, nor mourns for any publick or private calamity. Having once received a letter, and given it his servant to read, he was informed, that it was written by his brother, who, being shipwrecked, had swum naked to land, and was destitute of necessaries in a foreign country. Naked and destitute! says Gelidus, reach down the last volume of meteorological observations, extract an exact account of the wind, and note it carefully in the diary of the weather.

The family of Gelidus once broke into his study, to shew him that a town at a small distance was on fire; and in a few moments a servant came to tell him, that the flame had caught so many houses on both sides, that the inhabitants were confounded, and began to think of rather escaping with their lives, than saving their dwellings. What you tell me, says Gelidus, is very probable, for fire naturally acts in a circle.

Thus lives this great philosopher, insensible to every spectacle of distress, and unmoved by the loudest call of social nature, for want of considering that men are designed for the succour and comfort of each other; that though there are hours which may be laudably spent upon knowledge not immediately useful, yet the first attention is due to practical virtue; and that he may be justly driven out from the commerce of mankind, who has so far abstracted himself from the species, as to partake neither of the joys nor griefs of others, but neglects the endearments of his wife and the caresses of his children, to count the drops of rain, note the changes of the wind, and calculate the eclipses of the moons of Jupiter.

I shall reserve to some future paper the religious and important meaning of this epitome of wisdom, and only remark, that it may be applied to the gay and light, as well as to the grave and solemn parts of life; and that not only the philosopher may forfeit his pretences to real learning, but the wit and beauty may miscarry in their schemes, by the want of this universal requisite, the knowledge of themselves.

It is surely for no other reason, that we see such numbers resolutely struggling against nature, and contending for that which they never can attain, endeavouring to unite contradictions, and determined to excel in characters inconsistent with each other; that stock-jobbers affect dress, gaiety, and elegance, and mathematicians labour to be wits; that the soldier teazes his acquaintance with questions in theology, and the academick hopes to divert the ladies by a recital of his gallantries. That absurdity of pride could proceed only from ignorance of themselves, by which Garth attempted criticism, and Congreve waved his title to dramatick reputation, and desired to be considered only as a gentleman.

Euphues, with great parts, and extensive knowledge, has a clouded aspect, and ungracious form; yet it has been his ambition, from his first entrance into life, to distinguish himself by particularities in his dress, to outvie beaux in embroidery, to import new trimmings, and to be foremost in the fashion. Euphues has turned on his exterior appearance, that attention which would always have produced esteem, had it been fixed upon his mind; and though his virtues and abilities have preserved him from the contempt which he has so diligently solicited, he has, at least, raised one impediment to his reputation; since all can judge of his dress, but few of his understanding; and many who discern that he is a fop, are unwilling to believe that he can be wise.

There is one instance in which the ladies are particularly unwilling to observe the rule of Chilo. They are desirous to hide from themselves the advances of age, and endeavour too frequently to supply the sprightliness and bloom of youth by artificial beauty and forced vivacity. They hope to inflame the heart by glances which have lost their fire, or melt it by languor which is no longer delicate; they play over the airs which pleased at a time when they were expected only to please, and forget that airs in time ought to give place to virtues. They continue to trifle, because they could once trifle agreeably, till those who shared their early pleasures are withdrawn to more serious engagements; and are scarcely awakened from their dream of perpetual youth, but by the scorn of those whom they endeavoured to rival.

THE OLD AND THE NEW SCHOOL-MASTER

CHARLES LAMB
1775-1834

LAMB is one of the greatest of the English essayists: he is the most whimsical, the most delicately humorous, in a sense, the wisest. His fame rests chiefly upon the *Essays of Elia* from which this and the following paper are taken. The first collection of "Elia" was published in 1823; the second series appeared in 1833.

MY reading has been lamentably desultory and immethodical. Odd, out-of-the-way, old English plays and treatises, have supplied me with most of my notions and ways of feeling. In everything that relates to *science*, I am a whole Encyclopædia behind the rest of the world. I should have scarcely cut a figure among the franklins, or country gentlemen, in King John's days. I know less geography than a schoolboy of six weeks' standing. To me a map of old Ortelius is as authentic as Arrowsmith. I do not know whereabout Africa merges into Asia; whether Ethiopia lie in one or other of those great divisions; nor can form the remotest conjecture of the position of New South Wales, or Van Diemen's Land. Yet do I hold a correspondence with a very dear friend in the first-named of these two Terrae Incognitae. I have no astronomy. I do not know where to look for the Bear, or Charles's Wain; the place of any star; or the name of any of them at sight. I guess at Venus only by her brightness — and if the sun on some portentous morn were to make his first appearance in the West, I verily believe that, while all the world were gasping in apprehension about me, I alone should stand unterrified, from sheer incuriosity and want of observation. Of history and chronology I possess some vague points, such as one cannot help picking up in the course of miscellaneous study; but I never deliberately sat down to a chronicle, even of my own country. I have most dim apprehensions of the four great monarchies; and sometimes the Assyrian, sometimes the Persian, floats as *first* in my fancy. I make the widest conjectures concerning Egypt, and her shepherd kings. My friend M., with great painstaking, got me to think I understood the first proposition in Euclid, but gave me over in despair at the second. I am entirely unacquainted with the modern languages; and, like a better man than myself, have "small Latin and less Greek." I am a stranger to the shapes and texture of the commonest trees, herbs, flowers — not from the circumstance of my being town-born — for I should have brought the same inobservant spirit into the world with me, had I first seen it "on Devon's leafy shores," — and am no less at a loss among purely town objects, tools, engines, mechanic processes. — Not that I affect ignorance — but my head has not many mansions, nor spacious; and I have been obliged to fill it with such cabinet curiosities as it can hold without aching. I sometimes wonder, how I have passed my probation with so little discredit in the world, as I have done, upon so meagre a stock. But the fact is, a man may do very well with a very little knowledge, and scarce be found out, in mixed company; everybody is so much more ready to produce his own, than to call for a display of your acquisitions. But in a *tête-à-tête* there is no shuffling. The truth will out. There is nothing which I dread so much, as the being left alone for a quarter of an hour with a sensible, well-informed man, that does not know me. I lately got into a dilemma of this sort. —

In one of my daily jaunts between Bishopsgate and Shacklewell, the coach stopped to take up a staid-looking gentleman, about the wrong side of thirty, who was giving his parting directions (while the steps were adjusting), in a tone of mild authority, to a tall youth, who seemed to be neither his clerk, his son, nor his servant, but something partaking of all three. The youth was dismissed, and we drove on. As we were the sole passengers, he naturally enough addressed his conversation to me; and we discussed the merits of the fare, the civility and punctuality of the driver; the circumstance of an opposition coach having been lately set up, with the probabilities of its success — to all which I was enabled to return pretty satisfactory answers, having been drilled into this kind of etiquette by some years' daily practice of riding to and fro in the stage aforesaid — when he suddenly alarmed me by a startling question, whether I had seen the show of prize cattle that morning in Smithfield? Now as I had not seen it, and do not greatly care for such sort of exhibitions, I was obliged to return a cold negative. He seemed a little mortified, as well as astonished, at my declaration, as (it appeared) he was just come fresh from the sight, and doubtless had hoped to compare notes on the subject. However he assured me that I had lost a fine treat, as it far exceeded the show of last year. We were now approaching Norton Folgate, when the sight of some shop-goods *ticketed* freshened him up into a dissertation upon the cheapness of cottons this spring. I was now a little in heart, as the nature of my morning avocations had brought me into some sort of familiarity with the raw material; and I was surprised to find how eloquent I was becoming on the state of the India market — when, presently, he dashed my incipient vanity to the earth at once, by inquiring whether I had ever made any calculation as to the value of the rental of all the retail shops in London. Had he asked of me, what song the Sirens sang, or what name Achilles assumed when he hid himself among women, I might, with Sir Thomas Browne, have hazarded a "wide solution." My companion saw my embarrassment, and, the almshouses beyond Shoreditch just coming in view, with great good-nature and dexterity shifted his conversation to the subject of public charities; which led to the comparative merits of provision for the poor in past and present times, with observations on the old monastic institutions, and charitable orders; — but, finding me rather dimly impressed with some glimmering notions from old poetic associations, than strongly fortified with any speculations reducible to calculation on the subject, he gave the matter up; and, the country beginning to open more and more upon us, as we approached the turnpike at Kingsland (the destined termination of his journey), he put a home thrust upon me, in the most unfortunate position he could have chosen, by advancing some queries relative to the North Pole Expedition. While I was muttering out something about the Panorama of those strange regions (which I had actually seen), by way of parrying the question, the coach stopping relieved me from any further apprehensions. My companion getting out, left me in the comfortable possession of my ignorance; and I heard him, as he went off, putting questions to an outside passenger, who had alighted with him, regarding an epidemic disorder that had been rife about Dalston, and which, my friend assured him, had gone through five or six schools in that neighborhood. The truth now flashed upon me, that my companion was a schoolmaster; and that the youth, whom he had parted from at our first acquaintance, must have been one of the bigger boys, or the usher. — He was evidently a kind-hearted man, who did not seem so much desirous of provoking discussion by the questions which he put, as of obtaining information at any rate. It did not appear that he took any interest either, in such kind of inquiries, for their own sake; but that he was in some way bound to seek for knowledge. A greenish-coloured coat, which he had on, forbade me to surmise that he was a clergyman. The adventure gave birth to some reflections on the difference between persons of his profession in past and present times.

Rest to the souls of those fine old Pedagogues; the breed, long since extinct, of the Lilys, and Linacres; who believing that all learning was contained in the languages which they taught, and despising every other acquirement as superficial and useless, came to their task as to a sport! Passing from infancy to age, they dreamed away all their days as in a grammar-school. Revolving in a perpetual cycle of declensions, conjugations, syntaxes, and prosodies; renewing constantly the occupations which had charmed their studious childhood; rehearsing continually the part of the past; life must have slipped from them at last like one day. They were always in their first garden, reaping harvests of their golden time, among their *Flori* and their *Spici-legia;* in Arcadia still, but kings; the ferule of their sway not much harsher, but of like dignity with that mild sceptre attributed to King Basileus; the Greek and Latin, their stately Pamela and their Philoclea; with the occasional duncery of some untoward Tyro, serving for a refreshing interlude of a Mopsa, or a clown Damaetas!

With what a savour doth the Preface to Colet's, or (as it is sometimes called) Paul's Accidence, set forth! "To exhort every man to the learning of grammar, that intendeth to attain the understanding of the tongues, wherein is contained a great treasury of wisdom and knowledge, it would seem but vain and lost labour; for so much as it is known, that nothing can surely be ended, whose beginning is either feeble or faulty; and no building be perfect, whereas the foundation and ground-work is ready to fall, and unable to uphold the burden of the frame." How well doth this stately preamble (comparable to those which Milton commendeth as "having been the usage to prefix to some solemn law, then first promulgated by Solon, or Lycurgus") cor-

THE OLD AND THE NEW SCHOOLMASTER

respond with and illustrate that pious zeal for conformity, expressed in a succeeding clause, which would fence about grammar-rules with the severity of faith-articles! — "as for the diversity of grammars, it is well profitably taken away by the king's majesties wisdom, who foreseeing the inconvenience, and favourably providing the remedie, caused one kind of grammar by sundry learned men to be diligently drawn, and so to be set out, only everywhere to be taught for the use of learners, and for the hurt in changing of schoolmaisters." What a *gusto* in that which follows: "wherein it is profitable that he (the pupil) can orderly decline his noun, and his verb." *His* noun!

The fine dream is fading away fast; and the least concern of a teacher in the present day is to inculcate grammar-rules.

The modern schoolmaster is expected to know a little of everything, because his pupil is required not to be entirely ignorant of anything. He must be superficially, if I may so say, omniscient. He is to know something of pneumatics; of chemistry; of whatever is curious, or proper to excite the attention of the youthful mind; an insight into mechanics is desirable, with a touch of statistics; the quality of soils, &c.; botany; the constitution of his country, *cum multis aliis*. You may get a notion of some part of his expected duties by consulting the famous Tractate on Education addressed to Mr. Hartlib.

All these things — these, or the desire of them — he is expected to instil, not by set lessons from professors, which he may charge in the bill, but at school-intervals, as he walks the streets, or saunters through green fields (those natural instructors) with his pupils. The least part of what is expected from him is to be done in school-hours. He must insinuate knowledge at the *mollia tempora fandi*. He must seize every occasion — the season of the year — the time of the day — a passing cloud — a rainbow — a waggon of hay

— a regiment of soldiers going by — to inculcate something useful. He can receive no pleasure from a casual glimpse of nature, but must catch at it as an object of instruction. He must interpret beauty into the picturesque. He cannot relish a beggar-man, or a gipsy, for thinking of the suitable improvement. Nothing comes to him, not spoiled by the sophisticating medium of moral uses. The Universe — that Great Book, as it has been called — is to him indeed, to all intents and purposes, a book, out of which he is doomed to read tedious homilies to distasting schoolboys. — Vacations themselves are none to him, he is only rather worse off than before; for commonly he has some intrusive upper-boy fastened upon him at such times; some cadet of a great family; some neglected lump of nobility, or gentry; that he must drag after him to the play, to the Panorama, to Mr. Bartley's Orrery, to the Panopticon, or into the country, to a friend's house, or his favourite watering-place. Wherever he goes, this uneasy shadow attends him. A boy is at his board, and in his path, and in all his movements. He is boy-rid, sick of perpetual boy.

Boys are capital fellows in their own way, among their mates; but they are unwholesome companions for grown people. The restraint is felt no less on the one side, than on the other. — Even a child, that "plaything for an hour," tires *always*. The noises of children, playing their own fancies — as I now hearken to them by fits, sporting on the green before my window, while I am engaged in these grave speculations at my neat suburban retreat at Shacklewell — by distance made more sweet — inexpressibly take from the labour of my task. It is like writing to music. They seem to modulate my periods. They ought at least to do so — for in the voice of that tender age there is a kind of poetry, far unlike the harsh prose-accents of man's conversation. — I should but spoil their sport, and diminish my own sympathy for them, by mingling in their pastime.

I would not be domesticated all my days with a person of very superior capacity to my own — not, if I know myself at all, from any considerations of jealousy, or self-comparison, for the occasional communion with such minds has constituted the fortune and felicity of my life — but the habit of too constant intercourse with spirits above you, instead of raising you, keeps you down. Too frequent doses of original thinking from others, restrain what lesser portion of that faculty you may possess of your own. You get entangled in another man's mind, even as you lose yourself in another man's grounds. You are walking with a tall varlet, whose strides out-pace yours to lassitude. The constant operation of such potent agency would reduce me, I am convinced, to imbecility. You may derive thoughts from others; your way of thinking, the mould in which your thoughts are cast, must be your own. Intellect may be imparted, but not each man's intellectual frame.

As little as I should wish to be always thus dragged upwards, as little (or rather still less) is it desirable to be stunted downwards by your associates. The trumpet does not more stun you by its loudness, than a whisper teases you by its provoking inaudibility.

Why are we never quite at our ease in the presence of a schoolmaster? — because we are conscious that he is not quite at his ease in ours. He is awkward, and out of place, in the society of his equals. He comes like Gulliver from among his little people, and he cannot fit the stature of his understanding to yours. He cannot meet you on the square. He wants a point given him, like an indifferent whist-player. He is so used to teaching, that he wants to be teaching *you*. One of these professors, upon my complaining that these little sketches of mine were anything but methodical, and that I was unable to make them otherwise, kindly offered to instruct me in the method by which young gentlemen in *his* seminary were taught to compose English themes. — The jests of a schoolmaster are coarse, or thin. They do not tell out of school. He is under the restraint of a formal and didactive hypocrisy in company, as a clergyman is under a moral one. He can no more let his intellect loose in society, than the other can his inclinations. — He is forlorn among his co-evals; his juniors cannot be his friends.

"I take blame to myself," said a sensible man of this profession, writing to a friend respecting a youth who had quitted his school abruptly, "that your nephew was not more attached to me. But persons in my situation are more to be pitied, than can well be imagined. We are surrounded by young, and, consequently, ardently affectionate hearts, but we can never hope to share an atom of their affections. The relation of master and scholar forbids this. *How pleasing this must be to you, how I envy your feelings*, my friends will sometimes say to me, when they see young men, whom I have educated, return after some years' absence from school, their eyes shining with pleasure, while they shake hands with their old master, bringing a present of game to me, or a toy to my wife, and thanking me in the warmest terms for my care of their education. A holiday is begged for the boys; the house is a scene of happiness; I, only, am sad at heart. — This fine-spirited and warm-hearted youth, who fancies he repays his master with gratitude for the care of his boyish years — this young man — in the eight long years I watched over him with a parent's anxiety, never could repay me with one look of genuine feeling. He was proud, when I praised; he was submissive, when I reproved him; but he did never *love* me — and what he now mistakes for gratitude and kindness for me, is but a pleasant sensation, which all persons feel at revisiting the scene of their boyish hopes and fears; and the seeing on equal terms the man they were accustomed to look up to with reverence. My wife,

THE OLD AND THE NEW SCHOOLMASTER 303

too," this interesting correspondent goes on to say, "my once darling Anna, is the wife of a schoolmaster. — When I married her — knowing that the wife of a schoolmaster ought to be a busy notable creature, and fearing that my gentle Anna would ill supply the loss of my dear bustling mother, just then dead, who never sat still, was in every part of the house in a moment, and whom I was obliged sometimes to threaten to fasten down in a chair, to save her from fatiguing herself to death — I expressed my fears, that I was bringing her into a way of life unsuitable to her; and she, who loved me tenderly, promised for my sake to exert herself to perform the duties of her new situation. She promised, and she has kept her word. What wonders will not a woman's love perform?— My house is managed with a propriety and decorum, unknown in other schools; my boys are well-fed, look healthy, and have every proper accommodation: and all this performed with a careful economy, that never descends to meanness. But I have lost my gentle, *helpless* Anna! — When we sit down to enjoy an hour of repose after the fatigue of the day, I am compelled to listen to what have been her useful (and they are really useful) employments through the day, and what she proposes for her to-morrow's task. Her heart and her features are changed by the duties of her situation. To the boys, she never appears other than the *master's wife*, and she looks up to me as the *boys' master;* to whom all show of love and affection would be highly improper, and unbecoming the dignity of her situation and mine. Yet *this* my gratitude forbids me to hint to her. For my sake she submitted to be this altered creature, and can I reproach her for it?" For the communication of this letter, I am indebted to my cousin Bridget.

OLD CHINA
CHARLES LAMB

I HAVE an almost feminine partiality for old china. When I go to see any great house, I enquire for the china-closet, and next for the picture gallery. I cannot defend the order of preference, but by saying, that we have all some taste or other, of too ancient a date to admit of our remembering distinctly that it was an acquired one. I can call to mind the first play, and the first exhibition, that I was taken to; but I am not conscious of a time when china jars and saucers were introduced into my imagination.

I had no repugnance then — why should I now have? — to those little, lawless, azure-tinctured grotesques, that under the notion of men and women, float about, uncircumscribed by any element, in that world before perspective — a china tea-cup.

I like to see my old friends — whom distance cannot diminish — figuring up in the air (so they appear to our optics), yet on *terra firma* still — for so we must in courtesy interpret that speck of deeper blue, which the decorous artist, to prevent absurdity, has made to spring up beneath their sandals.

I love the men with women's faces, and the women, if possible, with still more womanish expressions.

Here is a young and courtly Mandarin, handing tea to a lady from a salver — two miles off. See how distance seems to set off respect. And here the same lady, or another — for likeness is identity on tea-cups — is stepping into a little fairy boat, moored on the hither side of this calm garden river, with a dainty mincing foot, which in a right angle of incidence (as angles go in our world) must infallibly land her in the midst of a flowery mead — a furlong off on the other side of the same strange stream!

Farther on — if far or near can be predicated of their world — see horses, trees, pagodas, dancing the hays.

Here — a cow and rabbit couchant, and co-extensive — so objects show, seen through the lucid atmosphere of fine Cathay.

I was pointing out to my cousin last evening, over our Hyson (which we are old fashioned enough to drink unmixed still of an afternoon), some of these *speciosa miracula* upon a set of extraordinary old blue china (a recent purchase) which we were now for the first time using; and could not help remarking, how favourable circumstances had been to us of late years, that we could afford to please the eye sometimes with trifles of this sort — when a passing sentiment seemed to overshade the brows of my companion. I am quick at detecting these summer clouds in Bridget.

"I wish the good old times would come again," she said, "when we were not quite so rich. I do not mean, that I want to be poor; but there was a middle state" — so she was pleased to ramble on, — "in which I am sure we were a great deal happier. A purchase is but a purchase, now that you have money enough and to spare. Formerly it used to be a triumph. When we coveted a cheap luxury (and, O! how much ado I had to get you to consent in those times!) — we were used to have a debate two or three days before, and to weigh the *for* and *against*, and think what we might spare it out of, and what saving we could hit upon, that should be an equivalent. A thing was worth buying then, when we felt the money that we paid for it.

"Do you remember the brown suit, which you made to hang upon you, till all your friends cried shame upon you, it grew so thread-bare — and all because of that folio Beaumont and Fletcher, which you dragged home late at night from Barker's in Covent Garden? Do you remember how we eyed it for weeks before we could make up our minds to the purchase, and had not come to a determination till it was near ten o'clock of the Saturday night, when you set off from Islington, fearing you should be too late — and when the old bookseller with some grumbling opened his shop, and by the twinkling taper (for he was setting bedwards) lighted out the relic from his dusty treasures — and when you lugged it home, wishing it were twice as cumbersome — and when you presented it to me — and when we were exploring the perfectness of it (*collating* you called it) — and while I was repairing some of the loose leaves with paste, which your impatience would not suffer to be left till daybreak — was there no pleasure in being a poor man? or can those neat black clothes which you wear now, and are so careful to keep brushed, since we have become rich and finical, give you half the honest vanity, with which you flaunted it about in that over-worn suit — your old corbeau — for four or five weeks longer than you should have done, to pacify your conscience for the mighty sum of fifteen — or sixteen shillings was it? — a great affair we thought it then — which you had lavished on the old folio. Now you can afford to buy any book that pleases you, but I do not see that you ever bring me home any nice old purchases now.

"When you came home with twenty apologies for laying out a less number of shillings upon that print after Lionardo, which we christened the 'Lady Blanch'; when you looked at the purchase, and thought of the money — and thought of the money, and looked again at the picture — was there no pleasure in being a poor man? Now, you have nothing to do but to walk into Colnaghi's, and buy a wilderness of Lionardos. Yet do you?

"Then, do you remember our pleasant walks to Enfield,

and Potter's Bar, and Waltham, when we had a holyday — holydays, and all other fun, are gone, now we are rich — and the little hand-basket in which I used to deposit our day's fare of savoury cold lamb and salad — and how you would pry about at noon-tide for some decent house, where we might go in, and produce our store — only paying for the ale that you must call for — and speculate upon the looks of the landlady, and whether she was likely to allow us a table-cloth — and wish for such another honest hostess, as Izaak Walton has described many a one on the pleasant banks of the Lea, when he went a-fishing — and sometimes they would prove obliging enough, and sometimes they would look grudgingly upon us — but we had cheerful looks still for one another, and would eat our plain food savorily, scarcely grudging Piscator his Trout Hall? Now, when we go out a day's pleasuring, which is seldom moreover, we *ride* part of the way — and go into a fine inn, and order the best of dinners, never debating the expense — which, after all, never has half the relish of those chance country snaps, when we were at the mercy of uncertain usage, and a precarious welcome.

"You are too proud to see a play anywhere now but in the pit. Do you remember where it was we used to sit, when we saw the Battle of Hexham, and the Surrender of Calais, and Bannister and Mrs. Bland in the Children in the Wood — when we squeezed out our shillings a-piece to sit three or four times in a season in the one-shilling gallery — where you felt all the time that you ought not to have brought me — and more strongly I felt obligation to you for having brought me — and the pleasure was the better for a little shame — and when the curtain drew up, what cared we for our place in the house, or what mattered it where we were sitting, when our thoughts were with Rosalind in Arden, or with Viola at the Court of Illyria? You used to say, that the gallery was the best place of all for enjoying a play socially — that the relish of such exhibitions must be in proportion to the infrequency of going — that the company we met there, not being in general readers of plays, were obliged to attend the more, and did attend, to what was going on, on the stage — because a word lost would have been a chasm, which it was impossible for them to fill up. With such reflections we consoled our pride then — and I appeal to you, whether, as a woman, I met generally with less attention and accommodation, than I have done since in more expensive situations in the house? The getting in indeed, and the crowding up those inconvenient staircases, was bad enough, — but there was still a law of civility to women recognised to quite as great an extent as we ever found in the other passages — and how a little difficulty overcome heightened the snug seat, and the play, afterwards. Now we can only pay our money and walk in. You cannot see, you say, in the galleries now. I am sure we saw, and heard too, well enough then — but sight, and all, I think, is gone with our poverty.

"There was pleasure in eating strawberries, before they became quite common — in the first dish of peas, while they were yet dear — to have them for a nice supper, a treat. What treat can we have now? If we were to treat ourselves now — that is, to have dainties a little above our means, it would be selfish and wicked. It is the very little more that we allow ourselves beyond what the actual poor can get at, that makes what I call a treat — when two people living together, as we have done, now and then indulge themselves in a cheap luxury, which both like; while each apologises, and is willing to take both halves of the blame to his single share. I see no harm in people making much of themselves in that sense of the word. It may give them a hint how to make much of others. But now — what I mean by the word —

OLD CHINA

we never do make much of ourselves. None but the poor can do it. I do not mean the veriest poor of all, but persons as we were, just above poverty.

"I know what you were going to say, that it is mighty pleasant at the end of the year to make all meet, — and much ado we used to have every Thirty-first Night of December to account for our exceedings — many a long face did you make over your puzzled accounts, and in contriving to make it out how we had spent so much — or that we had not spent so much — or that it was impossible we should spend so much next year — and still we found our slender capital decreasing — but then, betwixt ways, and projects, and compromises of one sort or another, and talk of curtailing this charge, and doing without that for the future — and the hope that youth brings, and laughing spirits (in which you were never poor till now), we pocketed up our loss, and in conclusion, with 'lusty brimmers' (as you used to quote it out of *hearty cheerful Mr. Cotton,* as you called him), we used to welcome in the 'coming guest.' Now we have no reckoning at all at the end of the old year — no flattering promises about the new year doing better for us."

Bridget is so sparing of her speech on most occasions, that when she gets into a rhetorical vein, I am careful how I interrupt it. I could not help, however, smiling at the phantom of wealth which her dear imagination had conjured up out of a clear income of poor — hundred pounds a year. "It is true we were happier when we were poorer, but we were also younger, my cousin. I am afraid we must put up with the excess, for if we were to shake the superflux into the sea, we should not much mend ourselves. That we had much to struggle with, as we grew up together, we have reason to be most thankful. It strengthened, and knit our compact closer. We could never have been what we have been to each other, if we had always had the sufficiency which you now complain of. The resisting power — those natural dilations of the youthful spirit, which circumstances cannot straighten — with us are long since passed away. Competence to age is supplementary youth, a sorry supplement indeed, but I fear the best that is to be had. We must ride, where we formerly walked: live better, and lie softer — and shall be wise to do so — than we had means to do in those good old days you speak of. Yet could those days return — could you and I once more walk our thirty miles a-day — could Bannister and Mrs. Bland again be young, and you and I be young to see them — could the good old one-shilling gallery days return — they are dreams, my cousin, now — but could you and I at this moment, instead of this quiet argument, by our well-carpeted fire-side, sitting on this luxurious sofa — be once more struggling up those inconvenient stair-cases, pushed about, and squeezed, and elbowed by the poorest rabble of poor gallery scramblers — could I once more hear those anxious shrieks of yours — and the delicious *Thank God, we are safe,* which always followed when the topmost stair, conquered, let in the first light of the whole cheerful theatre down beneath us — I know not the fathom line that ever touched a descent so deep as I would be willing to bury more wealth in than Crœsus had, or the great Jew R—— is supposed to have, to purchase it. And now do just look at that merry little Chinese waiter holding an umbrella, big enough for a bed-tester, over the head of that pretty insipid half-Madonnaish chit of a lady in that very blue summer-house."

THE OLD GENTLEMAN[1]
LEIGH HUNT

OUR Old Gentleman, in order to be exclusively himself, must be either a widower or a bachelor. Suppose the former. We do not mention his precise age, which would be invidious; — nor whether he wears his own hair or a wig; which would be wanting in universality. If a wig, it is a compromise between the more modern scratch and the departed glory of the toupee. If his own hair, it is white, in spite of his favourite grandson, who used to get on the chair behind him, and pull the silver hairs out, ten years ago. If he is bald at top, the hairdresser, hovering and breathing about him like a second youth, takes care to give the bald place as much powder as the covered; in order that he may convey to the sensorium within a pleasing indistinctness of idea respecting the exact limits of skin and hair. He is very clean and neat; and, in warm weather, is proud of opening his waistcoat half-way down, and letting so much of his frill be seen, in order to show his hardiness as well as taste. His watch and shirt-buttons are of the best; and he does not care if he has two rings on a finger. If his watch ever failed him at the club or coffee-house, he would take a walk every day to the nearest clock of good character, purely to keep it right. He has a cane at home, but seldom uses it, on finding it out of fashion with his elderly juniors. He has a small cocked hat for gala days, which he lifts higher from his head than the round one, when bowed to. In his pockets are two handkerchiefs (one for the neck at

[1] From *The Indicator*, 1820.

night-time), his spectacles, and his pocket-book. The pocket-book, among other things, contains a receipt for a cough, and some verses cut out of an odd sheet of an old magazine, on the lovely Duchess of A., beginning —

"When beauteous Mira walks the plain."

He intends this for a common-place book which he keeps, consisting of passages in verse and prose, cut out of newspapers and magazines, and pasted in columns; some of them rather gay. His principal other books are Shakespeare's Plays and Milton's Paradise Lost; the Spectator, the History of England, the Works of Lady M. W. Montague, Pope and Churchill; Middleton's Geography; the Gentleman's Magazine; Sir John Sinclair on Longevity; several plays with portraits in character; Account of Elizabeth Canning, Memoirs of George Ann Bellamy, Poetical Amusements at Bath-Easton, Blair's Works, Elegant Extracts; Junius as originally published; a few pamphlets on the American War and Lord George Gordon, etc., and one on the French Revolution. In his sitting-rooms are some engravings from Hogarth and Sir Joshua; an engraved portrait of the Marquis of Granby; ditto of M. le Comte de Grasse surrendering to Admiral Rodney; a humorous piece after Penny; and a portrait of himself, painted by Sir Joshua. His wife's portrait is in his chamber, looking upon his bed. She is a little girl, stepping forward with a smile, and a pointed toe, as if going to dance. He lost her when she was sixty.

The Old Gentleman is an early riser, because he intends to live at least twenty years longer. He continues to take tea for breakfast, in spite of what is said against its nervous effects; having been satisfied on that point some years ago by Dr. Johnson's criticism on Hanway, and a great liking for tea previously. His china cups and saucers have been broken since his wife's death, all but one, which is religiously kept for his use. He passes his morning in walking or riding, looking in at auctions, looking after his India bonds or some such money securities, furthering some subscription set on foot by his excellent friend Sir John, or cheapening a new old print for his portfolio. He also hears of the newspapers; not caring to see them till after dinner at the coffee-house. He may also cheapen a fish or so; the fish-monger soliciting his doubtful eye as he passes, with a profound bow of recognition. He eats a pear before dinner.

His dinner at the coffee-house is served up to him at the accustomed hour, in the old accustomed way, and by the accustomed waiter. If William did not bring it, the fish would be sure to be stale, and the flesh new. He eats no tart; or if he ventures on a little, takes cheese with it. You might as soon attempt to persuade him out of his senses, as that cheese is not good for digestion. He takes port; and if he has drunk more than usual, and in a more private place, may be induced by some respectful inquiries respecting the old style of music, to sing a song composed by Mr. Oswald or Mr. Lampe, such as —
"Chloe, by that borrowed kiss,"
or
"Come, gentle god of soft repose,"
or his wife's favourite ballad, beginning —
"At Upton on the hill,
There lived a happy pair."

Of course, no such exploit can take place in the coffee-room; but he will canvass the theory of that matter there with you, or discuss the weather, or the markets, or the theatres, or the merits of "my lord North" or "my lord Rockingham"; for he rarely says simply, lord; it is generally "my lord," trippingly and genteelly off the tongue. If alone after dinner, his great delight is the newspaper; which he prepares to read by wiping his spectacles, carefully adjusting them on his eyes, and drawing the candle close to him, so as to stand sideways betwixt his ocular aim and the small type. He then holds the paper at arm's length, and dropping his eyelids half down and his mouth half open, takes cognizance of the day's information. If he leaves off, it is only when the door is opened by a new-comer, or when he suspects somebody is over-anxious to get the paper out of his hand. On these occasions he gives an important hem! or so; and resumes.

In the evening, our Old Gentleman is fond of going to the theatre, or of having a game of cards. If he enjoys the latter at his own house or lodgings, he likes to play with some friends whom he has known for many years; but an elderly stranger may be introduced, if quiet and scientific; and the privilege is extended to younger men of letters; who, if ill players, are good losers. Not that he is a miser, but to win money at cards is like proving his victory by getting the baggage; and to win of a younger man is a substitute for his not being able to beat him at rackets. He breaks up early, whether at home or abroad.

At the theatre, he likes a front row in the pit. He comes early, if he can do so without getting into a squeeze, and sits patiently waiting for the drawing up of the curtain, with his hands placidly lying one over the other on the top of his stick. He generously admires some of the best performers, but thinks them far inferior to Garrick, Woodward, and Clive. During splendid scenes, he is anxious that the little boy should see.

He has been induced to look in at Vauxhall again, but likes it still less than he did years back, and cannot bear it in comparison with Ranelagh. He thinks everything looks poor, flaring, and jaded. "Ah!" says he, with a sort of triumphant sigh, "Ranelagh was a noble place! Such taste, such elegance, such beauty! There was the Duchess of A., the finest woman in England, Sir; and Mrs. L., a mighty fine creature; and Lady Susan what's her name, that had that unfortunate affair with Sir Charles. Sir, they came swimming by you like the swans."

The Old Gentleman is very particular in having his slippers ready for him at the fire, when he comes home. He is also extremely choice in his snuff, and delights to get a fresh boxful in Tavistock-street, in his way to the theatre. His box is a curiosity from India. He calls favourite young ladies by their Christian names, however slightly acquainted with them; and has a privilege also of saluting all brides, mothers, and indeed every species of lady, on the least holiday occasion. If the husband for instance has met with a piece of luck, he instantly moves forward, and gravely kisses the wife on the cheek. The wife then says, "My niece, Sir, from the country;" and he kisses the niece. The niece, seeing her cousin biting her lips at the joke, says, "My cousin Harriet, Sir;" and he kisses the cousin. He "never recollects such weather," except during the "Great Frost," or when he rode down with "Jack Skrimshire to Newmarket." He grows young again in his little grandchildren, especially the one which he thinks most like himself; which is the handsomest. Yet he likes best perhaps the one most resembling his wife; and will sit with him on his lap, holding his hand in silence, for a quarter of an hour together. He plays most tricks with the former, and makes him sneeze. He asks little boys in general who was the father of Zebedee's children. If his grandsons are at school, he often goes to see them; and makes them blush by telling the master or the upper-scholars, that they are fine boys, and of a precocions genius. He is much struck when an old acquaintance dies, but adds that he lived too fast; and that poor Bob was a sad dog in his youth; "a very sad dog, Sir; mightily set upon a short life and a merry one."

When he gets very old indeed, he will sit for whole evenings, and say little or nothing; but informs you, that there is Mrs. Jones (the housekeeper) — "*She'll* talk."

THE OLD LADY [1]

LEIGH HUNT

IF the Old Lady is a widow and lives alone, the manners of her condition and time of life are so much the more apparent. She generally dresses in plain silks, that make a gentle rustling as she moves about the silence of her room; and she wears a nice cap with a lace border, that comes under the chin. In a placket at her side is an old enamelled watch, unless it is locked up in a drawer of her toilet, for fear of accidents. Her waist is rather tight and trim than otherwise, and she had a fine one when young; and she is not sorry if you see a pair of her stockings on a table, that you may be aware of the neatness of her leg and foot. Contented with these and other evident indications of a good shape, and letting her young friends understand that she can afford to obscure it a little, she wears pockets, and uses them well too. In the one is her handkerchief, and any heavier matter that is not likely to come out with it, such as the change of a sixpence; in the other is a miscellaneous assortment, consisting of a pocket-book, a bunch of keys, a needle-case, a spectacle-case, crumbs of biscuit, a nutmeg and grater, a smelling-bottle, and, according to the season, an orange or apple, which after many days she draws out, warm and glossy, to give to some little child that has well behaved itself. She generally occupies two rooms, in the neatest condition possible. In the chamber is a bed with a white coverlet, built up high and round, to look well, and with curtains of a pastoral pattern, consisting alternately of large plants, and shepherds and shepherdesses. On the man-

[1] From *The Indicator*.

telpiece are more shepherds and shepherdesses, with dot-eyed sheep at their feet, all in coloured ware: the man, perhaps, in a pink jacket and knots of ribbons at his knees and shoes, holding his crook lightly in one hand, and with the other at his breast, turning his toes out and looking tenderly at the shepherdess: the woman holding a crook also, and modestly returning his look, with a gipsy-hat jerked up behind, a very slender waist, with petticoat and hips to *counteract*, and the petticoat pulled up through the pocket-holes, in order to show the trimness of her ankles. But these patterns, of course, are various. The toilet is ancient, carved at the edges, and tied about with a snow-white drapery of muslin. Beside it are various boxes, mostly japan; and the set of drawers are exquisite things for a little girl to rummage, if ever little girl be so bold, — containing ribbons and laces of various kinds; linen smelling of lavender, of the flowers of which there is always dust in the corners; a heap of pocket-books for a series of years; and pieces of dress long gone by, such as head-fronts, stomachers, and flowered satin shoes, with enormous heels. The stock of *letters* are under especial lock and key. So much for the bedroom. In the sitting-room is rather a spare assortment of shining old mahogany furniture, or carved arm-chairs equally old, with chintz draperies down to the ground; a folding or other screen, with Chinese figures, their round, little-eyed, meek faces perking sideways; a stuffed bird, perhaps in a glass case (a living one is too much for her); a portrait of her husband over the mantelpiece, in a coat with frog-buttons, and a delicate frilled hand lightly inserted in the waistcoat; and opposite him on the wall, is a piece of embroidered literature, framed and glazed, containing some moral distich or maxim, worked in angular capital letters, with two trees of parrots below, in their proper colours; the whole concluding with an A B C and numerals, and the name of the fair industrious, expressing it to be "her work, Jan. 14, 1762." The rest of the furniture consists of a looking-glass with carved edges, perhaps a settee, a hassock for the feet, a mat for the little dog, and a small set of shelves, in which are the *Spectator* and *Guardian*, the *Turkish Spy*, a *Bible* and *Prayer Book*, Young's *Night Thoughts* with a piece of lace in it to flatten, Mrs. Rowe's *Devout Exercises of the Heart*, Mrs. Glasse's *Cookery*, and perhaps *Sir Charles Grandison*, and *Clarissa*. *John Buncle* is in the closet among the pickles and preserves. The clock is on the landing-place between the two room doors, where it ticks audibly but quietly; and the landing-place is carpeted to a nicety. The house is most in character, and properly coeval, if it is in a retired suburb, and strongly built, with wainscot rather than paper inside, and lockers in the windows. Before the windows should be some quivering poplars. Here the Old Lady receives a few quiet visitors to tea, and perhaps an early game at cards: or you may see her going out on the same kind of visit herself, with a light umbrella running up into a stick and crooked ivory handle, and her little dog, equally famous for his love to her and captions antipathy to strangers. Her grandchildren dislike him on holidays, and the boldest sometimes ventures to give him a sly kick under the table. When she returns at night, she appears, if the weather happens to be doubtful, in a calash; and her servant in pattens, follows half behind and half at her side, with a lantern.

Her opinions are not many nor new. She thinks the clergyman a nice man. The Duke of Wellington, in her opinion, is a very great man; but she has a secret preference for the Marquis of Granby. She thinks the young women of the present day too forward, and the men not respectful enough; but hopes her grandchildren will be better; though she differs with her daughter in several points respecting their management. She sets little value on the new accomplishments; is a great though delicate connoisseur in butcher's meat and all sorts of housewifery; and if you mention waltzes, expatiates on the grace and fine breeding of the minuet. She longs to have seen one danced by Sir Charles Grandison, whom she almost considers as a real person. She likes a walk of a summer's evening, but avoids the new streets, canals, etc., and sometimes goes through the churchyard, where her other children and her husband lie buried, serious, but not melancholy. She has had three great epochs in her life: — her marriage — her having been at court, to see the King and Queen and Royal Family — and a compliment on her figure she once received, in passing, from Mr. Wilkes, whom she describes as a sad, loose man, but engaging. His plainness she thinks much exaggerated. If anything takes her at a distance from home, it is still the court; but she seldom stirs, even for that. The last time but one that she went, was to see the Duke of Wirtemburg; and most probably for the last time of all, to see the Princess Charlotte and Prince Leopold. From this beatific vision she returned with the same admiration as ever for the fine comely appearance of the Duke of York and the rest of the family, and great delight at having had a near view of the Princess, whom she speaks of with smiling pomp and lifted mittens, clasping them as passionately as she can together, and calling her, in a transport of mixed loyalty and self-love, a fine royal young creature, and "Daughter of England."

ROSALIND [1]

ANNA JAMESON

I COME now to Rosalind, whom I should have ranked before Beatrice, inasmuch as the greater degree of her sex's softness and sensibility, united with equal wit and intellect, give her the superiority as a woman; but that, as a dramatic character, she is inferior in force. The portrait is one of infinitely more delicacy and variety, but of less strength and depth. It is easy to seize on the prominent features in the mind of Beatrice, but extremely difficult to catch and fix the more fanciful graces of Rosalind. She is like a compound of essences, so volatile in their nature, and so exquisitely blended, that on any attempt to analyze them, they seem to escape us. To what else shall we compare her, all-enchanting as she is? — to the silvery summer clouds which, even while we gaze on them, shift their hues and forms dissolving into air, and light, and rainbow showers? — to the May-morning, flush with opening blossoms and roseate dews, and "charm of earliest birds?" — to some wild and beautiful melody, such as some shepherd boy might "pipe to Amarillis in the shade?" — to a mountain streamlet, now smooth as a mirror in which the skies may glass themselves, and anon leaping and sparkling in the sunshine — or rather to the very sunshine itself? for so her genial spirit touches into life and beauty whatever it shines on!

But this impression, though produced by the complete development of the character, and in the end possessing the whole fancy, is not immediate. The first introduction of Rosalind is less striking than interesting; we see her a de-

[1] From *Characteristics of Women*, 1832.

pendant, almost a captive, in the house of her usurping uncle; her genial spirits are subdued by her situation, and the remembrance of her banished father: her playfulness is under a temporary eclipse.

"I pray thee, Rosalind, sweet my coz, be merry!"
is an adjuration which Rosalind needed not when once at liberty, and sporting "under the green-wood tree." The sensibility and even pensiveness of her demeanor in the first instance, render her archness and gayety afterwards, more graceful and more fascinating.

Though Rosalind is a princess, she is a princess of Arcady; and notwithstanding the charming effect produced by her first scenes, we scarcely ever think of her with a reference to them, or associate her with a court, and the artificial appendages of her rank. She was not made to "lord it o'er a fair mansion," and take state upon her like the all-aecomplished Portia; but to breathe the free air of heaven, and frolic among green leaves. She was not made to stand the siege of daring profligacy, and oppose high action and high passion to the assaults of adverse fortune, like Isabel; but to "fleet the time carelessly as they did i' the golden age." She was not made to bandy wit with lords, and tread courtly measures with plumed and warlike cavaliers, like Beatrice; but to dance on the green sward, and "murmur among living brooks a music sweeter than their own."

Though sprightliness is the distinguishing characteristic of Rosalind, as of Beatrice, yet we find her much more nearly allied to Portia in temper and intellect. The tone of her mind is, like Portia's, genial and buoyant: she has something, too, of her softness and sentiment; there is the same confiding abandonment of self in her affections; but the characters are otherwise as distinct as the situations are dissimilar. The age, the manners, the circumstance in which Shakspeare has placed his Portia, are not beyond the bounds of probability; nay, have a certain reality and locality. We fancy her a contemporary of the Raffaelles and the Ariostos; the sea-wedded Venice, its merchants and Magnificos, — the Rialto, and the long canals, — rise up before us when we think of her. But Rosalind is surrounded with the purely ideal and imaginative; the reality is in the characters and in the sentiments, not in the circumstances or situation. Portia is dignified, splendid, and romantic; Rosalind is playful, pastoral, and picturesque; both are in the highest degree poetical, but the one is epic and the other lyric.

Every thing about Rosalind breathes of "youth and youth's sweet prime." She is fresh as the morning, sweet as the dew-awakened blossoms, and light as the breeze that plays among them. She is as witty, as voluble, as sprightly as Beatrice; but in a style altogether distinct. In both, the wit is equally unconscious; but in Beatrice it plays about us like the lightning, dazzling but also alarming; while the wit of Rosalind bubbles up and sparkles like the living fountain, refreshing all around. Her volubility is like the bird's song; it is the outpouring of a heart filled to overflowing with life, love, and joy, and all sweet and affectionate impulses. She has as much tenderness as mirth, and in her most petulant raillery there is a touch of softness — "By this hand, it will not hurt a fly!" As her vivacity never lessens our impression of her sensibility, so she wears her masculine attire without the slightest impugnment of her delicacy. Shakspeare did not make the modesty of his women depend on their dress, as we shall see further when we come to Viola and Imogen. Rosalind has in truth "no doublet and hose in her disposition." How her heart seems to throb and flutter under her page's vest! What depth of love in her passion for Orlando! whether disguised beneath a saucy playfulness, or breaking forth with a fond impatience, or half betrayed in that beautiful scene where she faints at the sight of his 'kerchief stained with his blood! Here her recovery of her self-possession — her fears lest she should have revealed her sex — her presence of mind, and quick-witted excuse

—"I pray you, tell your brother how well I counterfeited"—

and the characteristic playfulness which seems to return so naturally with her recovered senses, — are all as amusing as consistent. Then how beautifully is the dialogue managed between herself and Orlando! how well she assumes the airs of a saucy page, without throwing off her feminine sweetness! How her wit flutters free as air over every subject! With what a careless grace, yet with what exquisite propriety!

"For innocence hath a privilege in her
To dignify arch jests and laughing eyes."

And if the freedom of some of the expressions used by Rosalind or Beatrice be objected to, let it be remembered that this was not the fault of Shakspeare or the women, but generally of the age. Portia, Beatrice, Rosalind, and the rest, lived in times when more importance was attached to things than to words; now we think more of words than of things; and happy are we in these later days of super-refinement, if we are to be saved by our verbal morality. But this is meddling with the province of the melancholy Jaques and our argument is Rosalind.

The impression left upon our hearts and minds by the character of Rosalind — by the mixture of playfulness, sensibility, and what the French (and we for lack of a better expression) call naïveté — is like a delicious strain of music. There is a depth of delight, and a subtlety of words to express that delight, which is enchanting. Yet when we call to mind particular speeches and passages, we find that they have a relative beauty and propriety, which renders it difficult to separate them from the context without injuring their effect. She says some of the most charming things in the world, and some of the most humorous: but we apply them as phrases rather than as maxims, and remember them rather for their pointed felicity of expression and fanciful application, than for their general truth and depth of meaning.

WOUTER VAN TWILLER [1]
WASHINGTON IRVING

THE renowned Wouter (or Walter) Van Twiller was descended from a long line of Dutch burgomasters, who had successively dozed away their lives, and grown fat upon the bench of magistracy in Rotterdam; and who had comported themselves with such singular wisdom and propriety that they were never either heard or talked of — which, next to being universally applauded, should be the object of ambition to all sage magistrates and rulers.

His surname of Twiller is said to be a corruption of the original *Twijfler*, which in English means *doubter;* a name admirably descriptive of his deliberative habits. For though he was a man shut up within himself like an oyster, and of such a profoundly reflective turn that he scarcely ever spoke except in monosyllables; yet did he never make up his mind on any doubtful point. This was clearly accounted for by his adherents, who affirmed that he always conceived every subject on so comprehensive a scale that he had not room in his head to turn it over and examine both sides of it; so that he always remained in doubt, merely in consequence of the astonishing magnitude of his ideas!

There are two opposite ways by which some men get into notice — one by talking a vast deal and thinking a little, and the other by holding their tongues and not thinking at all. By the first, many a vapouring superficial pretender acquires the reputation of a man of quick parts — by the other, many a vacant dunderpate, like the owl, the stupidest of birds, comes to be complimented by a discerning world,

[1] From *Knickerbocker's History of New York* — 1809.

with all the attributes of wisdom. This, by the way, is a mere casual remark, which I would not for the universe have it thought I apply to Governor Van Twiller. On the contrary, he was a very wise Dutchman, for he never said a foolish thing; and of such invincible gravity that he was never known to laugh, or even to smile, through the course of a long and prosperous life. Certain, however, it is, there never was a matter proposed, however simple, and on which your common narrow-minded mortals would rashly determine at the first glance, but what the renowned Wouter put on a mighty mysterious, vacant kind of look, shook his capacious head, and having smoked for five minutes with redoubled earnestness, sagely observed, that "he had his doubts about the matter:" — which, in process of time, gained him the character of a man slow of belief, and not easily imposed on.

The person of this illustrious old gentleman was as regularly formed, and nobly proportioned, as though it had been moulded by the hands of some cunning Dutch statuary, as a model of majesty and lordly grandeur. He was exactly five feet six inches in height, and six feet five inches in circumference. His head was a perfect sphere, far excelling in magnitude that of the great Pericles (who was thence waggishly called *Schenocephalus,* or onion head) — indeed, of such stupendous dimensions was it, that dame Nature herself, with all her sex's ingenuity, would have been puzzled to construct a neck capable of supporting it; wherefore she wisely declined the attempt, and settled it firmly on the top of his back-bone, just between the shoulders; where it remained, as snugly bedded as a ship of war in the mud of Potowmac. His body was of an oblong form, particularly capacious at bottom; which was wisely ordered by providence, seeing that he was a man of sedentary habits, and very averse to the idle labor of walking. His legs, though exceeding short, were sturdy in proportion to the weight they had to sustain; so that when erect he had not a little the appearance of a robustious beer barrel, standing on skids. His face, that infallible index of the mind, presented a vast expanse perfectly unfurrowed or deformed by any of those lines and angles which disfigure the human countenance with what is termed expression. Two small gray eyes twinkled feebly in the midst, like two stars of lesser magnitude, in a hazy firmament; and his full-fed cheeks, which seemed to have taken toll of every thing that went into his mouth, were curiously mottled and streaked with dusky red, like a Spitzenberg apple.

His habits were as regular as his person. He daily took his four stated meals, appropriating exactly an hour to each; he smoked and doubted eight hours, and he slept the remaining twelve of the four-and-twenty. Such was the renowned Wouter Van Twiller — a true philosopher, for his mind was either elevated above, or tranquilly settled below, the cares and perplexities of this world. He had lived in it for years, without feeling the least curiosity to know whether the sun revolved round it, or it round the sun; and he had even watched for at least half a century, the smoke curling from his pipe to the ceiling, without once troubling his head with any of those numerous theories, by which a philosopher would have perplexed his brain, in accounting for its rising above the surrounding atmosphere.

In his council he presided with great state and solemnity. He sat in a huge chair of solid oak hewn in the celebrated forest of the Hague, fabricated by an experienced Timmerman of Amsterdam, and curiously carved about the arms and feet, into exact imitations of gigantic eagles' claws. Instead of a sceptre, he swayed a long Turkish pipe, wrought with jasmin and amber, which had been presented to a stadtholder of Holland, at the conclusion of a treaty with one of the petty Barbary powers. In this stately chair would he sit, and this magnificent pipe would he smoke, shaking his right knee with a constant motion, and fixing his eyes for hours together upon a little print of Amsterdam, which hung in a black frame against the opposite wall of the council chamber. Nay, it has even been said, that when any deliberation of extraordinary length and intricacy was on the carpet, the renowned Wouter would absolutely shut his eyes for full two hours at a time, that he might not be disturbed by external objects; and at such times the internal commotion of his mind was evinced by certain regular guttural sounds, which his admirers declared were merely the noise of conflict made by his contending doubts and opinions.

THE MICAWBERS [1]
CHARLES DICKENS

THE counting-house clock was at half-past twelve, and there was general preparation for going to dinner, when Mr. Quinion tapped at the counting-house window, and beckoned to me to go in. I went in, and found there a stoutish, middle-aged person, in a brown surtout and black tights and shoes, with no more hair upon his head (which was a large one and very shining) than there is upon an egg, and with a very extensive face, which he turned full upon me. His clothes were shabby, but he had an imposing shirt-collar on. He carried a jaunty sort of stick, with a large pair of rusty tassels to it; and a quizzing-glass hung outside his coat, — for ornament, I afterwards found, as he very seldom looked through it, and could n't see anything when he did.

"This," said Mr. Quinion, in allusion to myself, "is he."

"This," said the stranger, with a certain condescending roll in his voice, and a certain indescribable air of doing something genteel, which impressed me very much, "is Master Copperfield. I hope I see you well, sir?"

I said I was very well, and hoped he was. I was sufficiently ill at ease, Heaven knows; but it was not in my nature to complain much at that time of my life, so I said I was very well, and hoped he was.

"I am," said the stranger, "thank Heaven, quite well. I have received a letter from Mr. Murdstone, in which he mentions that he would desire me to receive into an apartment in the rear of my house, which is at present unoccupied — and is, in short, to be let as a — in short," said the stran-

[1] From *David Copperfield* — 1849-50.

ger, with a smile, and in a burst of confidence, "as a bedroom — the young beginner whom I have now the pleasure to —" and the stranger waved his hand, and settled his chin in his shirt-collar.

"This is Mr. Micawber," said Mr. Quinion to me.

"Ahem!" said the stranger, "that is my name."

"Mr. Micawber," said Mr. Quinion, "is known to Mr. Murdstone. He takes orders for us on commission, when he can get any. He has been written to by Mr. Murdstone, on the subject of your lodgings, and he will receive you as a lodger."

"My address," said Mr. Micawber, "is Windsor Terrace, City Road. I — in short," said Mr. Micawber, with the same genteel air, and in another burst of confidence — "I live there."

I made him a bow.

"Under the impression," said Mr. Micawber, "that your peregrinations in this metropolis have not as yet been extensive, and that you might have some difficulty in penetrating the arcana of the Modern Babylon in the direction of the City Road — in short," said Mr. Micawber, in another burst of confidence, "that you might lose yourself — I shall be happy to call this evening, and instal you in the knowledge of the nearest way."

I thanked him with all my heart, for it was friendly in him to offer to take that trouble.

"At what hour," said Mr. Micawber, "shall I —"

"At about eight," said Mr. Quinion.

"At about eight," said Mr. Micawber. "I beg to wish you a good day, Mr. Quinion. I will intrude no longer."

So he put on his hat, and went out with his cane under his arm: very upright, and humming a tune when he was clear of the counting-house. . . .

At the appointed time in the evening, Mr. Micawber

reappeared. I washed my hands and face, to do the greater honour to his gentility, and we walked to our house, as I suppose I must now call it, together; Mr. Micawber impressing the names of streets, and the shapes of corner houses upon me, as we went along, that I might find my way back, easily, in the morning.

Arrived at his house in Windsor Terrace (which I noticed was shabby like himself, but also, like himself, made all the show it could), he presented me to Mrs. Micawber, a thin and faded lady, not at all young, who was sitting in the parlour (the first floor was altogether unfurnished, and the blinds were kept down to delude the neighbours), with a baby at her breast. This baby was one of twins; and I may remark here that I hardly ever, in all my experience of the family, saw both the twins detached from Mrs. Micawber at the same time. One of them was always taking refreshment.

There were two other children; Master Micawber, aged about four, and Miss Micawber, aged about three. These, and a dark-complexioned young woman, with a habit of snorting, who was servant to the family, and informed me, before half-an-hour had expired, that she was "a Orfling," and came from St. Luke's workhouse, in the neighbourhood, completed the establishment. My room was at the top of the house, at the back: a close chamber; stencilled all over with an ornament which my young imagination represented as a blue muffin; and very scantily furnished.

"I never thought," said Mrs. Micawber, when she came up, twin and all, to show me the apartment, and sat down to take breath, "before I was married, when I lived with papa and mama, that I should ever find it necessary to take a lodger. But Mr. Micawber being in difficulties, all considerations of private feeling must give way."

I said: "Yes, ma'am."

"Mr. Micawber's difficulties are almost overwhelming just at present," said Mrs. Micawber; "and whether it is possible to bring him through them, I don't know. When I lived at home with papa and mama, I really should have hardly understood what the word meant, in the sense in which I now employ it, but experientia does it — as papa used to say."

I cannot satisfy myself whether she told me that Mr. Micawber had been an officer in the Marines, or whether I have imagined it. I only know that I believe to this hour that he *was* in the Marines once upon a time, without knowing why. He was a sort of town traveller for a number of miscellaneous houses, now; but made little or nothing of it, I am afraid.

"If Mr. Micawber's creditors *will not* give him time," said Mrs. Micawber, "they must take the consequences; and the sooner they bring it to an issue the better. Blood cannot be obtained from a stone, neither can anything on account be obtained at present (not to mention law expenses) from Mr. Micawber."

I never can quite understand whether my precocious self-dependence confused Mrs. Micawber in reference to my age, or whether she was so full of the subject that she would have talked about it to the very twins if there had been nobody else to communicate with, but this was the strain in which she began, and she went on accordingly all the time I knew her.

Poor Mrs. Micawber! She said she had tried to exert herself; and so, I have no doubt, she had. The centre of the street-door was perfectly covered with a great brass plate, on which was engraved "Mrs. Micawber's Boarding Establishment for Young Ladies:" but I never found that any young lady had ever been to school there; or that any young lady ever came, or proposed to come; or that the least preparation was ever made to receive any young lady. The only visitors I ever saw or heard of, were creditors. *They* used to come at all hours, and some of them were quite ferocious. One dirty-faced man, I think he was a boot-maker, used to edge himself into the passage as early as seven o'clock in the morning, and call up the stairs to Mr. Micawber — "Come! You ain't out yet, you know. Pay us, will you? Don't hide, you know; that's mean. I would n't be mean if I was you. Pay us, will you? You just pay us, d'ye hear? Come!" Receiving no answer to these taunts, he would mount in his wrath to the words "swindlers" and "robbers"; and these being ineffectual too, would sometimes go to the extremity of crossing the street, and roaring up at the windows of the second floor, where he knew Mr. Micawber was. At these times Mr. Micawber would be transported with grief and mortification, even to the length (as I was once made aware by a scream from his wife) of making motions at himself with a razor; but within half-an-hour afterwards, he would polish up his shoes with extraordinary pains, and go out, humming a tune with a greater air of gentility than ever. Mrs. Micawber was quite as elastic. I have known her to be thrown into fainting fits by the king's taxes at three o'clock, and to eat lamb-chops breaded, and drink warm ale (paid for with two tea-spoons that had gone to the pawnbroker's) at four. On one occasion, when an execution had just been put in, coming home through some chance as early as six o'clock, I saw her lying (of course with a twin) under the grate in a swoon, with her hair all torn about her face; but I never knew her more cheerful than she was, that very same night, over a veal-cutlet before the kitchen fire, telling me stories about her papa and mama, and the company they used to keep.

AHAB [1]

HERMAN MELVILLE

For several days after leaving Nantucket, nothing above hatches was seen of Captain Ahab. The mates regularly relieved each other at the watches, and for aught that could be seen to the contrary, they seemed to be the only commanders of the ship; only they sometimes issued from the cabin with orders so sudden and peremptory, that after all it was plain they but commanded vicariously. Yes, their supreme lord and dictator was there, though hitherto unseen by any eyes not permitted to penetrate into the now sacred retreat of the cabin.

Every time I ascended to the deck from my watches below, I instantly gazed aft to mark if any strange face were visible; for my first vague disquietude touching the unknown captain, now in the seclusion of the sea, became almost a perturbation. This was strangely heightened at times by the ragged Elijah's diabolical incoherences uninvitedly recurring to me, with a subtle energy I could not have before conceived of. But poorly could I withstand them, much as in other moods I was almost ready to smile at the solemn whimsicalities of that outlandish prophet of the wharves. But whatever it was of apprehensiveness or uneasiness — to call it so — which I felt, yet whenever I came to look about me in the ship, it seemed against all warranty to cherish such emotions. For though the harpooners, with the great body of the crew, were a far more barbaric, heathenish, and motley set than any of the tame merchant-ship companies which my previous experiences had made me acquainted

[1] From *Moby Dick* — 1851.

with, still I ascribed this — and rightly ascribed it — to the fierce uniqueness of the very nature of that wild Scandinavian vocation in which I had so abandonedly embarked. But it was especially the aspect of the three chief officers of the ship, the mates, which was most forcibly calculated to allay these colorless misgivings, and induce confidence and cheerfulness in every presentment of the voyage. Three better, more likely sea-officers and men, each in his own different way, could not readily be found, and they were every one of them Americans; a Nantucketer, a Vineyarder, a Cape man. Now, it being Christmas when the ship shot from out her harbour, for a space we had biting Polar weather, though all the time running away from it to the southward; and by every degree and minute of latitude which we sailed, gradually leaving that merciless winter, and all its intolerable weather behind us. It was one of those less lowering, but still grey and gloomy enough mornings of the transition, when with a fair wind the ship was rushing through the water with a vindictive sort of leaping and melancholy rapidity, that as I mounted to the deck at the call of the forenoon watch, so soon as I levelled my glance toward the taffrail, foreboding shivers ran over me. Reality outran apprehensions; Captain Ahab stood upon his quarter-deck.

There seemed no sign of common bodily illness about him, nor of the recovery from any. He looked like a man cut away from the stake, when the fire has overrunningly wasted all the limbs without consuming them, or taking away one particle from their compacted aged robustness. His whole high, broad form, seemed made of solid bronze, and shaped in an unalterable mould, like Cellini's cast Perseus. Threading its way out from among his grey hairs, and continuing right down one side of his tawny scorched face and neck, till it disappeared in his clothing, you saw a slender rod-like mark, lividly whitish. It resembled that perpendicular seam sometimes made in the straight lofty trunk of a great tree, when the upper lightning tearingly darts down it, and without wrenching a single twig, peels and grooves out the bark from top to bottom, ere running off into the soil, leaving the tree still greenly alive, but branded. Whether that mark was born with him, or whether it was the scar left by some desperate wound, no one could certainly say. By some tacit consent, throughout the voyage little or no allusion was made to it, especially by the mates. But once Tashtego's senior, an old Gay-Head Indian among the crew, superstitiously asserted that not till he was full forty years old did Ahab become that way branded, and then it came upon him, not in the fury of any mortal fray, but in an elemental strife at sea. Yet, this wild hint seemed inferentially negatived, by what a grey Manxman insinuated, an old sepulchral man, who, having never before sailed out of Nantucket, had never ere this laid eye upon wild Ahab. Nevertheless, the old sea-traditions, the immemorial credulities, popularly invested this old Manxman with preternatural powers of discernment. So that no white sailor seriously contradicted him when he said that if ever Captain Ahab should be tranquilly laid out — which might hardly come to pass, so he muttered — then, whoever should do that last office for the dead, would find a birth-mark on him from crown to sole.

So powerfully did the whole grim aspect of Ahab affect me, and the livid brand which streaked it, that for the first few moments I hardly noted that not a little of this overbearing grimness was owing to the barbaric white leg upon which he partly stood. It had previously come to me that this ivory leg had at sea been fashioned from the polished bone of the sperm whale's jaw. "Aye, he was dismasted off Japan," said the old Gay-Head Indian once; "but like his dismasted craft, he shipped another mast without coming home for it. He has a quiver of 'em."

I was struck with the singular posture he maintained. Upon each side of the Pequod's quarter-deck, and pretty close to the mizzen shrouds, there was an augur hole, bored about half an inch or so, into the plank. His bone leg steadied in that hole; one arm elevated, and holding by a shroud; Captain Ahab stood erect, looking straight out beyond the ship's ever-pitching prow. There was an infinity of firmest fortitude, a determinate, unsurrenderable wilfulness, in the fixed and fearless, forward dedication of that glance. Not a word he spoke; nor did his officers say aught to him; though by all their minutest gestures and expressions, they plainly showed the uneasy, if not painful, consciousness of being under a troubled master-eye. And not only that, but moody stricken Ahab stood before them with a crucifixion in his face; in all the nameless regal overbearing dignity of some mighty woe.

Ere long, from his first visit in the air, he withdrew into his cabin. But after that morning, he was every day visible to the crew; either standing in his pivot-hole, or seated upon an ivory stool he had; or heavily walking the deck. As the sky grew less gloomy; indeed, began to grow a little genial, he became still less and less a recluse; as if, when the ship had sailed from home, nothing but the dead wintry bleakness of the sea had then kept him so secluded. And, by and by, it came to pass, that he was almost continually in the air; but, as yet, for all that he said, or perceptibly did, on the at last sunny deck, he seemed as unnecessary there as another mast. But the Pequod was only making a passage now; not regularly cruising; nearly all whaling preparatives needing supervision the mates were fully competent to, so that there was little or nothing, out of himself, to employ or excite Ahab, now; and thus chase away, for that one interval, the clouds that layer upon layer were piled upon his brow, as ever all clouds choose the loftiest peaks to pile themselves upon.

Nevertheless, ere long, the warm, warbling persuasiveness of the pleasant, holiday weather we came to, seemed gradually to charm him from his mood. For, as when the red-cheeked, dancing girls, April and May, trip home to the wintry, misanthropic woods; even the barest, ruggedest, most thunder-cloven old oak will at least send forth some few green sprouts, to welcome such glad-hearted visitants; so Ahab did, in the end, a little respond to the playful allurings of that girlish air. More than once did he put forth the faint blossom of a look, which, in any other man, would soon have flowered out in a smile.

MRS. TOUCHETT [1]

HENRY JAMES

MRS. TOUCHETT was certainly a person of many oddities, of which her behaviour on returning to her husband's house after many months was a noticeable specimen. She had her own way of doing all that she did, and this is the simplest description of a character which, although it was by no means without benevolence, rarely succeeded in giving an impression of softness. Mrs. Touchett might do a great deal of good, but she never pleased. This way of her own, of which she was so fond, was not intrinsically offensive — it was simply very sharply distinguished from the ways of others. The edges of her conduct were so very clear-cut that for susceptible persons it sometimes had a wounding effect. This purity of outline was visible in her deportment during the first hours of her return from America, under circumstances in which it might have seemed that her first act would have been to exchange greetings with her husband and son. Mrs. Touchett, for reasons which she deemed excellent, always retired on such occasions into impenetrable seclusion, postponing the more sentimental ceremony until she had achieved a toilet which had the less reason to be of high importance as neither beauty nor vanity were concerned in it. She was a plain-faced old woman, without coquetry and without any great elegance, but with an extreme respect for her own motives. She was usually prepared to explain these — when the explanation was asked as a favour; and in such a case they proved totally different from those that had been attributed to her. She was virtually

[1] From *The Portrait of a Lady*. Reprinted by arrangement with Houghton Mifflin Company.

separated from her husband, but she appeared to perceive nothing irregular in the situation. It had become apparent, at an early stage of their relations, that they should never desire the same thing at the same moment, and this fact had prompted her to rescue disagreement from the vulgar realm of accident. She did what she could to erect it into a law — a much more edifying aspect of it — by going to live in Florence, where she bought a house and established herself; leaving her husband in England to take care of his bank. This arrangement greatly pleased her; it was so extremely definite. It struck her husband in the same light, in a foggy square in London, where it was at times the most definite fact he discerned; but he would have preferred that discomfort should have a greater vagueness. To agree to disagree had cost him an effort; he was ready to agree to almost anything but that, and saw no reason why either assent or dissent should be so terribly consistent. Mrs. Touchett indulged in no regrets nor speculations, and usually came once a year to spend a month with her husband, a period during which she apparently took pains to convince him that she had adopted the right system. She was not fond of England, and had three or four reasons for it to which she currently alluded; they bore upon minor points of British civilization, but for Mrs. Touchett they amply justified non-residence. She detested bread-sauce, which, as she said, looked like a poultice and tasted like soap; she objected to the consumption of beer by her maid-servants; and she affirmed that the British laundress (Mrs. Touchett was very particular about the appearance of her linen) was not a mistress of her art. At fixed intervals she paid a visit to her own country; but this last one had been longer than any of its predecessors.

DOÑA RITA[1]

JOSEPH CONRAD

THE woman of whom I had heard so much, in a sort of way in which I had never heard a woman spoken of before, was coming down the stairs, and my first sensation was that of profound astonishment at this evidence that she did really exist. And even then the visual impression was more of colour in a picture than of the forms of actual life. She was wearing a wrapper, a sort of dressing gown of pale blue silk embroidered with black and gold designs round the neck and down the front, lapped round her and held together by a broad belt of the same material. Her slippers were of the same colour, with black bows at the instep. The white stairs, the deep crimson of the carpet and the light blue of the dress made an effective combination of colour to set off the delicate carnation of that face, which, after the first glance given to the whole person, drew irresistibly one's gaze to itself by an indefinable quality of charm beyond all analysis and made you think of remote races, of strange generations, of the faces of women sculptured on immemorial monuments and of those lying unsung in their tombs. While she moved downwards from step to step with slightly lowered eyes there flashed upon me suddenly the recollection of words heard at night, of Allègre's words about her, of there being in her "something of the women of all time."

At the last step she raised her eyelids, treated us to an exhibition of teeth as dazzling as Mr. Blunt's and looking even stronger; and indeed, as she approached us she brought home to our hearts (but after all I am speaking only for

[1] From *The Arrow of Gold*. Reprinted by permission of Doubleday, Page and Company, the owners of the copyright.

myself) a vivid sense of her physical perfection in beauty of limb and balance of nerves, and not so much of grace, probably, as of absolute harmony.

She said to us, "I am sorry I kept you waiting." Her voice was low pitched, penetrating, and of the most seductive gentleness. She offered her hand to Mills very frankly as to an old friend. Within the extraordinary wide sleeve, lined with black silk, I could see the arm, very white, with a pearly gleam in the shadow. But to me she extended her hand with a slight stiffening, as it were a recoil of her person, combined with an extremely straight glance. It was a finely shaped, capable hand. I bowed over it, and we just touched fingers. I did not look then at her face.

THE MISER [1]

FRANK NORRIS

THE interior of the junk shop was dark and damp, and foul with all manner of choking odors. On the walls, on the floor, and hanging from the rafters was a world of débris, dust-blackened, rust-corroded. Everything was there, every trade was represented, every class of society; things of iron and cloth and wood; all the detritus that a great city sloughs off in its daily life. Zerkow's junk shop was the last abiding-place, the almshouse, of such articles as had outlived their usefulness.

Maria found Zerkow himself in the back room, cooking some sort of a meal over an alcohol stove. Zerkow was a Polish Jew — curiously enough his hair was fiery red. He was a dry, shrivelled old man of sixty odd. He had the thin, eager, cat-like lips of the covetous; eyes that had grown keen as those of a lynx from long searching amidst muck and débris; and claw-like, prehensile fingers — the fingers of a man who accumulates, but never disburses. It was impossible to look at Zerkow and not know instantly that greed — inordinate, insatiable greed — was the dominant passion of the man. He was the Man with the Rake, groping hourly in the muck-heap of the city for gold, for gold, for gold. It was his dream, his passion; at every instant he seemed to feel the generous solid weight of the crude fat metal in his palms. The glint of it was constantly in his eyes; the jangle of it sang forever in his ears as the jangling of cymbals.

[1] From *McTeague*. Reprinted by permission of Doubleday, Page and Company, the owners of the copyright.

MR. HASTINGS [1]

WILLIAM GILPIN

MR. HASTINGS was low of stature, but strong, and active; of a ruddy complexion, with flaxen hair. His cloaths were always of green cloth. His house was of the old fashion; in the midst of a large park, well stocked with deer, rabbits, and fish-ponds. He had a long narrow bowling-green, in it; and used to play with round sand-bowls. Here too he had a banquetting-room built, like a stand, in a large tree. He kept all sorts of hounds, that ran buck, fox, hare, otter, and badger; and had hawks of all kinds, both long, and short winged. His great hall was commonly strewed with marrow-bones; and full of hawk-perches, hounds, spaniels, and terriers. The upper end of it was hung with fox-skins of this, and the last year's killing. Here, and there a pole-cat was intermixed; and hunter's poles in great abundance. The parlour was a large room, compleatly furnished in the same stile. On a broad hearth, paved with brick, lay some of the choicest terriers, hounds, and spaniels. One or two of the great chairs, had litters of cats in them, which were not to be disturbed. Of these three or four always attended him at dinner; and a little white wand lay by his trencher, to defend it, if they were too troublesome. In the windows, which were very large, lay his arrows, cross-bows, and other accoutrements. The corners of the room were filled with his best hunting and hawking poles. His oister-table stood at the lower end of the room, which was in constant use twice a day, all the year round; for he never failed to eat oisters both at dinner, and supper; with which the neigh-

[1] From *Forest Scenery* — 1790.

bouring town of Pool supplied him. At the upper end of the room stood a small table with a double desk; one side of which held a church-bible; the other, the book of martyrs. On different tables in the room lay hawk's hoods; bells; old hats, with their crowns thrust in, full of pheasant eggs; tables; dice; cards; and store of tobacco-pipes. At one end of this room was a door, which opened into a closet; where stood bottles of strong beer, and wine; which never came out but in single glasses, which was the rule of the house; for he never exceeded himself; nor permitted others to exceed. Answering to this closet, was a door into an old chapel; which had been long disused for devotion; but in the pulpit, as the safest place, was always to be found a cold chine of beef, a venison-pasty, a gammon of bacon, or a great apple-pye, with thick crust, well-baked. His table cost him not much, tho it was good to eat at. His sports supplied all, but beef and mutton; except on Fridays, when he had the best of fish. He never wanted a London pudding; and he always sang it in with, "*My part lies therein-a.*" He drank a glass or two of wine at meals; put syrup of gilly-flowers into his sack; and had always a tun-glass of small-beer standing by him, which he often stirred about with rosemary. He lived to be an hundred; and never lost his eyesight nor used spectacles. He got on horse-back without help; and rode to the death of the stag, till he was past fourscore.

JAMES BOSWELL [1]
THOMAS CARLYLE

BOSWELL was a person whose mean or bad qualities lay open to the general eye; visible, palpable to the dullest. His good qualities, again, belonged not to the Time he lived in; were far from common then; indeed, in such a degree, were almost unexampled; not recognizable therefore by every one; nay, apt even (so strange had they grown) to be confounded with the very vices they lay contiguous to and had sprung out of. That he was a wine-bibber and gross liver; gluttonously fond of whatever would yield him a little solacement, were it only of a stomachic character, is undeniable enough. That he was vain, heedless, a babbler; had much of the sycophant, alternating with the braggadocio, curiously spiced too with an all-pervading dash of the coxcomb; that he gloried much when the Tailor, by a court-suit, had made a new man of him; that he appeared at the Shakspeare Jubilee with a riband, imprinted "Corsica Boswell," round his hat; and in short, if you will, lived no day of his life without doing and saying more than one pretentious ineptitude: all this unhappily is evident as the sun at noon. The very look of Boswell seems to have signified so much. In that cocked nose, cocked partly in triumph over his weaker fellow-creatures, partly to snuff up the smell of coming pleasure, and scent it from afar; in those bag-cheeks, hanging like half-filled wine-skins, still able to contain more; in that coarsely protruded shelf-mouth, that fat dewlapped chin: in all this, who sees not sensuality, pretension, boisterous imbecility enough; much that could not have been orna-

[1] From the essay "Boswell's Life of Johnson"— 1832.

mental in the temper of a great man's overfed great man (what the Scotch name *flunky*), though it had been more natural there? The under part of Boswell's face is of a low, almost brutish character.

Unfortunately, on the other hand, what great and genuine good lay in him was nowise so self-evident. . . .

The world, as we said, has been but unjust to him; discerning only the outer terrestrial and often sordid mass; without eye, as it generally is, for his inner divine secret; and thus figuring him no wise as a god Pan, but simply of the bestial species, like the cattle on a thousand hills. Nay, sometimes a strange enough hypothesis has been started of him; as if it were in virtue even of these same bad qualities that he did his good work; as if it were the very fact of his being among the worst men in this world that had enabled him to write one of the best books therein! Falser hypothesis, we may venture to say, never rose in human soul. *Bad* is by its nature negative, and can do *nothing;* whatsoever enables us to *do* any thing is by its very nature *good*. Alas, that there should be teachers in Israel, or even learners, to whom this world-ancient fact is still problematical, or even deniable! Boswell wrote a good Book because he had a heart and an eye to discern Wisdom, and an utterance to render it forth; because of his free insight, his lively talent, above all, of his Love and childlike Open-mindedness. His sneaking sycophancies, his greediness and forwardness, whatever was bestial and earthly in him, are so many blemishes in his Book, which still disturb us in its clearness; wholly hindrances, not helps. Towards Johnson, however, his feeling was not Sycophancy, which is the lowest, but Reverence, which is the highest of human feelings. None but a *reverent* man (which so unspeakably few are) could have found his way from Boswell's environment to Johnson's: if such worship for real God-made superiors showed itself also as worship for apparent Tailor-made superiors, even as hollow interested mouth-worship for such, — the case, in this composite human nature of ours, was not miraculous, the more was the pity! But for ourselves, let every one of us cling to this last article of Faith, and know it as the beginning of all knowledge worth the name: That neither James Boswell's good Book, nor any other good thing, in any time or in any place, was, is, or can be performed by any man in virtue of his badness, but always and solely in spite thereof.

TENNYSON[1]

THOMAS CARLYLE

I THINK he must be under forty, not much under. One of the finest looking men in the world. A great shock of rough dusty-dark hair; bright, laughing hazel eyes; massive aquiline face, most massive yet most delicate; of sallow-brown complexion, almost Indian-looking; clothes cynically loose, free-and-easy; smokes infinite tobacco. His voice is musical — metallic — fit for loud laughter and piercing wail, and all that may lie between; speech and speculation free and plenteous; I do not meet, in these late decades, such company over a pipe!

[1] From a letter to Emerson — 1844.

BOERHAAVE

SAMUEL JOHNSON

HERMANN BOERHAAVE (1668–1738), a famous Dutch physician, was Professor of Botany, Chemistry and Medicine at the University of Leyden. The sketch of his life from which this characterization is taken was contributed by Johnson to the *Gentleman's Magazine* in 1739.

THUS died Boerhaave, a man formed by nature for great designs, and guided by religion in the exertion of his abilities. He was of a robust and athletick constitution of body, so hardened by early severities, and wholesome fatigue, that he was insensible of any sharpness of air, or inclemency of weather. He was tall, and remarkable for extraordinary strength. There was, in his air and motion, something rough and artless, but so majestick and great, at the same time, that no man ever looked upon him without veneration, and a kind of tacit submission to the superiority of his genius.

The vigour and activity of his mind sparkled visibly in his eyes; nor was it ever observed, that any change of his fortune, or alteration in his affairs, whether happy or unfortunate, affected his countenance.

He was always cheerful, and desirous of promoting mirth by a facetious and humorous conversation; he was never soured by calumny and detraction, nor ever thought it necessary to confute them; "for they are sparks," said he, "which, if you do not blow them, will go out of themselves."

Yet he took care never to provoke enemies by severity of censure, for he never dwelt on the faults or defects of others, and was so far from inflaming the envy of his rivals, by dwelling on his own excellencies, that he rarely mentioned himself or his writings.

He was not to be overawed or depressed by the presence, frowns, or insolence of great men, but persisted, on all occasions, in the right, with a resolution always present and always calm. He was modest, but not timorous, and firm without rudeness.

He could, with uncommon readiness and certainty, make a conjecture of men's inclinations and capacity by their aspect.

His method of life was to study in the morning and evening, and to allot the middle of the day to his publick business. His usual exercise was riding, till, in his latter years, his distempers made it more proper for him to walk: when he was weary, he amused himself with playing on the violin.

His greatest pleasure was to retire to his house in the country, where he had a garden stored with all the herbs and trees which the climate would bear; here he used to enjoy his hours unmolested, and prosecute his studies without interruption.

The diligence with which he pursued his studies, is sufficiently evident from his success. Statesmen and generals may grow great by unexpected accidents, and a fortunate concurrence of circumstances, neither procured nor foreseen by themselves; but reputation in the learned world must be the effect of industry and capacity. Boerhaave lost none of his hours, but, when he had attained one science, attempted another; he added physick to divinity, chymistry to the mathematicks, and anatomy to botany. He examined systems by experiments, and formed experiments into systems. He neither neglected the observations of others, nor blindly submitted to celebrated names. He neither thought so highly of himself, as to imagine he could receive no light from books, nor so meanly, as to believe he could discover nothing but what was to be learned from them. He examined the observations of other men, but trusted only to his own.

Nor was he unacquainted with the art of recommending truth by elegance, and embellishing the philosopher with polite literature: he knew that but a small part of mankind will sacrifice their pleasure to their improvement, and those authors who would find many readers, must endeavor to please while they instruct.

He knew the importance of his own writings to mankind, and lest he might, by a roughness and barbarity of style, too frequent among men of great learning, disappoint his own intentions, and make his labours less useful, he did not neglect the politer arts of eloquence and poetry. Thus was his learning, at once, various and exact, profound and agreeable.

But his knowledge, however uncommon, holds, in his character, but the second place; his virtue was yet much more uncommon than his learning. He was an admirable example of temperance, fortitude, humility, and devotion. His piety, and a religious sense of his dependance on God, was the basis of all his virtues, and the principle of his whole conduct.

ENGLISH FOR COLLEGE COURSES

EXPOSITORY WRITING
By MERVIN J. CURL.
Gives freshmen and sophomores something to write about, and helps them in their writing.

SENTENCES AND THINKING
By NORMAN FOERSTER, University of North Carolina, and J. M. STEDMAN, Jr., Emory University.
A practice book in sentence-making for college freshmen.

A HANDBOOK OF ORAL READING
By LEE EMERSON BASSETT, Leland Stanford Junior University.
Especial emphasis is placed on the relation of thought and speech, technical vocal exercises being subordinated to a study of the principles underlying the expression of ideas. Illustrative selections of both poetry and prose are freely employed.

ARGUMENTATION AND DEBATING (*Revised Edition*)
By WILLIAM T. FOSTER, Reed College.
The point of view throughout is that of the student rather than that of the teacher.

THE RHETORICAL PRINCIPLES OF NARRATION
By CARROLL LEWIS MAXCY, Williams College.
A clear and thorough analysis of the three elements of narrative writing, viz.: setting, character, and plot.

REPRESENTATIVE NARRATIVES
Edited by CARROLL LEWIS MAXCY.
This compilation contains twenty-two complete selections of various types of narrative composition.

THE STUDY AND PRACTICE OF WRITING ENGLISH
By GERHARD R. LOMER, Ph.D., and MARGARET ASHMUN.
A textbook for use in college Freshman courses.

HOW TO WRITE SPECIAL FEATURE ARTICLES
By WILLARD G. BLEYER, University of Wisconsin.
A textbook for classes in Journalism and in advanced English Composition.

NEWSPAPER WRITING AND EDITING
By WILLARD G. BLEYER.
This fully meets the requirements of courses in Journalism as given in our colleges and universities, and at the same time appeals to practical newspaper men.

TYPES OF NEWS WRITING
By WILLARD G. BLEYER.
Over two hundred typical stories taken from representative American newspapers are here presented in a form convenient for college classes in Journalism.

HOUGHTON MIFFLIN COMPANY

FOR COURSES ON THE DRAMA

DRAMATIC TECHNIQUE
   By George Pierce Baker, Harvard University.

THE TUDOR DRAMA
   By C. F. Tucker Brooke, Yale University.
   An illuminating history of the development of English Drama during the Tudor Period, from 1485 to the close of the reign of Elizabeth.

CHIEF CONTEMPORARY DRAMATISTS, First Series
   Edited by Thomas H. Dickinson, formerly of the University of Wisconsin.

CHIEF CONTEMPORARY DRAMATISTS, Second Series
   Edited by Thomas H. Dickinson.
   This book supplements the *First Series* by making available in a companion volume plays which represent the later tendencies in the drama of Europe and America.

CHIEF EUROPEAN DRAMATISTS
   Edited by Brander Matthews, Columbia University, Member of the American Academy of Arts and Letters.
   This volume contains one typical play from each of the master dramatists of Europe, with the exception of the English writers.

A STUDY OF THE DRAMA
   By Brander Matthews.
   Devoted mainly to an examination of the structural framework which the great dramatists of various epochs have given to their plays; it discusses only incidentally the psychology, the philosophy, and the poetry of these pieces.

THE CHIEF ELIZABETHAN DRAMATISTS
   Edited by W. A. Neilson, President of Smith College, formerly Professor of English Literature in Harvard University.

   This volume presents typical examples of the work of the most important of Shakespeare's contemporaries, so that, taken with Shakespeare's own works, it affords a view of the development of the English drama through its most brilliant period.

A HISTORY OF THE ELIZABETHAN DRAMA
   By Felix E. Schelling, University of Pennsylvania. 2 vols.

SHAKESPEAREAN PLAYHOUSES
   By Joseph Quincy Adams, Cornell University.
   A History of English Theatres from the Beginnings to the Restoration. Fully illustrated.

SHAKESPEARE QUESTIONS
   By Odell Shepard, Trinity College. *Riv. Lit. Series.* No. 246.
   An outline for the study of the leading plays.

HOUGHTON MIFFLIN COMPANY

Riverside Literature Series

LIBRARY BINDING

Sir Gawain and the Green Knight, and Piers the Ploughman. WEBSTER AND NEILSON.

Chaucer's The Prologue, The Knight's Tale, and The Nun's Priest's Tale. MATHER.

Ralph Roister Doister. CHILD.

The Second Shepherds' Play, Everyman, and Other Early Plays. CHILD.

Bacon's Essays. NORTHUP.

Shakespeare Questions. SHEPARD.

Milton's Of Education, Areopagitica, The Commonwealth. LOCKWOOD.

Boswell's Life of Johnson. JENSEN.

Goldsmith's The Good-Natured Man, and She Stoops to Conquer. DICKINSON.

Sheridan's The School for Scandal. WEBSTER.

Shelley's Poems. (Selected.) CLARKE.

Huxley's Autobiography, and Selected Essays. SNELL.

Selections from the Prose Works of Matthew Arnold. JOHNSON.

Selected Literary Essays from James Russell Lowell. HOWE and FOERSTER.

Howells's A Modern Instance.

Briggs's College Life.

Briggs's To College Girls.

Perry's The American Mind and American Idealism.

Burroughs's Studies in Nature and Literature.

Newman's University Subjects.

Bryce's Promoting Good Citizenship.

Eliot's The Training for an Effective Life.

English and American Sonnets. LOCKWOOD.

The Little Book of American Poets. RITTENHOUSE.

The Little Book of Modern Verse. RITTENHOUSE.

High Tide. An Anthology of Contemporary Poems. RICHARDS.

Minimum College Requirements in English for Study.

The Second Book of Modern Verse. RITTENHOUSE.

Abraham Lincoln. A Play. DRINKWATER.

RIVERSIDE ESSAYS
Edited by ADA L. F. SNELL
Associate Professor of English, Mount Holyoke College

The purpose of the Riverside Essays is to present to students of English composition essays by modern authors which deal in a fresh way with such subjects as politics, science, literature, and nature. The close study of vigorous and artistic writing is generally acknowledged to be the best method of gaining a mastery of the technique of composition.

In the Riverside Essays the material consists of essays which, with few exceptions, have been printed entire. Other advantages of the Riverside Essays for both instructor and student lie in the fact that the material is presented in separate volumes, each of which is devoted to a single author and contains two or more representative essays.

Finally, the series has none of the earmarks of the ordinary textbook which the student passes on, marked and battered, to the next college generation. The books are attractively printed, and bound in the Library Binding of the Riverside Literature Series. The student will therefore be glad to keep these books for his own library.

PROMOTING GOOD CITIZENSHIP
By JAMES BRYCE. With an Introduction. *Riverside Literature Series*, No. 227, Library Binding.

STUDIES IN NATURE AND LITERATURE
By JOHN BURROUGHS. *Riverside Literature Series*, No. 226, Library Binding.

UNIVERSITY SUBJECTS
By JOHN HENRY NEWMAN. *Riverside Literature Series*, No. 225, Library Binding.

THE AMERICAN MIND AND AMERICAN IDEALISM
By BLISS PERRY. With an Introduction. *Riverside Literature Series*, No. 224, Library Binding.

HOUGHTON MIFFLIN COMPANY

This book is **DUE** on the last date stamped below

SEP 5 1942

SEP 14 1945

NOV 12 1958

DEC 22 1960

Form L-9-10m-2,'31

PR
285   Smith -
640
       Essays and
       studies.

UC SOUTHERN REGIONAL LIBRARY FACILITY

AA   000 296 195 1

PR
1285
S64e

Lightning Source UK Ltd.
Milton Keynes UK
UKHW020827291118
333183UK00011B/733/P